The Democracy of Knowledge

About the Series

The **Political Theory and Contemporary Philosophy** series stages an ongoing dialogue between contemporary European philosophy and political theory. Following Hannah Arendt's and Leo Strauss's repeated insistence on the qualitative distinction between political theory and political philosophy, the series showcases the lessons each discipline can draw from the other. One of the most significant outcomes of this dialogue is an innovative integration of 1) the findings of twentieth- and twenty-first-century phenomenology, existentialism, hermeneutics, psychoanalysis, and deconstruction (to name but a few salient currents) and 2) classical as well as modern political concepts, such as sovereignty, polity, justice, constitution, statehood, self-determination, etc.

In many instances, the volumes in the series both re-conceptualize age-old political categories in light of contemporary philosophical theses and find broader applications for the ostensibly non- or apolitical aspects of philosophical inquiry. In all cases, political thought and philosophy are featured as equal partners in an interdisciplinary conversation, the goal of which is to bring about a greater understanding of today's rapidly changing political realities.

The series is edited by Michael Marder, Ikerbasque Research Professor in the Department of Philosophy at the University of the Basque Country, Vitoria-Gasteiz.

Other volumes in the series include:

Deconstructing Zionism by Michael Marder and Santiago Zabala
Heidegger on Hegel's Philosophy of Right by Marcia Sa Cavalcante Schuback, Michael Marder and Peter Trawny
The Metaphysics of Terror by Rasmus Ugilt
The Negative Revolution by Artemy Magun
The Voice of Conscience by Mika Ojakangas

The Democracy of Knowledge

Daniel Innerarity

Translated by Sandra Kingery

BLOOMSBURY
NEW YORK • LONDON • NEW DELHI • SYDNEY

Bloomsbury Academic
An imprint of Bloomsbury Publishing Plc

1385 Broadway	50 Bedford Square
New York	London
NY 10018	WC1B 3DP
USA	UK

www.bloomsbury.com

First published 2013
Paperback edition first published 2015

© Daniel Innerarity, 2013

All rights reserved. No part of this publication may be reproduced or transmitted in any form or by any means, electronic or mechanical, including photocopying, recording, or any information storage or retrieval system, without prior permission in writing from the publishers.

No responsibility for loss caused to any individual or organization acting on or refraining from action as a result of the material in this publication can be accepted by Bloomsbury Academic or the author.

Library of Congress Cataloging-in-Publication Data
Innerarity, Daniel, 1959-
The democracy of knowledge/by Daniel Innerarity.
pages cm
Includes bibliographical references and index.
ISBN 978-1-62356-275-5 (hardcover: alk. paper) 1. Knowledge, Sociology of. 2. Knowledge management–Economic aspects. 3. Knowledge economy. 4. Democracy. I. Title.
HM651.I56 2013
306.4'2–dc23
2013005982

ISBN: HB: 978-1-6235-6275-5
PB: 978-1-5013-0278-7
ePUB: 978-1-6235-6033-1
ePDF: 978-1-6235-6664-7

Typeset by Fakenham Prepress Solutions, Fakenham, Norfolk NR21 8NN

For Juan Arana, a mathematician who does not calculate, anarchistic in values, and methodical in friendship.

Contents

Introduction: Governing Knowledge ... ix

Part 1 Overburdened Intelligence ... 1

1 Well-Informed Ignorance ... 3
2 Order and Disorder: A Poetics of Exception ... 17

Part 2 The Organization of Uncertainty ... 31

3 Knowledge and Non-Knowledge Societies ... 33
4 Knowledge in the Knowledge Society ... 47
5 The Dialogue between Knowledge and Power ... 65
6 Scientific Citizenship ... 81

Part 3 The Cognitive Challenge of the Economy ... 99

7 The Intelligence of the Economic Crisis ... 101
8 An Economy for an Incalculable World ... 119

Part 4 Geography of Creativity ... 139

9 The Value of Creativity ... 141
10 On the Concept of Social Innovation ... 161
11 The Governance of Smart Territories ... 183

Index ... 201

Introduction: Governing Knowledge

Knowledge is not merely a means of understanding reality, but a tool that allows us to live together. Its most important function is not to mirror a presumed objective truth or to adjust our perceptions to external reality, but to serve as our most powerful instrument when it comes to fostering democratic coexistence among human beings. In contrast to what is generally assumed, our most significant collective problems do not arise because of a lack of willpower, decisiveness, or morality. Instead, we should understand them as failures of cognition or as knowledge that is poorly organized from the point of view of its democratic legitimacy.

I do not share Richard Rorty's provocative thesis that democracy is more important than truth. There is no need to rank one above the other, much less declare them incompatible. What I am arguing in this book is, instead, an expansion of democracy to knowledge in two ways: 1) the issues that science seeks to clarify are relevant for all citizens; and 2) the fundamental problems facing any democracy—such as our solution to the economic crisis—are not problems of political will as much as they are cognitive failures that must be resolved with both a greater knowledge of the complex realities over which we govern and a fine tuning of the tools of governance. I began the exploration of this topic in my previous book, *The Future and its Enemies*,[1] where I addressed the idea that reflecting on the future is the best way to improve democracy. This book will extend that research by arguing that knowledge and other fields related to it (the politics of science and innovation, the advice given to governments, the assessment of public policy, the understanding of current social transformations, or the cognitive competence of regulators) are spheres where not only economic prosperity but, even more fundamentally, democratic quality is determined. Politics *of* knowledge and *through* knowledge has become a question of democratic citizenship, where numerous theoretical problems, especially the quality of our public space, are at stake.

The starting point of this book is the hypothesis that a knowledge and innovation society is characterized by a considerable increase in the number

---

[1] Daniel Innerarity (2012), *The Future and its Enemies: In Defense of Political Hope*, Sandra Kingery (trans.), Stanford: Stanford University Press.

of possibilities it faces and a corresponding increase in the contingent nature of its primary activities. Whenever we have to choose, decide, anticipate or entrust a task, the range of options tends to be so large that we can never be entirely satisfied that no relevant possibilities have been overlooked. Both individuals and societies as a whole are compelled to manage this explosion of opportunities in all its myriad forms (information overload, diversity of opinions, contradictory demands for legitimation, increasing options, a proliferation of risks, innovations with unforeseeable consequences, etc.), which is why the astute management of this excess of options occupies the majority of their time. The main challenge confronting individuals, organizations and society as a whole is to manage that excess of possibilities fairly and intelligently. The primary anthropological experience at the root of many of our social and political problems is an *overburdened intelligence*, which I analyze in the first section of this book. This section serves as an anthropological introduction to the concept of governing knowledge.

In this context, the most important political action is the *collective organization of uncertainty*, which is the subject of the second part of the book. A democratic society depends not only on legitimate decisions, but also on adequate knowledge. Problems of knowledge are political issues, and political problems are also, to some extent, cognitive problems. Questions about the legitimacy of a political oversight of knowledge and about the quality of knowledge underpinning that supervision are not mere theoretical concerns, but central dilemmas of what I call the democracy of knowledge. The reason I am addressing not only the governance of knowledge but also the organization of uncertainty is that what we celebrate as an explosion of knowledge and information must also be considered—given the lack of proportion between our limited knowledge and the problems we need to confront—a society of ignorance. It is safe to say that the principal controversies of the coming years will revolve around these types of issues: questions about what we know, what we do not know and all the incomplete knowledge on which we base our collective decisions.

The specific effort to create learning processes, a typical demand in knowledge societies, is particularly pressing in the economic sector. In the third part of the book, I develop the idea of the *cognitive challenge of the economy*, which the current economic crisis reveals. I believe it is most useful to consider the crisis as a sign of a huge collective failure when it comes to anticipating and managing risks generated by economic activity that is, in a manner of speaking, more intelligent than our regulatory instruments. We can only recover necessary cognitive competence by conceptually renovating the field and instruments of economics that are meant to be precise measures of something of which we are not entirely certain. If the economic sciences still aim to present a general theory about the social order, then they do not need precise calculation as much as a systemic vision. Our goal in this regard should follow the Keynesian axiom that it is better to be roughly right than precisely wrong. This is what I will call an economy for an incalculable world.

A knowledge and innovation society replaces the traditional educational ideals—to be perfect, to be well informed, to have a critical eye—with a new skill that we generally call *creativity*, which could be understood as the ability to modify our expectations when reality contradicts them rather than trying to convince reality to change. The last section of the book analyzes the multiple paradoxes engendered by this concept. *The Geography of Creativity* examines the distribution of creativity throughout society and the possibility that a society or place may be more intelligent than each of us individually. The cognitive turning point in the politics of space and in the government in general depends precisely on the fact that humanity's greatest challenge is no longer taming nature but ensuring that information and organization progress at the same rate.

Part One

Overburdened Intelligence

1

Well-Informed Ignorance

We talk about the knowledge society with great enthusiasm, without noting the new challenges and demands it entails or the skills that people and organizations need to acquire within it. Rhetoric about the knowledge society is endlessly optimistic, since knowledge is a resource that never seems to run out. We are accustomed to celebrating the accessibility of information as if it made us automatically wise, and we overlook the new ignorance to which the complexity of information seems to condemn us. I would like to emphasize the difficulties that having too many celebrations causes—and it is never a bad thing to have some spoilsport remind us of existing problems. I will also discuss some of the challenges of a knowledge society and some strategies for surviving within it. Only by confirming the paradoxes inherent to the knowledge society can we understand how it requires a particular management of ignorance.

1. Paradoxes inherent to the knowledge society

It is said that we live in an information or knowledge society, but we should admit just the opposite: ours is a society of disinformation and ignorance. In what sense? Not in the sense that there is some perverse booby trap designed to confuse us, but in a way that is simultaneously both more complex and more banal. Our ignorance is a consequence of three characteristics found in contemporary societies: the non-immediate nature of our experience of the world, the concentration of information, and the technology that intervenes between us and reality. Let us take a look at each of these in turn.

a) A second-hand world

The fundamental problem of the knowledge society is that, amazingly enough, it makes us all a little dumber; the contrast between what we know and what can and, especially, should be known is so marked that it would make more sense to call it a society of ignorance. Max Weber formulated it like this: "The 'savage' knows infinitely more about the economic and social conditions of his own existence than does the 'civilized man'" (2012, 301). We are more ignorant in the sense that, in other cultures, human beings knew very little, but that little bit was practically everything they could and should know. The knowledge that primitive people had was first-hand, immediate, and verifiable, while we enjoy the strange privilege of being surrounded by a series of things that are *known*, that *someone* knows, that are theoretically within our grasp, but that we ourselves do not know.

For people in other time periods, the world was more comprehensible and transparent than it is for us. Scientific progress makes it not easier but harder to comprehend the world, since knowledge makes information more complex. Furthermore, in a complex society, there are more things—devices, information, processes—that we have simply to accept as rational. The more complex a system, the more inevitable it is to have acceptance without understanding. Scientific knowledge has less and less to do with the way we live in the world, and the explanations science offers us do not mesh with our common sense. Black holes are as incomprehensible as nanoseconds; financial derivatives are as distant from our normal experience as are statistics on infant mortality in Ethiopia. We could say that the more we know as a species, the greater the distance between the world and common sense.

Our world is second-hand and mediated. It cannot be any other way: we would know very little if we only knew what we know personally. We make use of innumerable epistemological prostheses. Our cognitive growth is dependent on trusting and delegating. Secondary experiences have at least as much, if not more, of an impact as primary experiences when it comes to determining human lives. Almost everything we know about the world is known through specific intermediations. That is why the criticism that we are manipulated and poorly informed has a certain degree of plausibility, even if this criticism ignores the benefits of complexity and stems from nostalgia for a world that no longer exists.

b) Excessive information

One of the uncomfortable discrepancies in our world is a type of ignorance that is typical in advanced societies. It is produced by an excess of information and is designated by neologisms such as "infotrash" or "infotoxication." The specialization and fragmentation of knowledge has produced a plethora of information that is accompanied by a very slight increase in our comprehension of the world. Human knowledge doubles every five years. But in proportion to the available knowledge, we are increasingly less wise. We also find that the knowledge we have is not divisible, but demands an overarching perspective, which is increasingly difficult to attain. Connections between things frequently become unmanageable. Software designers call this "overlinking," an excess of references between different areas of knowledge. We know that everything is linked to everything and, therefore, nothing more is known. This theoretical perplexity finds its practical counterpart in the surfeit of options that complicate decision making, to the extent that we may be immobilized.

Enormous amounts of information and communication inform without giving any sense of direction. It is a paradox of privation in the midst of abundance. We live in the midst of such a bounty of information and our subjective capacity to assimilate it is so limited that our perplexity could be captured by Arnold Gehlen's statement that we live in a strange world about which we are only too well informed (1978, 310).

In a knowledge society, excess is the enemy. The American poet Donald Hall is right when he says that "information is the enemy of intelligence." Badly managed complexity is the new ignorance. Or better yet, as Weick (1995) says: "the problem is confusion, not ignorance." There is a type of impasse that stems from the very accumulation of information, because information does not distinguish between what makes sense and what does not. So what do we do when we do not know what we should do? We accumulate data, offer too many explanations, assume greater responsibilities, take more time, and so on. Accumulating information is a way of freeing ourselves from the uncomfortable task of thinking, because the instantaneity of information impedes reflection.

We live in an informative environment filled with a massive amount of data that does not provide direction. There is an excess of stimuli that have the appearance of information, but we are forced to make individual decisions whether to consider them information or not. There is no information without interpretation. Anyone who is wandering aimlessly through the media maze and accepting everything he or she hears or reads as information is not informed. The informed person is one who has learned to filter messages out of the flood of data that are relevant for his or her personal situation.

c) The submissive user

All the paradoxes of the knowledge society are summarized in the following statement: we live in a society that is more intelligent than each one of us. Knowledge is everywhere; there is more knowledge than we can know. We are surrounded by experts in whom we must trust, intelligent machines whose inner workings are a mystery to us, news we cannot personally confirm … In a world full of intermediaries, knowledge is presented to us in the form of indirect experience; rumors are the norm when knowledge is media-based (Marquard 1989, 94). Cyberspace is a giant rumor cooker, a consumer of other people's knowledge. Managing rumors and making use of other people's knowledge are habitual ways for us to experience reality.

In this respect, Kant described a common, concrete experience in an abstract manner: the I think must be able to accompany all my representations (2008, 94). One can spend one's whole life driving cars and typing on computers without ever having looked inside of one. The act, for example, of opening the hood of our car when it breaks down is simply a show of pride before we give in completely. It expresses nothing more than a primal resistance toward recognizing what we knew from the very beginning: we must call an expert as soon as possible. The self-mobility of our auto-mobiles has turned into other-mobility.

In the age of microelectronics, we find ourselves surrounded by black boxes into which there is no intuitive access. We have all felt the familiar desperation that comes from the incomprehensible language of the user guides for domestic appliances. We have long since abandoned a relationship with the world that Heidegger defined as "*Zuhandenheit*": an unproblematic, daily part of reality, ready-to-hand (1986, SZ 55). The things we had on hand would run out as we used them and were never thought of as objects. Compare that to any household appliance. Gadgets in a multimedia society are, in Hermann Sturm's precise expression, "prostheses of the no-longer-understood," declarations of the surrender of personal experience. In this world, use is no longer sovereign and obvious. We all embody the voluntary status of enslaved users. We give in to what we do not understand in order to make use of it. As with the world of economics and politics, in the world of technical objects, comprehension has been replaced by acceptance. Fortunately, the user surface removes the logical and mechanical depth of appliances from sight.

Use and comprehension of an instrument are two different things. Knowing how to use something is not the same as understanding it; one thing is "know-how" and another is knowledge. In the contemporary world, knowledge that is used but not understood is on the rise. The division of work that was typical in the industrial society has now been replaced by the division of knowledge in the knowledge society. The user is a client of simplicity. We do not want to know anything about the deeper logic of processors and programs; we prefer to remain on the pleasant surface of functionality. This affects our lifestyle in many ways. We have gotten used to taking things at the "interface value" (Turkle 1995); in other words, we trust them at a surface level. We do not search hidden depths for some essential core; we simply enjoy using the media. We accept not knowing what is inside the black box of the things and devices we use, whether they are cars or computers. This is what Helmut Schelsky called "fake familiarity," which we could call "consumer fideism." We are reminded of this at every turn (e.g. "only to be opened by an expert"; "consult your pharmacist"), which keeps us in our place as mere users and avoids complaints about being cheated. Paradoxically, our submissiveness affords us much more freedom. Being able to use more than we understand means that technology frees us from having to think and decide at every step. In the end, what technology does is introduce an automatism that is not "interrupted by decision" (Luhmann 2000, 370).

A product is intelligent when it is capable of concealing this chasm of ignorance in such a way that the user does not see it and is seduced by the simplicity of use. This is the idea behind all the advertizing that insists on ease of use, tactile or visual proximity. Instruments are comprehensible when they hide their technology. The success of many instruments depends specifically on the fact that they employ technology that is easier to use than to explain. In this way, they are similar to games, which explains why children are so comfortable in the universe of the new media and quickly become more competent than their parents—competence is not achieved by reading the instruction manual, but through the pleasure of use.

Only someone suffering from nostalgia could believe that this type of informed ignorance is fundamentally negative. By using tools that do our thinking for us, we have accomplished things we would never renounce. To say it in a slightly provocative manner: if it were necessary, our civilization could renounce intelligent people, but not intelligent objects. The progress of civilization is not driven by what people think, but by what they no longer have to think. The American philosopher Alfred Whitehead expressed it like this: "civilization advances by extending the number of important operations which we can perform without thinking about them" (1948, 41–2). Civilization advances to the extent that there are objects and procedures that allow us to act without having to reflect. This constitutes user confidence. The foundation of our civilization is submissiveness to that which is not understood. In this way, technology permits an ignorance that is not only inoffensive, but that we can even consider beneficial.

2. The management of knowledge

To understand how the aforementioned knowledge and its paradoxes are handled, we must distinguish between data, information, and knowledge. Only in this way will we understand that the management of knowledge requires more than producing data and exchanging information; it demands a design of knowledge.

a) The universe of data

An organization should have observational instruments that make it possible to generate data that concern the organization and its context. This is why people make an effort to obtain things such as satellite photos, economic indicators, census data, or a record of the state of world stock markets.

Although an excess of data is the most common situation, organizations may sometimes lack the data they need or the necessary observational instruments. For a few years now, there has been an emphasis on the practical relevance of data about the future possibilities of organizations. There tends to be little data about this because there are no useful observational instruments. In this sense, the development of new instruments such as the "Balanced Scorecard" is very promising. These new tools not only reflect hard, quantitative data, but also customer satisfaction, the quality of processes, the EFQM management model (which requires an annual review of its members), or the model of "rating," which indicates future capacity for payment, financial solidity, and future vulnerability.

The management of knowledge only prepares us for innovation if there are adequate instruments to measure the quality of organizations. Double-entry bookkeeping had a revolutionary effect on the economy because it modified the criteria for measuring a company's value. At a time of continuous changes, having criteria to measure quality is especially important, since only that which can be measured can be changed and because changes are only possible if we can take measurements with indicators that are relevant to the organization and its members. If, for example, the success of a business is measured by the value of its market shares, this means the company considers that measure relevant and will position itself in such a way that it can increase its market value. If the success of a particular public administration agency is measured by the number of cases it resolves, then the organization will try to increase that number and will pay scant attention to other possible indicators. When a university is considered successful because it maintains order and prevents problems, it will be managed in accordance with those criteria of relevance.

So the data depend on what the particular instruments and processes of observation allow us to "see." Strictly speaking, there is no data in and of itself, only data that depend on observations—in other words, data produced or constructed by observation.

In general, the biggest problem is not a lack of data, but a use of trivial indicators and a surfeit of irrelevant or senseless data. The majority of the data generated by organizations (e.g. records, balances, annual reports) are nothing more than a collection of "unintelligent" data. The data makes sense and is useful only when it is transformed into information.

b) Preparing information

The management of data demands mechanisms and routines for the reduction of its quantity and complexity. We must, then, move from data to information. Data becomes information when it is first introduced into a relevant context. Data must be codified in some way in order to exist. Given that relevance does not exist in and of itself, since every relevancy depends on a system, all information must be relative to a system. Different systems (teams, people, departments, organizations) can extract completely different information from the same set of data. There is only information when a system of observation has criteria of relevance at its disposal and is capable of conferring concrete relevance onto the data.

An organization should possess observation procedures and criteria of relevance for the construction of information; that is the only way it can take the ocean of data and generate information that is useful for the strategy and goals of the organization in any particular context. Many organizations have not understood this, and they talk about an exchange of information when they are actually referring to a mere transfer of data. The "exchange of information" that is so often talked about tends to be nothing more than an exchange of data that the actors in question transform into *different* information. A productive exchange of information is only possible when the actors and systems that are involved have first gone to the trouble of coordinating their criteria of relevance so they are speaking the same language.

What was said about data is also true for information, increasingly so as time goes by: there is an excess of relevant information, to such an extent that it is not easy to have a general vision or to understand or assimilate all the information. This increases the risk of choosing irrelevant or secondary information and not paying attention to what is truly important. That is why it is necessary to manage the search and selection of information in accordance with specific criteria and principles. This defines whether an organization remains a mere collector of information or whether it is capable of transforming the management of information into the management of knowledge.

Databanks are not the solution to the problem of information but the problem in and of itself. For some time now, we have had at our disposal all the information that is necessary, but accessing the stored knowledge is a difficult act of selection. In a knowledge society, problems generally do not stem from a lack of information but a lack of criteria when it comes to looking for information. Anyone can use Google to secure information, whether or not it is relevant. The gathering of information frequently discourages the person who needs to make a decision. It may well be that the more the person knows, the harder it is to make a decision. Another example to illustrate this difficulty stems from the policies of transparency. Transparency and access to documents are frequently invoked, but if one wants to know what is going on, what documents should be requested (Weiler 1999, 349)? Transparency is only real if those who govern, in addition to making data available, provide information.

c) The value of knowledge

Under pressure from information and communication technologies, we tend to think all problems stem from a lack of information. But questions of meaning cannot be answered by information. The transfer of information is only one part of human communication.

Information and knowledge are not the same, and information can even impede knowledge. This is because, first of all, new information does not necessarily lead to new knowledge. Information is only transformed into knowledge when it is properly processed, when it is used to make comparisons, draw conclusions, and establish connections. Knowledge can be understood as information that is accompanied by experience, judgment, intuition, and values. The mere accumulation of information with no coherent order or practical relevance does not constitute useful knowledge. "Knowledge is a structure that makes possible and facilitates the management of information" (Luhmann 1997, 124)—in other words, it accepts information as new or as irrelevant.

Information does not distinguish between what makes sense and what does not. An encyclopedia contains more information than the most intelligent person in the world. What it does not contain is knowledge. Knowledge is information with value, with a high degree of reflexivity. "Knowledge is not something you have. Knowledge is an activity. Knowledge demands appropriation rather than mere consumption. Information is something you have, and access to it demands little cognitive effort" (Stehr 2003, 47). Information "travels" and is transmitted without excessive impediments; it is more mobile than knowledge, less sensitive to context, more self-sufficient. "Information is reported; knowledge is produced" (Krohn 2003, 99). That is why the transfer of information should not be confused with the transfer of knowledge, because knowledge, in and of itself, cannot be transferred; it is actively generated.

We should adjust the quantity of information that is at our disposal. We must link data, facts, and opinions with recognized knowledge and elaborate a coherent image of the world. This is a skill that can be acquired; the world need not be buried beneath a garbage heap of information. Information must be converted into knowledge by assessing it with criteria of meaning. Access, ease of connection, availability should not be seen only as a threat, but also an opportunity. In a society that no longer depends on unquestionable traditions, people and organizations must get used to filtering any information that is meaningful to their lives and reformulating their routines on the basis of that personal appropriation. This is why we need innovation.

The principal difficulty that organizations confront in a knowledge society is not, paradoxically speaking, obtaining knowledge. It is freeing themselves from knowledge, combating the excess of information. More than anything, organizations must create systems that articulate knowledge, not systems that simply contain data.

d) Informative design

In this context of intermediaries, excessive information, and users, what is our most important skill? When direct experience is very limited, when the accumulation of data seems inconvenient and does not require knowing how devices work in order to use them, what we need are knowledge designers who make the information we have into something intelligible, converting it into knowledge. The most creative task is that of processing information. Programming and designing communicative spaces is much more valuable than mechanical work. The worker of the future, in a knowledge society, is a designer of information, someone who opens doors within the labyrinth of information. A knowledge manager forges new paths that can be traveled through the maze of stored material. His or her main service is "info-mapping": knowing where knowledge is found. Once we reach a specific point, information does nothing for us; it needs to be filtered, configured, and structured.

We continuously send, receive, store, and manipulate information. We are exposed to a stream of data about which we must ask what is important and what can be ignored. Data supply networks afford no answers to these questions. For that reason, in order to avoid drowning in information, we need techniques for selection and cognitive discrimination. That is the purpose of "cognitive maps" (Axelrod 1976), and we can presume that the demand for these knowledge maps will increase in the future. People's greatest skill will be their ability to choose. What we need are significant reductions in complexity. This is always a risky task because we know that any attempt at simplification reaches a critical limit when necessary reduction turns into excessive simplicity. But the need for intelligible simplification of the world continues to be our main challenge. This is why we can presume that books will continue to have a great future: books work as filters that choose information.

In this context, we should think, for example, about the use of media. Skill in using media is not only a question of knowing how to use devices and technology, as if that were enough to understand the world and act properly within it. These skills are necessary, but not sufficient. It is not only a question of knowing how to use media but of using them to create greater understanding and communication. This demands a thoughtful relationship with media, the ability to choose, a comprehension of symbols, the interpretation of signs, an economy of time.

In the end, a knowledge designer is someone who is dedicated to the search for correct questions. More interesting than searching for the answers to questions is formulating the questions to which those answers might apply. We must learn the art of questioning as the best technique for reducing complexity and determining that which is truly significant.

3. Reducing complexity, managing excess

A knowledge society is, as I have tried to show, a society that is more intelligent than we are. This means that the individual is, in a manner of speaking, the "bottleneck" of the information and knowledge society. We have at our disposal a variety of options that no longer correspond to our time resources. Possibilities and skills are in complete disproportion. In this situation, a type of fast-food thinking is imposed. The human measure today is transferred to the concepts of filtering and selection. Filtering reduces complexity to the extent that it disqualifies a certain amount of information as "noise." Noise is information about which you do not want to know anything. The primary difficulty is being accurate with the things you discredit as mere noise so you do not ignore something relevant. We are forced to make choices that are contingent and risky because we are confronted with the complexity of an enormous world.

Within the current flood of data, a correct reduction in information is our most valuable asset. Which are the best strategies to defend ourselves from the particular excesses that threaten us? What will the main educational goals be in a knowledge and innovation society? They could be summarized into two basic skills: managing attention and wiping out information.

Human beings have to manage attention because we are systems that elaborate information, not in a parallel fashion, but sequentially, one thing after another. We cannot normally do many things at the same time. In a situation of social complexity, the limits to the interactions between simultaneous subsystems are quickly revealed. We cannot talk on the phone and write a novel concurrently; it is impossible to pay attention to all sources of information with the same intensity. Those who have any organizational experience are familiar with a combination of procedures that stem from our limited ability to pay attention. That limitation forces a selectivity that can sometimes be painful.

Comparing all our resources, attention is the most scare, and managing it properly depends on a lot of factors. One simple technique consists of differentiating urgent tasks from less urgent ones; another method is not trying to control everything. At the same time, everyone knows that excessive information makes it very easy to waste time and that there is a point when the only thing an accumulation of data does is delay decisions. In organizations, the effective management of attention is especially important for those who need to see the big picture.

Richness of information and poverty of attention are two sides of the same coin. The greater the available information, the more important it is to manage our attention and the more limited the time we can dedicate to unmanageable amounts of information. The design of organizational communications has to do first of all with screening out irrelevant information when there is uncertainty and a lack of time. It is not a question of giving managers more information but, instead, protecting them from distractions. To fully understand this typical attribute of a knowledge society, we must keep in mind that acting in a world in which information is scarce is completely different from acting in a world in which, in contrast, it is attention that is hard to access.

The struggle against complexity frequently takes the form of an elimination of information. Human beings, through evolution or by specific techniques, are only capable of expanding their memory to a very small degree. That is why the greater the amount of what is, in principle, available knowledge, the greater the desire and even the necessity to not pay attention to specific information and to implement procedures to separate what deserves to be known from what does not. The art of properly forgetting is more important every day; it is the rationally justified rejection of information. The fact that the ability to prepare information is limited does not mean that there is no relevant difference between accidental "incompleteness," the result of bad preparation, and deliberate, designed incompleteness (Lindblom 1965, 519). Selectivity in the elaboration of information is certainly inevitable, but it can be structured in a way that makes sense.

In any case, we need to move from the excessive management of knowledge, developed with an eye toward perfection and completeness, to selective management. We need techniques that make it possible for us to move forward with incomplete knowledge. Society needs forms of culture to reduce that which is possible to that which can be developed (Luhmann 1997, 405). This is the reason for the idea of "rational ignorance" that stems from Anthony Downs and his economic theory of democracy (1957) or the incrementalist idea of the "-minded search" (Cyert and March 1963, 170) that refuses to engage in an exhaustive search of every possible alternative that could be considered for a specific problem.

Not knowing is rational when the costs of dealing with additional information are higher than their usefulness. The procedures to significantly reduce relevant information make it easier to focus on the most important things and ignore details and interconnections. Procedures like categorization, authentication, normalization, typification relieve us from the enormous effort that comes from treating every situation as if it were unique. As with stereotypes and categories, these procedures allow us to move through the world without making continuous decisions (Perrow 1970, 58).

It is not true that it never hurts to obtain more information. Excess is harmful; it distracts from what is most important; it can even get in the way of decision making. That is why we must destroy information, although it might seem to challenge the modern desire for knowledge.

But daily experience reveals that we are continuously establishing filters of relevance and selection. From the "no ads" notice on mailboxes to ordering the daily special at a restaurant, reduced-length instruction manuals, or turning to the canon of essential books, our life is full of ways in which to disregard certain information as noise that distracts us from that which is most crucial. Anyone with any work experience has learned that a waste basket is any organization's most essential tool. Or as Bateson said, "You cannot live without an eraser." The fundamental problem we face is that of intelligent discrimination: what must be omitted, disregarded, ignored. The most worthwhile knowledge is knowing what we do not need to know. Added value today means less information. We are looking for synthesis, general visions, the heart of the matter.

We cannot process all the information that comes to us. To make it possible to pay attention, we are forced to wipe out information. To that end, there is, first, the dynamic of forgetting and of organized ignorance, which are essential as filters of relevance and agents of selection. Of course, there is an element of risk when we destroy information, since the decision about whether the knowledge is worthwhile or not has to be made without knowing for sure.

Being well prepared in the current knowledge society means having developed a special ability to destroy information, not to think about, to forget. This, incidentally, is something that computers cannot do. Their preference is always to save; they resist forgetting. We can see this by the fact that, when given almost any order to delete, they insistently ask us "Are you sure you want to delete document X?" and by the fact that it is almost always possible to recover information that we thought had been deleted. Information is converted into something useful and meaningful by the specifically human way of processing information: by forgetting.

Bibliography

Axelrod, Robert (ed.) (1976), *Structure of Decision: The Cognitive Maps of Political Elites*, Princeton, NJ: Princeton University Press.
Cyert, Richard M. and March, James G. (1963), *A Behavioral Theory of the Firm*, Cambridge, MA: Blackwell.
Downs, Anthony (1957), *An Economic Theory of Democracy*, New York: Harper.
Gehlen, Arnold (1978), *Einblicke*, Frankfurt: Suhrkamp.
Heidegger, Martin (1986), *Sein und Zeit*, Tübingen: Niemeyer.
Kant, Immanuel (2008 [1787]), *Critique of Pure Reason*, J. M. D. Meiklejohn (trans.), Charleston, SC: Forgotten Books.
Krohn, Wolfgang (2003), "Das Risiko des (Nicht-)Wissen: Zum Funktionswandel der Wissenschaft in der Wissensgesellschaft", in Stefan Böschen and Ingo Schulz-Schaeffer (eds), *Wissenschaft in der Wissensgesellschaft*, Wiesbaden: Westdeutscher Verlag, 87–118.
Lindblom, Charles (1965), *The Intelligence of Democracy: Decision Making through Mutual Adjustment*, New York: Free Press.
Luhmann, Niklas (1997), *Die Gesellschaft der Gesellschaft*, Frankfurt: Suhrkamp.
—(2000), *Organisation und Entscheidung*, Opladen: Westdeutscher Verlag.
Marquard, Odo (1989), *Aesthetica und Anaesthetica: Philosophische Überlegungen*, Paderborn: Schöningh.
Perrow, Charles (1970), *Organizational Analysis*, London: Tavistock.
Stehr, Nico (2003), *Wissenspolitik: Die Überwachung des Wissens*, Frankfurt: Suhrkamp.
Turkle, Sherry (1995), *Life on the Screen: Identity in the Age of the Internet*, New York: Simon & Schuster.
Weber, Max (2012), *Collected Methodological Writings*, Hans Henrik Bruun and Sam Whimster (eds), Hans Henrik Bruun (trans.), New York: Routledge.
Weick, Karl (1995), *Sensemaking in Organizations*, London: Sage.
Weiler, Joseph (1999), *The Constitution of Europe*, Cambridge: Cambridge University Press.
Whitehead, Alfred N. (1948 [1911]), *An Introduction to Mathematics*, New York: Oxford University Press.

2

Order and Disorder: A Poetics of Exception

While working, the mind proceeds from disorder to order. It is important that it maintain resources of disorder until the end, and that the order it has begun to impose on itself does not bind it so completely, does not become such a rigid master, that it cannot change it and make use of its initial liberty.
(Valéry 1960, 714)

We live at a time when nothing—neither knowledge nor skills—is conquered with absolute security. Newness, the ephemeral, the rapid turnover of information, of products, of behavioral models, the need for frequent adaptations, the demand for flexibility all give the impression that we live only in the present in a way that hinders stabilization. Imprinting something on to the long term seems less important that valuing the instant and the event. That being said, thought has always been connected to the task of organizing and classifying, with the goal of conferring stability on the disorganized multiplicity of the manifestations of reality. In order to continue making sense, this articulation of the disparate must understand the paradoxes of order and organization. That is what has been going on recently: there has been a greater awareness of disorder and irregularity at the level of concepts and models for action and in everything from science to the theory of organizations. This difficulty is as theoretical as it is practical; it demands that we reconsider disorder in all its manifestations, as disorganization, turbulence, chaos, complexity or entropy.

These new trains of thought are meant to tackle non-linear dynamics, dissipative structures, fluctuation-induced order, habitual imbalance, complex and open systems, the emergence of new ideas, and relative stabilizations. Considering these matters requires the realization that order is hidden within disorder, randomness is perpetual, and the consideration of movement and its fluctuations is more meaningful than structures and constants. That is why, against a maximalist conception of order and against a definitive taxonomy according to which things find stable positions as part of a harmonic whole, we must elaborate something like a poetic epistemology of exception, based on the experience that order is often disadvantageous for life, that disorder and exceptions are cognitively rich, and that all classification is limited.

1. Disorganized knowledge

The most famous statement about the disorder of knowledge springs from Borges' imagination. There is, on the one hand, the oft-quoted text that cites the strange classification of animals in a particular Chinese encyclopedia; this text became the springboard for Foucault's *The Order of Things* (2012). The animals were divided into

> (a) those that belong to the Emperor, (b) embalmed ones, (c) those that are trained, (d) suckling pigs, (e) mermaids, (f) fabulous ones, (g) stray dogs, (h) those that are included in this classification, (i) those that tremble as if they were mad, (j) innumerable ones, (k) those drawn with a very fine camel's hair brush, (l) others, (m) those that have just broken a flower vase, (n) those that resemble flies from a distance. (Borges 1968, 103)

Borges has other stories about the impossible nature of libraries understood as exact memories of humanity or faithful representations of what is known. In "The Congress," for example, we are told of the unsuccessful efforts of a group of Latin Americans who decide to create a Congress of the World with a corresponding library but cannot come to an agreement about its composition. Enormous packages of uncataloged books pile up in a cellar. They finally decide to set fire to them and abandon the project after realizing that it has encompassed the entire universe (Borges 1977). Reality and the representation of reality came head to head over an insurmountable divide.

It is possible that Borges' insight is the source for many other stories that have made the classification of knowledge into a paradoxical, absurd, and impossible task. Among all the fanciful classifications that have been suggested to librarians in the postmodern era, Paul Braffort's *Les Bibliothèques invisibles* [*Invisible Libraries*] deserves mention. He proposes organizing books based on their literal titles, according to criteria such as colors (allowing the classification of books such as Simenon's *The Yellow Dog* or Queneau's *The Blue Flowers*), the calendar (which would unite titles like Bossuet's *Maundy Thursday*, Marx's *The Eighteenth Brumaire*, and Huizinga's *The Autumn of the Middle Ages*), or relatives (where we would find, for example, Dostoyevsky's *The Brothers Karamazov*, Harriet Beecher Stowe's *Uncle Tom's Cabin*, Bernhard's *Wittgenstein's Nephew*). Another criterion, more precise, but equally unsuitable for classifying and organizing knowledge, is found in Vladimir Nabokov's *Invitation to a Beheading*, where a prison librarian maintained a catalog that classified books according to their number of pages. These and other similar stories arise from the same cultural experience: when we emphasize the way useless or ridiculous aspects of order lead to arbitrariness, knowledge is seen as something that cannot be meaningfully organized, as something monstrous.

In this way, literature registers a problem that reveals some of the properties of knowledge in the contemporary world; it shows the humor of the situation faced by people in so-called knowledge societies. These stories would barely make sense in a more limited universe, without the quantity of knowledge we are forced to manage and the enormous difficulties that entails. Libraries and archives are clearly not merely places that store books and documents; more than anything, they are systems of classification and ordering based on a logic that evolves with the passing of time but that always tries to make knowledge available. These systems of order constitute classifications of the representation of knowledge. One example is the Porphyrian tree that persisted until Diderot, reflecting the complexity of knowledge and its articulation. There are new models now, like the net, the mind map, or the rhizome, that seem to have surpassed the previous model, which was rendered unusable by excessive hierarchy and simplicity. These models try to respond to the problem of how to think about the order and articulation of knowledge within a more complex scenario that cannot be handled with traditional library systematics. No internet search engine needs a hierarquization of concepts. The articulation of themes and content avoids any metastructure of logic without thus being reduced to chaos or complete boundlessness. Knowledge seems to float freely, beyond titles and rubrics. Its growing accessibility seems connected to the loss of meaning of all possible structures.

These and similar difficulties encourage us to rethink the organization of knowledge without hiding behind a comfortable ignorance of paradoxes engendered by any classificatory system. We will most likely be forced to abandon the idea of a cultural order in which every thing has its place, a transcendental and unquestioned order. Knowledge, like the social order, is always unstable, unprotected, and threatened; it is anything but an imperturbable conquest, protected in the face of all instability. Tranquility is also always deceitful in the ordering of knowledge, a truce with a limited lifespan. Stability has long deserved distrust and suspicion, even declarations of impossibility. At the same time, we seem to need a certain amount of order so we can come to an agreement with reality, and it is impossible to act without presuming that the conditions of the world will persevere, even if only to a small degree. With these conflicting demands and in the face of the growing complexity that a knowledge society poses, is it still possible to talk about regularity, order, and classification, and under what circumstances can we do so?

2. The inaccuracy of rules

The whole question of order and its complexity and possibility plays out in the clarification of what it means to follow a rule. There is already a longstanding debate about this question of rule following which, in more recent philosophy, has generated a series of concepts that to some extent attempt to problematize the simple distinction between order and disorder, between following a rule and breaking it, between the prohibited and the required. Thinkers like Luhmann (1964), Waldenfels (1987), Elster (1989), and Bourdieu (1987) coincide in talking about an ambiguous zone, a threshold, a space for play and maneuvering, for in-difference regarding the dichotomy of rule vs exception.

This question originated with Kant, who may have been the first to recognize the inevitable inaccuracy of the rules guiding human actions. His formulation centers on the problem of moving from theory to practice, which seems to symbolize the nucleus containing more general inaccuracies about human life. Kant understood that the idea of prescribing the application of the rule within the rule itself would lead to an infinite regress. In "On the Common Saying: That May Be Correct in Theory, But It Is of No Use in Practice" (1996, 280), he rejects the presumption that the step from theory to practice can be regulated with complete precision; there are no rules to determine if the rules apply in any given case. It is impossible to create an unambiguous rule about when and how to apply the rules. Answering that question requires a specific ability to make judgments; the application of rules always demands interpretation, creativity, and decision making, which implies a certain amount of inaccuracy similar to artistic intuition, ingenuity, or subtlety that Kant addresses in *Anthropology from a Pragmatic Point of View* (2006) as an ability regarding concrete matters. It is something that cannot truly be taught since teaching always depends on rules.

The other milestone on the topic is Wittgenstein's well-known analysis of rule-following. Wittgenstein claims that there are sometimes rules about applying rules (1958, 90; Arregui 1988); in other words, although there are times when we can use a second-order rule to regulate the application of first-order rules, the process of justifying an action with reference to rules has its limits. In this process of justification, there comes a time when subsequent rules can no longer be invoked and only action remains. The chain of reasons we can invoke to justify the way we are following a rule has a limit. At the end of the series of reasons or the end of the chain of rules that regulate how the rules must be applied, there is spontaneity in the action. A rule, no matter how many times it has been applied in the past, does not determine a particular way of acting in the present.

On the most fundamental level, this inaccuracy of rules is caused by their minimal ability to understand context. Rules can specify contexts, but that determination is always incomplete because, in the first place, contexts overlap and intertwine and, secondly, the contexts for the application of rules cannot be defined completely. Many of the errors we commit depend on a mistaken identification of context (Bateson 1983, 374). If, for example, an audience member decided to call the police or a doctor after hearing Hamlet talk to Ophelia about suicide, that would be a confusion of contexts. A librarian who catalogues *El santo al cielo* [*The Saint to Heaven*], Sánchez Ostiz's poetry collection, alongside religious books is making the typical mistake of paying attention to the literal meaning of words without observing the context surrounding them. Machine translation is of limited use for a similar reason. Understanding context requires intelligence, which cannot be replaced by machinery or a specific rule.

The truth we desire, as with goodness or justice, is not a matter of mathematical precision; instead, it is inscribed within a vital context without which it is unintelligible. Context gives human affairs a meaning that is richer and more complex than anything that will be achieved by the exactitude of automatic processes. There are things that are true, but inconvenient; others that used to be true, but no longer are; some are true, yet no one knows it; and in addition to what is true, there are things that are relevant, meaningful, interesting, and so on. The partiality and inevitability of contexts stems from locating things within areas of meaning that do not have exact rules. It is the same imprecision as we find in life, which makes us continually have to choose, interpret, and apply norms to any given situation. But the relationship between the rule and its application is subject to some paradoxes—noted in the philosophical tradition bookmarked by Kant and Derrida—according to which the application of rules not only fulfills the rules, but also complements, modifies, and suspends them. There is something like a self-deconstruction of the rules that corresponds with what Derrida called *différance*: the infringement of norms is a condition of possibility for their application, which also allows for the freedom to find something new. Following a rule always implies choosing between a selection of rules and, therefore, deciding which of them is the most relevant. The correct decision is not guaranteed by the rules themselves, and following one rule often means breaking others.

Any application of rules includes some breaking of those rules. There are traditional beliefs about the exception proving the rule; the end justifying the means; the rudeness of excessive punctuality and agreed-upon delays, *cum tempore*; *epikeia* in moral theology; allowing discretion in the application of norms and rules; etc. Why does the exception confirm the rule by breaking it? Because rules are not meant to be valid without exception; because the exception is not found outside the rule, but within it. In some ways, rules must foresee their own exceptions in order to maintain their elasticity and strength.

The idea of an infinite regress comes up again, in practice, when a system has to do something to regulate exceptions; many institutions have instructions in this regard. In these cases, the idea is to learn to handle events that are unusual, in other words, to extract the last hint of regularity out of irregular cases, creating something like a routine for the exceptional. It is a question of determining, for example, what we should do when faced with a catastrophe or how to regulate extraordinary circumstances. Regulating what needs to be done in extraordinary circumstances is, however, somewhat paradoxical, since it tends to make the exception into a regular situation, to normalize it: providing a rule for all exceptions, which would no longer be an exception for *that* rule. But any rule generates exceptions. And the exception cannot be regulated because an exception, to the extent it is unforeseen, is not fully anticipatable. In spite of that, in practice, we can create some explicit rules for extraordinary circumstances. This is the goal of "patterned evasions": establishing norms that regulate the breaking of norms. Its inevitable paradox becomes apparent in the special case of false alarms. When alarms become too frequent, they end up being ignored on a regular basis. They become routine, which can be fatal when the alarm ends up not being false. The sinking of the *Titanic* is one of the most notorious cases of this routine lack of concern in spite of the insistence of the alarm. Determining when we are faced with "extraordinary circumstances" is something that must necessarily remain somewhat unspecified, requiring the judgment discussed by Kant or, to say it with Gadamer, *sensus communis* (1989, 22).

If the application of rules is so imprecise, it makes sense to define creativity as a poetics of exception. The application of rules is an aesthetic activity to the extent that no rule contains the method of its application within itself. If a law contained the method of its application, then there would be no free play between the action and the law, and following a norm would be pure mechanical automatism that would leave no room for freedom in any relevant sense. In reality, we find it quite natural and obvious that rules are broken. Language is one example; its abilities cannot be reduced to a series of rules or procedures, as poetry or metaphoric processes remind us. Similarly, lawyers talk about "constructive interpretations," which attests to the fact that interpretation is always creative. The heuristic moment of reason indicates that there is a certain amount of knowledge involved in any application of a law, rule or order, and that rule following is mediated by the interpretation of the norm and presumes a specific ability that derives precisely from knowing how to use it. The fact that no rule contains its method of application within itself means that following a rule always implies a certain type of knowledge, an inventive ability that can be explained by analogy with the procedures of the poetic imagination. In the end, we will see that without imagination there is no good behavior or reasonable order, that goodness and truth have more to do with aesthetics than we thought.

3. Impossible repetition

A rule is a general procedure that implies a certain amount of repetition. The pursuit or application of rules is part of everyone's daily experience, from the tasks of a librarian to the decisions of a judge. Repetition plays a very important role for societies and groups in the organization of knowledge, the formation of conscience, and learning. Schütz discussed the anthropological usefulness of the "etcetera," without which we would incapable of any action (1971, 153). Rules and norms are a must for institutional stability because we need to know what to pay attention to in life, the expectation of repetition. "Doing the same thing under the same circumstances" means repeating; institutions and organizations establish repetition; rules are repeatable procedures.

This principle of repetition is still aporetic. Following a rule means acting in the same way under the same circumstances. "The use of the word 'rule' and the use of the word 'same' are interwoven" (Wittgenstein 2009, §225). But neither the circumstances nor the way of acting can ever be exactly the same. So we need to add "the same from a relevant point of view" or "the same in the essential," without being able to indicate what "relevant" or "essential" means here. This leads to areas of indeterminacy: criteria of similarity, proportion, relevance can only be obtained in a practical context and cannot be articulated as a definitive set of rules. Practice overcomes, exceeds, and deconstructs prescriptions. Wittgenstein, Bourdieu, and Derrida have shown this in the context of play. Peter Winch (1990), striving to make parts of Wittgenstein's philosophy relevant for the social sciences, affirmed that we can only know if two things should be treated the same way if we are told the context in which that question is raised.

This paradox makes repetition impossible. Kierkegaard, Deleuze, and Derrida have called attention to this fact by stating that repetition, action that is submitted to rules, is false: institutional assurance always implies fragility, the application of rules or imitation always presumes a singular creation, legislation always comes later. Kierkegaard declared: "The dialectic of repetition is easy, because that which is repeated has been, otherwise it could not be repeated; but precisely this, that it has been, makes repetition something new" (2009). Freud said something similar: repetition makes fixed something that cannot be fixed (2011). The pleasure children get from listening to the same story or repeating the same game stems from not having experienced cessation or the irretrievable; repetitions are still pure for them. Maturity seems to be a type of consciousness of the unrepeatable and, to use one of Lacan's expressions, repetition is a meeting that falls through, something like a missed encounter.

If all repetition—all regularity—is inevitably flawed, no matter how small this anomaly might seem, this would mean that something similar can be discovered in all apparent repetition. In cybernetics and systems theory, there is a concept used to explain this type of thing: recursivity. Conditions are set, then applied, but the application itself is reintroduced in the process of definition. There is an insistence on the particular, on the individual case, an idiosyncratic resistance that converts all science and all practice into an interpretive task. There is an interpretative moment that limits subsumption and relativizes generalizations; it recontextualizes. Referring specifically to the law, Derrida says that every case is other; each case needs a completely different interpretation; it cannot and should not be substituted by any existing, registered or codified rule (Derrida

1992). Otherwise, we would be confronting a mechanical operation. There has been, since at least the time of Heraclitus, some agreement about what repetition cannot, strictly speaking, be: identical reproduction. Repetition is never pure; it carries within it the mark of a constituent difference. There must be an increase, something additional, posterior, given that the application of rules is never a repetition in the sense of a guaranteed replica, or a mere reproduction.

4. Managing exceptions

The fundamental experience produced by the aforementioned themes is the consciousness of the finiteness of order and a radicalization of the idea of contingency. The most radical form of contingency refers to the very idea of order; not only is the place that something occupies within the established order contingent, but that very order could be different. The crisis of large mechanisms, the totalities according to which everything could be ordered, demands that we think about order and disorder differently. The discovery of complexity situates us before a panorama in which things are less and less describable and action becomes more conscious of its limits. Knowledge no longer constitutes a system of interpretation or a system of unifying action: it is fragmented and becomes more complex and more abstract. There is also a greater consciousness of the lability of constructions and orderings, which is expressed in experiences like fragility, loss of meaning, ambiguity, contingency, paradoxes, indetermination, zones where one cannot distinguish between the rule and its exception, between the rule and its violation, between normality and chaos.

Even though we do not possess common denominators, hierarchical principles or stable foundations that would allow us to unify the world in an orderly fashion, we can be sure that the time of simple organizational systems has already passed. Those who conceive of order only as a triumph over disorder and of disorder as a fault or a lack, as something essentially negative, display their unsuitability for managing complex matters adequately. People and institutions are divided between those who cannot stand order and those who cannot stand disorder. But intelligent behavior always moves between the two extremes, even beyond the opposition itself. There are many experiences that are not explained by this simplifying dichotomy. This is neither a question of ignoring the distinction between order and disorder or of hypostatizing it, but of treating it as a distinction that one must learn to negotiate. It is essential to think and act beyond a simple opposition between order and disorder, which attempts to force us to choose between rigidity and anarchy, as if there were no space for regulated anarchy or the articulation of independent elements between the two poles.

It is possible to conceive of disorder as something that allows handling in high contingency situations, in the midst of complicated and contradictory groupings. Dynamic contexts do not accept too much order; it ends up being punished as stagnation, perplexity, and a lack of creativity. "Order, if it wants to be considered a complex order, must be enriched with elements of disorder, with the strength of anarchy, with the resources of chaos" (Willke 2003, 9). Complex systems are precisely those that have "acquired the ability to bring order and chaos into a special kind of balance" (Waldrop 1994, 12). In the midst of that complexity, there is no choice but to risk being disorganized in order to articulate an architecture of order within complex systems. The fact is that a disorder within which one can still maintain control is already a type of order. There are established disorders; they become consolidated and give some direction. Following the Hegelian idea that identity comes from articulating identity and non-identity (Hegel 1986, 96), Luhmann has proposed defining order as the combination of order and disorder; systems are accidental places and routines (2002, 109) where heterogeneous coherences are established.

For that reason, order implies a partial domestication of disorder, which demands a certain amount of tolerance toward exception. This is why all management today is understood as "management by exception," and this ability is more and more in demand. There is a tacit breaking of the rules that is necessary for thought, action, and social organization. Not all rule breaking is an expression of arbitrariness or selfishness on the part of the actors, just as following the rules does not necessarily imply their correct assimilation (we can see this with outdated laws whose very fulfillment contradicts the spirit of the law, labor strikes that consist of fulfilling work obligations to the extreme, or appealing to the fact that one was obeying orders to escape responsibility for one's decisions; in addition, rules and procedures can allow one to apologize). There are deviations from the rules that help accomplish exactly what the rules are meant to achieve, in the same way that a literal application of the rules leads to a falsification of the logic of those very rules. Breaking the rules is a part of order in the same way holes make up fabric, like the net that is, according to the definition found in *Flaubert's Parrot* by Julian Barnes, a combination of intertwined holes. What if order was nothing other than the management of disorder and rules a collection of exceptions?

Everything seems to indicate that thought, action, society have no choice but to support a certain breaking of the rules, a transgression of the norm. The paradox could be softened if we added that the breaking of the rules can take place within certain limits, with the goal of assuring the flexibility of the whole. In that case, we could define some means for exceptions that, as is often said, would prove the rule: occasional carnivals that subvert order and hierarchies, introducing chaos into the territory of order and, by this means, affording it stability. Or localized and harmless deviations, rebellious spaces that do not create excessive pressure on the whole, etc. But exceptions specifically resist functionalization. This type of strategy does not constitute a definitive solution, since it demands that the exception be regulated, as if it were possible to escape from the threat that that particular regulation would be broken in turn. The marginal existence of areas of deviation, abnormality, and discrepancy are part of the nature of any cultural order regarding the officially regulated, and those marginal areas must necessarily remain fuzzy.

But absolutizing exceptions does not constitute a solution in the face of these imprecisions. The extrapolation of the idea that repetition is impossible leads to the hypostatization of difference, which returns us to the starting point. As Nietzsche already warned, the value of the exception would be lost if it were to become a rule (1980, 76). We cannot even console ourselves by believing, with Benjamin (1977, 697), that the exception is the true rule, because in that case, one would simply replace the other, and the way of thinking would remain the same. Converting the exception into a rule implies perpetuating the problem and abandoning the attempt to be less rigid in our articulation of the difference between order and individual cases. If disorder were absolute and everything an exception, there would be no exceptions, strictly speaking, because exceptions presume something anomalous from the established order. As with false alarms, an exception that becomes a norm ends up destroying its exceptional nature.

The peculiarities of order reveal the fundamentally heuristic nature of knowledge. If every individual case of a rule is always an *individual* case, in other words, a "special" case because it never stops being a singular example of a general rule, then every case is unique and contains something exceptional. In all knowledge, there is a practical exercising that is not practical training with specific routines and skills, but the acquisition of judgment about what is implied. In the end, it is nothing but what has, since Aristotle, been called prudence, and it could be interpreted as the management of the unexpected, the capacity for organization and improvisation, for articulating the general and the particular, creativity. The tradition ranging from Kant to Gadamer refers to this ability to conceive of judgment as an activity that contains a level of precision, of enhancement, constructive, creative, or brilliant. "At issue is always something more than the correct application of general principles" (Gadamer 1989, 34). The question about order ends up always referring to personal creativity and organizational inventiveness.

How, then, do we manage the unexpected? How do we prepare ourselves for the unexpected? How do we give order to exceptions? We do so in a quite limited fashion, because it is a fact of life and life's very flexibility that the use of norms, orders, and rules is open to the novelty and singularity of every situation. That is why the integration of organizations cannot be absolutely guaranteed through rules, institutional design, normative intentions, but does in fact end up being largely contingent, depending on that concurrence of emergency and self-organization to which modern theories of complexity allude. Complex, adaptive, dynamic systems realize order through fluctuation (Prigogine) with extremely unstable material (Luhmann). The difficulties of order also represent a possibility: better understanding the fluidity of the present, recognizing the ways in which order and disorder are intertwined, and giving way to new types of order that are more flexible. That type of order is not something that is conserved by protecting it from change. The management of disorder is not a defensive action or a restorative operation, but a conquest, a constant creation. Order represents the continuity of chaos by other means.

Bibliography

Arregui, Jorge V. (1988), "El papel de la estética en la ética," in *Pensamiento* (1988/44), 439–53.

Balandier, Georges (1988), *Le Desordre: Eloge du mouvement*, Paris: Fayard.

Bateson, G. (1983), *Ökologie des Geistes: Anthropologische, psychologische, biologische und epistemologische Perspektiven*, Frankfurt: Suhrkamp.

Benjamin, Walter (1977), *Gesammelte Schriften*, Frankfurt: Suhrkamp.

Borges, Jorge Luis (1968), "The Analytical Language of John Wilkins, in *Other Inquisitions* 1937–52, Ruth L. C. Simms (trans.), New York: Simon & Schuster, 101–5.

—(1977), "The Congress," in *The Book of Sand*, Norman Thomas di Giovanni (trans.), New York: Dutton, 27–49.

Bourdieu, Pierre (1987), *Choses dites*, Paris: Minuit.

Braffort, Paul (1990), "Les Bibliothèques invisibles," in *La Bibliothèque oulipienne*, 3, Paris: Seghers, 241–66.

Derrida, Jacques (1992), "Force of Law," Mary Quaintance (trans.), in *Deconstruction and the Possibility of Justice*, Drucilla Cornell, Michael Rosenfeld, and David Gray Carlson (eds), New York: Routledge, 3–67.

Elster, John (1989), *The Cement of Society*, Cambridge: Cambridge University Press.

Foucault, Michel (2012), *The Order of Things: An Archaeology of Human Sciences*, New York City: Knopf Doubleday.

Freud, Sigmund (2011), *Beyond the Pleasure Principle*, Todd Dufresne (ed.), Gregory C. Richter (trans.), Buffalo, NY: Broadview.

Gadamer, Hans-Georg (1989), *Truth and Method*, Joel Weinsheimer and Donald G. Marshall (trans), New York: Continuum.

Hegel, Georg W. F. (1986), *Jenaer Schriften 1801–1807: Werke 2*, Frankfurt: Suhrkamp.

Kant, Immanuel (1996), "On the Common Saying: That May Be Correct in Theory, But It Is of No Use in Practice," in *Practical Philosophy*, Vol. 8 of *The Cambridge Edition of the Works of Immanuel Kant in English*, Mary J. Gregor (trans.), New York: Cambridge University Press, 289–306.

—(2006), *Anthropology from a Pragmatic Point of View*, Robert B. Louden (ed. and trans.), New York: Cambridge University Press.

Kaulbach, Friedrich (1985), "Aspectos vigentes de la estética kantiana," *Themata* (1985/2), 5–10.

Kierkegaard, Søren (2009), *Repetition and Philosophical Crumbs*, Edward F. Mooney (ed.), M. G. Piety (trans.), New York: Oxford.

Luhmann, Niklas (1964), *Funktionen und Folgen formaler Organisation*, Berlin: Duncker & Humboldt.

—(1995), *Soziale Systeme: Grundriss einer allgemeine Theorie*, Frankfurt: Suhrkamp.

—(2002), *Das Erziehungssystem der Gesellschaft*, Frankfurt: Suhrkamp.

Morin, Edgar (1990), "Le dialogue de l'ordre et du desordre," in K. Pomian, *La Querelle du déterminisme*, Gallimard: Paris, 79–101.

Nabokov, Vladimir (1959), *Invitation to a Beheading*, Dmitri Nabokov (trans.), New York: Vintage.

Nietzsche, Friedrich (1980), *Die fröhliche Wissenschaft, Kritische Studienausgabe* 3, G. Colli and M. Montinari (eds), Berlin: Walter de Gruyter.

Schütz, Alfred (1971), *Gesammelte Aufsätze I: Studien zur phänomenologischen Philosophie*, Den Haag: Nijhoff.

Valéry, Paul (1960), *Tel quel*, Oeuvres II, Paris: la Pléiade.

Waldenfels, Bernhard (1987), *Ordnung im Zwielicht*, Frankfurt: Suhrkamp.

Waldrop, Mitchell (1994), *Complexity: The Emerging Science at the Edge of Order and Chaos*, London: Penguin.

Willke, Helmut (2003), *Heterotopia: Studien zur Krisis der Ordnung moderner Gesellschaften*, Frankfurt: Suhrkamp.

Winch, Peter (1990), *The Idea of a Social Science and its Relation to Philosophy*, London: Routledge & Kegan Paul.

Wittgenstein, Ludwig (1958), *The Blue and the Brown Books*, Oxford: Blackwell.

—(2009), *Philosophical Investigations* I, 4th edn, G. E. M. Anscombe, P. M. S. Hacker and Joachim Schulte (trans), Malden, MA: Wiley Blackwell.

Part Two

The Organization of Uncertainty

3

Knowledge and Non-Knowledge Societies

Knowledge, to the extent that it is considered crucial in the knowledge society, constitutes one of the fundamental questions of democratic citizenship. To address these issues, we must begin by analyzing the nature of the knowledge society and, concretely, the form of knowledge that has been generalized in it. How can we know if we are looking at a knowledge society or simply something that resembles it? If there is science and fashion, changes and novelties, patents and derived products, entrepreneurship and transgression, is that sufficient to call it a society of knowledge and innovation? There is an initial complication with celebrating the knowledge society as something new if we keep in mind that knowledge is a general human attribute and not a specific difference at a concrete point in time. Knowledge, understood as the ability to comprehend the surrounding environment through abstract reflection and the intentional accumulation of concrete experiences, is a property belonging to *homo sapiens* as such, and it explains our success relative to other living creatures. When does it make sense, then, to talk about the "knowledge society"? How can one identify the new role of knowledge in a society that could be distinguished from all previous societies precisely by knowledge? What is different about the particularly close relationship that exists between the economy and knowledge, a relationship so frequently referenced nowadays that it seems we are revealing a historically unprecedented combination?

Correctly answering these questions is divisive, but it is equally vital to understand the function of ignorance in a knowledge society, the importance of ignorance for the acquisition and reproduction of knowledge, for the emergence and change of institutions. Ignorance is not merely a shortfall when it comes to decision making but an opportunity for creative action. A knowledge society is, from the start, a society that "produces" ignorance to the extent that it questions and destabilizes traditional positions; the flipside of innovation is the production of superseded knowledge and obsolete practices. Science and research are no longer authoritative or definitive but, to the extent that they articulate new knowledge, they are producers of uncertainty and instability. A knowledge society is a society in which collective intelligence consists of prudently and rationally managing the ignorance in which we are forced to live; in other words, it is, in the end, a non-knowledge or ignorance society. We could formulate it less dramatically by affirming that it is a society in which we have no choice but to learn to operate with incomplete knowledge.

1. A world made of knowledge

Although there are reasons for skepticism when a change of epoch is announced, no one will dispute that we can observe gradual changes toward a centrality of knowledge in our societies. The transition of organizations and societies toward knowledge in the emphatic sense is revealed by the fact that, alongside the traditional infrastructures of power and money, knowledge is gaining importance as a government resource and mode of operation. The traditional factors of production (land, labor, capital) lose importance in the face of expert knowledge; knowledge management is becoming the most relevant form of labor in advanced societies, while more traditional forms of labor are carried out by machines or delocalized to destinations with lower salaries. For this reason, we talk about a knowledge society when new forms of knowledge and symbolization pervade all essential social sectors qualitatively, when a society's structures and processes of reproduction are filled by so many activities dependent on knowledge that operations that elaborate information, symbolic analysis, and expert systems are more important than other factors of production.

But reducing knowledge to an economic resource does not do justice to the full complex meaning of knowledge in today's society. This is because the cognitive components of action are more and more important. In the end, we live in a *world made of knowledge*: the majority of what we currently call knowledge or learning does not entail a direct relationship with things, but objectified knowledge—in other words, the knowledge that mediates between people and nature, in language, databases, books, devices, etc.

The growing intensity of knowledge asserts itself in diverse areas of work and organization. From the social point of view, the emergence of a knowledge society is explained by the presence of different phenomena: the advent of intensive knowledge (patents, advising, training, new media, financial services) or new business spaces in the third sector, the birth and expansion of new technologies (information technology and bio- and nanotechnologies), the spread and application of technical scientific research, the acceleration of innovative processes (with a corresponding decrease in the length of time knowledge is valid), the growing importance of calculation procedures (rating, auditing, benchmarking), the change in the form and content of qualifications (lifetime learning, new abilities like "soft skills").

The origin of the knowledge society is linked to the transformation of the social production of knowledge. From this perspective, the knowledge society is not merely characterized by the growth and application of knowledge or caused by the increasing importance of science. More distinctive than all that is the generalization of the type of scientific research activities in the sense of systematic and controlled reflections and revisions of knowledge. The knowledge society is defined by the institutionalization of reflexive mechanisms in all the different social fields that become instruments of learning in society. The principle of research, of manipulating information in order to learn, has become a generalized way of acting in today's society. If the knowledge of previous societies rested on rules that were transmitted without question and if learning took place in an unplanned or informal manner, today's society finds itself increasingly controlled by the imperative of a learning driven by active experience. The generalization of research means that hypothetical thought and experimental activity have left the isolated world of the laboratory; they have spread throughout society and are practiced in many places where action is based on knowledge. No cultural space, no institution or ideology can survive without research, in other words, without the willingness to delve into an area with few certainties, but rich in arguments, risk, and creativity.

What is most important, then, when it comes to characterizing a society as a knowledge society are not devices or people's qualifications, not even the value of the knowledge of products and services. What is decisive is *the type of knowledge* that is considered central in knowledge societies, concretely, the creation and organization of knowledge that is particularly active and reflexive (Giddens 1991). There are societies that have known a lot but do not deserve to be called knowledge societies because their knowledge was generally passive and non-critical, transmitted through authorized tradition. The knowledge that is currently modifying our societies is not old knowledge, accumulated and non-reflexive, but *new* knowledge. We are undergoing a change of emphasis that is making us switch from the application of *existing* knowledge to the creation of *new* knowledge. A knowledge society is characterized by the fact that the knowledge that is necessary for its operation is no longer principally based on experience; it is generated through active learning processes. The knowledge on which we must focus our efforts is a revisable and revised knowledge, inseparably accompanied by ignorance, which means it always contains specific risks.

Reflection is distinguished from the mechanisms of recalling experiences by other social forms of the past, as well as by modern rationalization as understood by Max Weber. Experiences are no longer carried out passively, but prospectively, through an investigative attitude, in a systematic and reflexive manner. The means of reproducing knowledge is not carried out through application but through the strategic production of knowledge. That is why it is situated at the epicenter of the category of innovation, in which new technologies, organization and communication, and the solution to ecological problems all play an important role.

Instead of defining knowledge as something people own or something they can dispose of—which is more closely aligned with the concept of information—knowledge should be considered action, something that human beings do. Knowledge is an activity; it presumes appropriation and not only consumption. Information is possessed, and accessing it does not impose special cognitive demands. We talk about the *transfer* of information, but the idea that something like a transfer of knowledge can exist is rather doubtful. Information "travels" without too many impediments; it is mobile, general and unaffected by context. The true transfer of knowledge, on the other hand, is connected to a process of discovery and learning, which is not at all automatic, despite what the concept of transference seems to imply.

In a knowledge society, managing learning processes is more important than administering knowledge. In highly differentiated systems, which confront enormously complex problems, the need arises to transform chance learning processes into an organized conquest of knowledge. This reflexivity of knowledge modifies the style of knowing, which stops being a mere application of transmitted knowledge and becomes the discovery of prospective knowledge.

Luhmann described this same process in a different manner when he established a supremacy of knowledge over prescription: in large parts of society, such as science, technology, the economy, or the media, there is an increase in the meaning of a type of expectations we could call *cognitive*, adaptive, focused on learning, while normative and prescriptive expectations are decreasing. He summarized the contrast in this way: "cognitive expectations try to change themselves; normative expectations want to change their objects" (Luhmann 1991, 55). Cognitive expectations contrast with normative expectations in the ways in which they consider and manage deceptions; this presumes a completely different consideration of learning. From this point of view, we can only call a society a knowledge society if modes of learning guided by cognitive expectations are widespread.

For this reason, a knowledge society is not only characterized by better education, more intelligent products, or knowledge-based organizations. A knowledge society also implies a change in the meaning of knowledge and intelligence at the level of its diverse social systems, such as politics, law, education or health care. One of the characteristics of the modern age was that science had exclusive competence when it came to producing, assessing, and reviewing knowledge. Other social systems incorporated new knowledge in a manner influenced by, for example, political advising or expert opinions. Currently, on the other hand, this strict division of labor has dissipated, and there is a proliferation of "centers of expertise" (Jasanoff 1990). The scientific system is no longer in any position to control the production and application of specialized knowledge that is produced in "other" contexts. The disappearance of the conventional division of labor between those who produce knowledge and those who apply it, between designers and users, has led to what we could call a reintroduction of peripheral knowledge in the creation of knowledge.

This is why universities, which have augmented their degree of importance in the knowledge society, have lost their monopoly as a central institution for the production of knowledge; other institutions that produce knowledge and that have a more immediate relationship with practice compete with them. Of course, universities are still the principal institutions of institutionalized knowledge, which has particular relevance in an unstable society. But knowledge production at universities is polycentric. This explains why, for example, the greatest innovations of corporate governments or financial institutions are not produced in the research centers designed for that purpose, but in hybrid spaces of reflection and action. In comparison to these spaces, universities are slower or on the defensive. The production and legitimation of knowledge has been liberated from the academic system.

The knowledge society is defined as one in which reflexive mechanisms have been institutionalized in all social arenas. These reflexive mechanisms are differentiated from the way experience was typically accumulated in past social systems by the fact that experiences are not carried out or received "passively," but in a prospective fashion, with innovation, selectivity, and reflection. Social innovations are developed under the imperative of learning that is directed by active experience. To allow for strategic action, the future is anticipated through models and simulations, deviations from expected results are researched systematically, data is processed and explained, etc. Systematic knowledge and methods for its production have acquired a central role in contemporary societies. This type of society identifies itself by the centrality that active learning and the generalization of scientific research has acquired within it.

A knowledge society is characterized by a generalization of the type of activities that make up scientific research. Systematic, controlled reflection (which used to be almost exclusively the purview of science and the university) becomes a generalized principle of action throughout society. The positions, norms, and values that used to be transmitted without question are offered up for reflection with a view to the future production of knowledge in all social systems (the economy, art, law and politics, but even religion). This feature of contemporary societies can be characterized as the "scientification" (Weingart 1983) of society or, more exactly, as "reflexive modernization" (Beck 1996). That being said, it is important to clarify that a knowledge society is not a science society. In modern societies, no social system—whether it be politics, the economy, or science—can represent every aspect of society without deforming society as a whole. The procedures of science, especially its methodical work with innovative knowledge, have been generalized, but this does not mean that the specificity of diverse social systems has disappeared.

The biggest challenge of a knowledge society is the creation of collective intelligence. What used to be a division of labor in industrialized societies is now a division of knowledge, in other words, the articulation of knowledge that is spread throughout society. A knowledge society is, from this point of view, a society that is particularly interested not so much in whether its component parts are intelligent as whether the society as a whole is. Forms of collective intelligence are found in the crystalized experience of technological instruments or in social practices, in memories of "epistemic communities," in institutions and organizations, in common procedures and rules, in languages, cultures, and symbols. Collective intelligence designs an emerging attribute of social systems that does not stem from the mere aggregate of individual intelligences; it is, instead, an intelligence that belongs to the system as a whole.

2. The non-knowledge society

That being said, it is important not to mistakenly believe that the knowledge society is a celebration of knowledge and forget that the other side of this reality is a form of ignorance that is also very typical of it. If we think about questions like financial governance or climate change, maintaining the label "knowledge society" may be too pretentious or should be understand not so much as an achievement but as a demand to confront our principal problems by improving our cognitive capabilities. Knowledge societies have transformed the idea of knowledge so radically that one might rightfully now call them "non-knowledge societies." In other words, these are societies that are increasingly aware of their store of non-knowledge, and they make progress not by increasing their knowledge but by learning to manage various forms of ignorance: doubt, probability, risk, and uncertainty. There is uncertainty about the risks and consequences of our decisions, but also about rules and legitimacy. New and diverse forms of uncertainty are making an appearance; these refer not just to that which is not yet known, but also to things that cannot be known. We cannot generate appropriate knowledge for every potential problem. A small portion of existing knowledge is supported by unquestionable facts, but the rest of it depends on hypotheses, premonitions, or circumstantial evidence.

But there is another more dramatic aspect of this ignorance that has to do with the fact that the tasks that are undertaken include unknown and partially unknowable dimensions: side effects and unforeseen consequences that must be managed in environments of great complexity, interdependence, and deterritorialization in future scenarios that are difficult to anticipate. One of the fundamental questions about collective ignorance refers to "systemic ignorance" (Willke 2002, 29). This involves social risks, futures, a collection of actors, and too many events related to too many events, in such a way that the ability of individual actors to make decisions is overwhelmed.

This return to uncertainty does not mean that contemporary societies depend less on knowledge. Quite the opposite. Their dependence on it is greater than ever; what has changed is science and knowledge in general. For some time now, more and more attention has been given to a series of things that could be interpreted as "the weakness of science": uncertainty, contextuality, interpretive flexibility, non-knowledge. At the same time, the problems we are confronting are different, thus changing the type of knowledge we need. In many areas, we must resort to theories that make use of models of probability but have no precise long-term forecasts. When it comes to the most serious issues affecting nature or the fate of humankind, we face risks for which science provides no definitive solution. What science does do is transform ignorance into doubt and uncertainty (Heidenreich 2003, 44). Science is in no position to free politics from the responsibility of having to make decisions under conditions of uncertainty.

Even though the sciences have helped greatly expand the quantity of reliable knowledge, when it comes to highly complex systems such as the climate, human behavior, the economy or the environment, it is becoming increasingly more challenging to obtain causal explanations or accurate predictions. This is because our cumulative knowledge also brings to light the infinite universe of non-knowledge. This process of the weakening and pluralizing of knowledge is probably what is behind the crisis in politics and the erosion of state authority. We will not be able to recover knowledge's ability to configure the world until we manage to reformulate power alongside the new forms of knowledge. A society of risk demands a culture of risk.

Modern society has long relied on being able to adopt political and economic decisions on the basis of rational and socially legitimated (scientific) knowledge. Persistent disputes about risk, uncertainty, and non-knowledge, as well as continuous infighting among experts, have increasingly and irreversibly destroyed this confidence. Instead, we are aware that science is very often not sufficiently consistent and reliable to make objectively indisputable decisions that can be socially legitimized. Consider, for example, risks related to health or the environment, which can generally only be identified with great uncertainty. For this reason, decisions about these matters must not depend on knowledge as much as on a justified, rational, and legitimate handling of ignorance.

The knowledge model, which has been in use until now, was naïvely cumulative; the assumption was that new knowledge could be added to previous knowledge without undermining it, thereby gradually diminishing the boundaries of the unknown and increasing the calculability of the world. But this is no longer the case. Society's dynamic principle is no longer a continuing increase of knowledge and a corresponding decrease of the unknown. There is an entire set of non-knowledge produced by science itself, a "science-based ignorance" (Ravetz 1990, 26). This non-knowledge does not stem from a temporary lack of information, but is the result of the advancement of knowledge. That very non-knowledge (regarding the consequences, scope, limits, and reliability of knowledge) is increasing at a more than proportional rate (Luhmann 1997,

1106). If the dominant means of combating ignorance used to demand eliminating it, the current approach assumes that there is an irreducible dimension to ignorance. Thus, we must understand, tolerate, and even make use of ignorance, viewing it as a resource (Smithson 1989; Wehling 2006). We have one example in the fact that in a knowledge society, the risk posed by "confidence in other peoples' knowledge" has become a key issue (Krohn 2003, 99). Knowledge societies can be specifically characterized as societies that must learn to manage this ignorance.

The boundaries between knowledge and non-knowledge are neither unquestionable nor obvious nor stable. In many cases, questions about how much we can still know, what can no longer be known, or what will never be known are still unanswered. This has nothing to do with typical Kantian humility about how little we know and how limited the scope of human knowledge. It is less precise than Merton's "specified ignorance," which focuses on weak forms of ignorance, such as the ignorance that is assumed or feared, the ignorance of not knowing *what* we do not know or *the extent to which* we do not know. We are often ignorant about what might happen, but also even about "the area of possible outcomes" (Faber and Proops 1993, 114).

The appeal to "unknown unknowns" that are beyond the scientifically established hypotheses of risk has become a powerful and controversial argument in social debates on new research and technologies. Of course, it is still important to expand the range of expectation and relevance so as to distinguish the areas of non-knowledge that we had not seen until now and to begin discovering "unknown ignorance." But this goal should not make us slip into the fantasy of believing that the problem of unknown unknowns can be resolved in a traditional manner, such as making it completely disappear through more and better knowledge. Even when the relevance of unknown unknowns has been explicitly acknowledged, we still do not know *what* is not known and *whether* anything that is unknown is crucial. Knowledge societies have to accept the idea that they will always need to face the issue of unknown unknowns; they will never be in a position of knowing whether or the extent to which the "unknown unknowns" they are necessarily faced with are relevant.

As Ulrich Beck cautions, this "time of side effects" is characterized not by knowledge, but by non-knowledge (1996, 298). This is the real social battleground: those who know and those who do not, and the ability to recognize and challenge knowledge and non-knowledge. If we look closely, the most important political confrontations nowadays stem from distinct assessments of non-knowledge or the uncertainty of knowledge. Society disagrees over appraisals of fear, hope, illusion, expectations, confidence, crises, none of which have an indisputable, objective correlation. The effect of this controversy is to place emphasis on those dimensions of non-knowledge that accompany the development of science; on its unknown consequences, issues that are left unresolved, limitations on validity, and so on. These controversies generally revolve not around knowledge itself, but the non-knowledge that inevitably accompanies it. When people discuss contrary or dominant knowledge, this is precisely what they are doing: "drawing attention to ignorance," (Stocking 1998), emphasizing the things we do not know.

This "politicization of non-knowledge" (Wehling 2006) has, for example, become apparent within the framework of disputes on technology policy that have taken place since the 1970s. Not only did we become more aware of the importance of the unknown, but this perception and its corresponding assessment became increasingly more disparate. What essentially inspired fear in some people inspired high expectations in others. While some people spoke about a short-term cognitive deficiency, others understood that there were things we could never know. This all took place at a time when we were realizing that science produced not only knowledge but also uncertainty, "blind spots," and non-knowledge. The fears and anxieties that flavor a good deal of public opinion are not entirely unfounded, as advocates of zero-risk technology tend to assume. Behind society's rejection of some technical options, there is often a perception of a particular uncertainty or lack of knowledge that science and technology should acknowledge. In this and other similar conflicts, divergent and even incompatible perceptions of non-knowledge collide.

From this point forward, our biggest dilemmas will revolve around "decision-making under ignorance" (Collingridge 1980). Making decisions under ignorance requires new forms of justification, legitimation, and observation of consequences. How can we protect ourselves from threats against which, by definition, we do not know what to do? And how can we do justice to the plurality of the perceptions of non-knowledge if we do not know the scope and relevance of what we do not know? How much non-knowledge can we afford without unleashing uncontrollable threats? What ignorance should we consider relevant and how much can we ignore as harmless? What particular balance of control and chance is acceptable in terms of responsibility? Regarding what we do not know, is it a carte blanche for taking action, or conversely, a warning that maximum precautions should be in place?

Societies confront non-knowledge in different ways. From a social standpoint, they react with disagreement; f rom a temporal standpoint, with provisional understanding; f rom an objective standpoint, with imperatives to try to prevent the worst case scenario. Consider the case of the "precautionary principle," now a part of European Union treaties and international agreements such as the Rio Declaration on Environment and Development. These agreements suggest that there should be no delay in the adoption of efficient measures to avoid serious, irreversible damage such as climate change, even though the scientific evidence is not complete. However, the precautionary principle remains a controversial rule with widely divergent interpretations. In any case, such an approach is interesting in so far as it explores the consequences of certain decisions, the likelihood a particular type of destruction will take place, the criteria under which these negative consequences may be acceptable, and the search for possible alternatives.

We are now living with the paradox that knowledge societies have destroyed the authority of knowledge. Knowledge is becoming pluralized and decentralized; it is more fragile and debatable. But this has a necessary effect on power because, following Bacon's principle, we were accustomed to the idea that knowledge strengthens power, whereas the exact opposite is true today: knowledge weakens power. There has been a growing pluralization and diffusion of knowledge, de-monopolizing it and opening it to dispute. Along with the scientific research that has traditionally taken place at universities, new ways of knowing are appearing from a diverse set of social agents, such as the knowledge of NGOs, the professional skills of citizens, the knowledge of various social subsystems, the accessibility of information, the multiplication of expert knowledge, and so on. To the extent that the production of knowledge is diversified, the possibility of controlling these processes decreases. Knowledge societies are characterized by the fact that more stakeholders also wield increasingly diverse background knowledge; these informed participants are in a position to assert their own knowledge when confronting government projects. Instead of an increase in certainty, we have a multitude of cacophonous voices discussing their claims to knowledge and their definitions of non-knowledge.

Jasanoff uses the term "technologies of humility" (2005, 373) to talk about an institutionalized way of thinking about the frontiers of human knowledge—that which is unknown, uncertain, ambiguous, and uncontrollable—acknowledging the limits on prediction and control. A similar approach encourages us to consider the possibility of unforeseen consequences, to make explicit the normative features that are buried within technical decisions, to recognize the need for collective learning and multiple points of view.

In this context, rather than the traditional image of a science that produces objective "hard" facts, pushing back ignorance and telling politics what to do, we need a type of science that will cooperate with politics in the management of uncertainty. For this reason, we must develop a reflexive culture of uncertainty that does not perceive non-knowledge as the outer edge of the yet-to-be investigated (Wehling 2004, 101), but as an essential part of knowledge and science. We shall not regard that which is not known, uncertain knowledge, the merely plausible, non-scientific forms of knowledge, and ignorance as imperfect phenomena but as resources (Bonss 2003, 49). There are times when, in the absence of safe and secure knowledge, cognitive strategies must be developed in order to take action within the bounds of uncertainty. Among the most important types of knowledge are risk assessment, management, and communication. We must learn to operate in an environment where the relationship between cause and effect is not clear, but fuzzy and chaotic.

These are the profound reasons for which a democracy of knowledge is not governed by expert systems but by the integration of those expert systems into larger government procedures, which necessarily include decisions in areas where ignorance is unyielding. Our principal democratic controversies revolve around determining precisely what ignorance we can accept, how we can reduce ignorance through precautionary measures, or the risks we would be wise to assume. We are faced with the challenge of learning to manage the uncertainties that can never be completely eliminated, transforming them into calculable risks and learning possibilities. Societies today must develop not only the ability to solve problems but also the ability to respond appropriately to the unexpected. It will not be an easy task, but we can console ourselves by remembering that we are a "non-knowledge society," not because we know little, but because what we know pales in relation to the size of the issues we have decided to undertake.

Bibliography

Beck, Ulrich (1996), "Wissen oder Nicht-Wissen? Zwei Perspektiven reflexiver Modernisierung," in Ulrich Beck, Anthony Giddens and Scott Lash, *Reflexive Modernisierung: Eine Kontroverse*, Frankfurt: Suhrkamp.

Bonss, Wolfgang (2003), "Jenseits von Verwendung und Transformation," in H. W. Franz, J. Howaldt, H. Jacobsen and R. Kopp (eds), *Forschen — lernen — beraten: Der Wandel von Wissensprodukction und transfer in der Sozialwissenschaften,* Berlin: Sigma, 37–52.

Collingridge, D. (1980), *The Social Control of Technology,* New York: St. Martin's Press.

Faber, Malte and Proops, John L. (1993), *Evolution, Time, Production and the Environment,* Berlin: Springer.

Giddens, Anthony (1991), *Modernity and Self-identity: Self and Society in the Late Modern Age,* Cambridge: Polity Press.

Heidenreich, Martin (2003), "Die Debatte um die Wissensgesellschaft," in Stefan Böschen and Ingo Schulz-Schaeffer (eds), *Wissenschaft in der Wissensgesellschaft,* Wiesbaden: Westdeutscher Verlag, 25–51.

Japp, Klaus P. (1997), "Die Beobachtung von Nichtwissen," *Soziale Systeme* 3 (2), 289–312.

Jasanoff, Sheila (1990), *The Fifth Branch,* Cambridge, MA: Harvard University Press.

—(2005), "Technologies of Humility: Citizen Participation in Governing Science," in Alexander Bogner and Helge Torgersen (eds), *Wozu Experten? Ambivalenzen der Beziehung von Wissenschaft und Politik,* Wiesbaden: Verlag für Sozialwissenschaften, 370–89.

Krohn, Wolfgang (2003), "Das Risiko des (Nicht-)Wissen: Zum Funktionswandel der Wissenschaft in der Wissensgesellschaft," in Stefan Böschen and Ingo Schulz-Schaeffer (eds), *Wissenschaft in der Wissensgesellschaft,* Wiesbaden: Westdeutscher Verlag, 87–118.

Luhmann, Niklas (1991), *Soziologische Aufklärung* 2, Opladen: Westdeutscher Verlag.

—(1997), *Die Gesellschaft der Gesellschaft,* Frankfurt: Suhrkamp.

Ravetz, Jerome R. (1990), *The Merger of Knowledge with Power: Essays in Critical Science,* London and New York: Mansell.

Smithson, Michael (1989), *Ignorance and Uncertainty: Emerging Paradigms,* New York: Springer.

Stocking, S. Holly (1998), "Drawing Attention to Ignorance," *Science Communication* 20, 165–78.

Wehling, Peter (2006), *Im Schatten des Wissens? Perspektiven der Soziologie des Nichtwissens,* Konstanz: UVK Verlagsgesellschaft.

Weingart, Peter (1983), "Verwissenschaftlichung der Gesellschaft, Politisierung der Wissenschaft," *Zeitschrift für Soziologie* 12 (3), 225–41.

Willke, Helmut (2002), *Dystopia: Studien zur Krisis des Wissens in der modernen Gesellschaft,* Frankfurt: Suhrkamp.

4

Knowledge in the Knowledge Society

All human progress is accompanied by the dark shadows where the imagery of disasters is cultivated. As knowledge increases, the corresponding fear of a secret threat lying in ambush right behind that knowledge also grows. We have an increased ability to travel, communicate, understand, and make our opinion heard, but we are increasingly convinced by the suspicion that our power is illusory and drawn to speeches denouncing the repressive measures employed by powerful institutions against helpless individuals. We buy into rhetoric about the way the biggest and most powerful institutions (the state, education, means of communication, or medicine) oppress the individual, represented as a defenseless individual (a citizen, worker, voter, student, patient). Apocalyptic descriptions of contemporary society make it seem normal to imagine helpless victims, manipulated consumers, deceived tourists, confused voters, and ignorant workers. Within this worldview, science and technology are unmasked as accomplices of the powerful or as instruments of a class that exercises new repressions. If these accusations were as true as they are absorbing, we would find ourselves in the paradoxical situation of living in a society where greater overall rationality causes greater political irrationality.

The notion of the knowledge society I am going to describe here is incompatible with the scientific naïveté that believed that both scientific knowledge and our ability to manipulate social reality were unlimited. I do not share the vision—utopian for some and terrifying for others—of the complete rationalization of irrationality, of the disappearance of local identities, of the destruction of other forms of knowledge that could be considered non-scientific or non-traditional. It is true that there is no social, economic or cultural reality that is immune to scientific and technical knowledge. But the unprecedented significance of scientific knowledge in contemporary society does not mean that all other attitudes and forms of life are suppressed.

My goal will be to defend an opinion that, while not very pleasing to those who traffic in great expectations—of an optimistic or pessimistic nature—strikes me as more reasonable than the alternative: namely, the knowledge society allows for more personal freedom than any previous social arrangement. This freedom is, to a large extent, the flipside of the fact that, fortunately or unfortunately, human beings are incapable of doing much good or causing much damage. We place too much trust in science and technology; this is true both for those of us who expect science and technology to solve all problems and for those who blame science and technology for all misfortunes, up to and including mortgages. Life is not easily malleable; it does not adapt as well to technology as its supporters desire or its detractors fear. There are many limits and obstacles when we try to apply science to reality; some of these roadblocks can be overcome, and others, fortunately, do not seem likely to disappear. In fact, the growth and expansion of science is not necessarily accompanied by a reduction in uncertainty, risk, and unpredictability. That is why the basic problem in today's societies is the governability of complex frameworks, which is the most convincing antithesis to the conspiratorially controllable society featured in the new *cyber-epic*.

1. The criticism of technological and scientific civilization

In the 1960s, social theorists of very diverse political orientations—from conservatives to neo-Marxists, from Schelsky (1961) to Marcuse ([1964], 1989)—carried out a relentless criticism of technological and scientific civilization, denouncing the imminent creation of a culture controlled by science and the dangers of a technological state. The general tone of these criticisms was that instrumental rationality was the starting point for social manipulation and control. Those were propitious times for the creation of dark future scenarios: science seemed to have turned the apocalyptical nightmare of world destruction into a concrete possibility. There were predictions of unstoppably differentiated evolutionary laws, a reduction in the operative ability of individual actors, an inability to elaborate one's own opinion and defend one's identity, a conspiracy of the elites involving systematically veiled self-interest, a threat to personal autonomy, repressive systems, a breakdown in the private sector, extremely efficient control over every aspect of life, the introduction of ever more numerous and detailed restrictions, increasing regulation, etc.

From that point on, criticism of the growing power of science and technology became routine. Competition for the most accurate epithet assumed an identifiable target group. The most imaginative speeches made use of formulas such as the threat of *the imperialism of instrumental reason* (Weizenbaum), the danger of an aggressive *colonization of the lifeworld* (Habermas) or the inevitability of a new *Taylorization of the working world* (Volpert). This is the context that allowed for the development of ideas such as Bell's thesis (1960) regarding the end of ideologies or Robert Lane's prognosis (1966) that we were at the beginning of a new era in which scientific knowledge would reduce the significance of politics. At the same time, there was discussion of a new type of society; it was denounced as a technical state or a "scientific–technological civilization" (Mumford 1962; Schelsky 1961). Later, with greater subtlety, these were called "registration societies" (Böhme 1984, 15) because the authorities would wield an enormous amount of data about its citizens.

These and other similar analyses from the same time period suffered from a mistaken confidence in the practical efficiency of technology and science. Looking back, we can now say that after fifty years of theories about postindustrial societies, we have become more cautious and more skeptical, regarding to both hope and fear. Neither technocratic expectations nor humanist hopes have been fulfilled. Perhaps the observation by Jean Jacques Salomon (1973, 60) is true, and the myth of human progress through scientific progress is, paradoxically, laid to rest by scientific progress itself.

The now-clichéd criticism of science deserves some revision, in part because it stems largely from poorly understood science. The social power of science and technology is not a causal determinant of all aspects and phases of human life, as hoped or feared by those who see this as one of modernity's inexorable destinies. This assumption is based on a mistaken understanding of the social power of scientific knowledge; it fails to consider the fact that there are limits on scientific knowledge, even in modern societies. Max Weber and Karl Mannheim already pointed out the fact that the capitalist–rationalist process had its limits and was only capable of prevailing under certain circumstances.

The dramatic effects that science has on the lifeworld do not necessarily imply that everyone interiorizes a scientific vision of the world, that common sense is replaced by scientific thought, that political power is exercised in a central and authoritarian manner, that there are no limits for the discovery and implementation of scientific knowledge, or that these discoveries are risk-free. Planning can also lead to an increase in things such as flexibility, alternative actions, non-anticipatable practical consequences, and so on, which do not justify fears of some kind of calculating control.

On the other hand, the concept of technology being considered here includes some questionable premises. In the first place, it assumes that, unlike technology, social processes have a type of unlimited elasticity and malleability. This idea is based on the questionable thesis of a radical availability of history that would docilely obey our technical objectives. In the second place, technical development is seen as a self-sustaining autonomous process. But I find it very unlikely that the development of technology will be exclusively propelled by a single, self-referential logic of growth, in other words, by the best or most efficient solution to a concrete problem. It is not the case that technological preferences help improve processes by, for example, deeming one of the possible technological solutions the best and implementing it (Krohn and Rammert 1985). The introduction of new technologies or the rejection of new technological developments is not determined by technological criteria alone. Technology cannot impose itself absolutely when the reasons we prefer a particular technological solution are found in other areas of life; this happens when the decision is based on political, aesthetic or moral opportunities.

One of the principal assumptions of modern science was that it could act as a replacement for other types of knowledge. Both those in favor and those opposed to modern science and technology shared the conviction that scientific knowledge eliminated any other kind of knowledge (Marcuse [1964] 1989; Schelsky 1965; Bell 1973). They believed that the rationalization of social action would make traditional or irrational beliefs disappear. The first theories of the knowledge society were also marked by the weight of the positivist conception of science. Lane (1966) reflected the optimism of the early 1960s when he expressed his conviction that scientific thought would reduce and replace previous knowledge in its entirety, deeming it inappropriate or even irrational. But this supposed gradual elimination of traditional certainties, identities, ideologies, and expectations is more of a desire or a fear than a reality. Science and technology also guarantee the survival of existing forms of action; it could even be said, to a certain extent, that they are responsible for the fact that a lot of conventional ways of thinking and acting are not invalidated.

One of the truisms used to criticize the technology and science society is the supposedly unstoppable concentration of power that is revealed by the sophistication of the control wielded over society. In the last analysis, new technologies could strengthen the conditions of the *panopticon* extolled by

Bentham in 1791 as an example of control (Foucault 1977). It is unquestionable that the new information technologies allow much more efficient surveillance than in premodern societies (Giddens 1990, 22). But it is still unclear whether contemporary society will turn toward a perfectly organized authoritarian state or whether that same evolution will establish the possibility of a radical democratization instead. On the one hand, certain technologies can be starting points for alarming developments because, as many people fear, they allow for flawless centralized surveillance. At the same time, this technological development allows for a significant amount of decentralization, local initiatives, and even effective and accessible surveillance of the people in charge of surveillance.

The specific social constraints of a knowledge society are not the same as the constraints analyzed by the traditional theories of power relationships in general and political power specifically. In the traditional concept of power, power is consciously sought out and implemented; responsibilities can be assigned, the usefulness or costs of exercising power are generally clearly shared and calculable. But the starting point of any investigation into the exercise of power in a knowledge society must be the obscuring of the decision centers in our societies, as well as the fact that the type of power afforded by knowledge has changed substantially when compared to the power that was expected from science and technology at the beginning of the modern era.

In knowledge societies, human action is strongly conditioned by the circumstances that stem from scientific knowledge and technological devices. But at the same time, ways of thinking and acting in that society can be more effectively protected from the influence of science, to the extent that the conditions allowing resistance are decisively improved. Science and technology is becoming more influential at the same time as social action is becoming increasingly contingent and fragile; this does not provide the "rationality" produced by science a definitive triumph over "irrationality."

What most characterizes the knowledge society is the fact that science and technology provide possible action for a growing number of actors, who can even decisively perfect the resistance against homogenized behavior in that society. Science and technology multiply and intensify the possibilities of opposing the evolutions they themselves have unleashed. They not only configure powers that limit possibilities of choice, afford more efficient controls, and solidify existing relationships of dominance and inequality; they can also, thanks to that same knowledge, increase the possibilities for action, influence those who are powerful, demythologize authority figures, and configure new groups and actors. In reference to power, knowledge should not only be considered a means of coercion—as it appears, at least implicitly, in many conceptions of power–but also a possibility of defending against and avoiding power as well as organizing opposition. That is why it is not contradictory to affirm that in knowledge societies there is an increase in stability and constancy that parallels the increase in insecurity and fragility.

The difficulties that oppose the concentration of knowledge lead to the disappearance of a central authority in society. To make use of one of Alain Touraine's (1984) metaphors, we can say that actors, in the knowledge society, do not focus their attention on a central location but address separate decision centers that form a mosaic rather than a pyramid. In spite of the denouncements of homogenization, today's society no longer has a few influential (or monolithic) political parties, family structures, labor unions, religious communities, ethnic groups, social strata or classes. We can observe a process of decentralization or relaxation in every one of these types of social organization. The reason for this process must be found in the very nature of the knowledge that was established in the paradigm of understanding contemporary society, the type of power it offers, and the weakness that defines it.

2. Power and weakness of knowledge

It is now common for theorists to affirm that in the knowledge society collective influence and the exercise of power and control are increasingly influenced by knowledge. Knowledge increasingly assumes the function of the classic factors of production, like property, labor, and land. The application of knowledge has replaced the traditional power apparatus as the dominant and preferred means of power for social action. This change forces us to rethink the social organization by examining the characteristics of a knowledge that is not the same as the knowledge studied by classic sociologists. Classic social theories were overly dependent on a rather deterministic conception of social evolution; they had not thought enough about the power and impotence of scientific knowledge.

The knowledge in knowledge societies is fundamentally scattered. The competence conferred by knowledge is so diversified and can so easily be substituted and combined that concrete social distinctions in a knowledge society are less coherent, one-dimensional, and homogenous than the distinctions in an industrial society. Knowledge is more and more accessible, directly or indirectly, to ever-larger sectors of the population.

The flexibility of knowledge is also revealed by the fact that its practical applications are less evident, unquestioned, and explicit than in traditional societies. Knowledge is less connected to definitive social structures. The most recent changes in social structure depend on the fact that the social construction of knowledge has been modified. I am referring to the growing importance of the (re)interpretation of knowledge and, therefore, the loss of its typical descriptors: safe, trustworthy, definitive, non-controversial, etc. The interpretation and reproduction of knowledge have become decisive social tasks (Stehr 1994, 223).

For this very reason, scientific progress does not mean that planning, prediction, and political control are facilitated. In specific circumstances, scientific progress goes hand and hand with developments in the opposite direction, along the lines of a growing fragility in society, a greater consciousness of the limits that necessarily accompany all knowledge. The limits I am referring to are of an epistemological nature; they are limits put in place by scientific knowledge itself. The very machinery of science—as Gehlen (1949, 12) observed—coerces scientists. I do not believe the limits of the power of science should be understood as irreducible irrationality, as a lack of erudition among certain social groups, or even as the result of a conscious attempt by science to keep people in the dark in order to secure its own power. The most important thing for understanding the society in which we live would be to discover the cognitive and social qualities that explain why non-scientific knowledge continues to occupy a significant social niche in modern societies.

The supposed dynamic of replacing all forms of non-scientific rationality has been questioned for a long time. Durkheim did not accept Comte's view that scientific truths would dismantle mythological expression. Mythological truths are accepted without any proof, while scientific truths must be submitted to a verification process. That being said, social action is continually under time pressure and cannot wait for social problems to be solved scientifically. The production of scientific knowledge is only possible when the time crunch and the overriding need for action are overcome. Scientific knowledge has generally emerged when there is delay, distance, examination, and an interruption of the constraints of life. Science has even managed to make these restrictions essential for the validation of scientific knowledge. But "life cannot wait" (Durkheim [1912] 1994). Society should work with certain conceptions of itself. The uncertainty within which science works is not appropriate for life itself. As Pierre Bourdieu says, we should assign a logic to practice that raises less severe logical demands than the logic of logic. The peculiarity of practice consists of not allowing theoretical considerations, because the truth of practice is blindness regarding its own truth (Bourdieu 1990). In Durkheim's view, the delay of scientific development and the fact that sociologists always have a cultural lag permit the survival of what could be considered mythologies. In societies in which scientific knowledge is dominant, mythological truths do not lose their social function.

The idea of a triumphant march of scientific knowledge and the resulting decline of traditional knowledge implicitly presumes that, strictly speaking, only scientific knowledge progresses while non-scientific knowledge lacks any progressive dynamic. The feebleness of non-scientific knowledge finds its parallel in the assumption that science continually reduces the field of traditional knowledge but does not increase or even enrich it in any way. However, scientific knowledge references other forms of knowledge, especially common sense knowledge, which it cannot replace (Luckmann 1981). Furthermore, science itself is a source of growth and the evolution of non-scientific knowledge (Brzezinski 1970). "While our knowledge continues to grow exponentially, our relevant ignorance does so even more rapidly. This is the ignorance generated by science" (Ravetz 1987, 100). The progress of scientific knowledge and especially its practical application carry within themselves new unresolved problems, side effects, and risks. From this point of view, scientific discourse produces ignorance, even if it is "certified ignorance."

The expansion of knowledge is not necessarily accompanied by a parallel reduction of non-knowledge and by an improvement in our ability to take it all in. Quite the opposite—the growth of knowledge may very well imply an explosion of confusion, uncertainty, and an inability to foresee future action. Science establishes a plurality of possibilities; but "with each satisfaction, with every bit of knowledge, science produces a series of new questions, a whole new trend of human dissatisfaction" (Richta 1972, 249).

Among the new ignorances, one that is most self-evident stems from the unpredictability of initiated movements. Many of the changes that have scientific causes resist, paradoxically, rational control, planning, programming or foresight. Dangerous, unforeseen consequences and risks that are hard to recognize are now more relevant than in so-called industrial societies. Hermann Lübbe's observation about our collective capacity to anticipate the future is very pertinent: the inaccuracy of predictions has increased more than the amount of knowledge we wield. "In contrast to the present time, all previous presents enjoyed the extraordinary cultural advantage of being able to say things about their future with much more exactitude than we can about our own" (1987, 95). Lübbe is fundamentally referring to technological knowledge in his observations about the relationship between uncertainty and quantities of knowledge. The number of situations that modify structural conditions of life increases proportionally to the amount of available knowledge. The exactness and validity of predictions are not improved by the progress of knowledge; they are reduced. Modern society is increasingly fragile. This tendency is accentuated even though—or precisely because—our knowledge about nature and society increases. We are confronting the paradox that an increase in knowledge can provide us with better knowledge of its limits. Knowledge is never absolute, and as its scope increases, it stops claiming that it is.

One possible reservation in the face of this panorama of liberating possibilities about the knowledge society consists of appealing to a "tyranny of the experts" (Lieberman 1970). There are those who claim that technology creates its own politics and that its demands serve the interests of the dominant elites (McDermott 1969). This warning deserves to be analyzed because it often rests on an inaccurate vision of the social significance of the growth of the professions based on knowledge. This does not mean, for example, that the difference between scientific knowledge and common sense knowledge is getting larger. Habermas maintains that rationalization progressively weakens the lifeworld and increases the distance between the culture of the experts and the public. But this development is not inevitable. The need for increasing surrender to the experts does not necessarily have to be linked to an impoverishment of daily life or a weakening of the forms and knowledge we cultivate in our lives or a strengthening of the ability to manipulate and control individuals. In addition, ease of access to specialized advice has emancipating consequences for the individual.

The traditional comparison between knowledge and power saw knowledge as something that can be controlled privately, thus limiting its access. Traditional political power includes the possibility of limiting individual freedoms, imposing one's own will against others' resistance, forcing obedience, threatening coercion and administrative persecution without excluding the possibility of physical violence. These are not the types of knowledge and power that are specific to knowledge societies. It is not a question of power passing to other hands, but of modifying the mode and content of power and, therefore, also its methods and reach.

On the other hand, the social control awarded to science presupposes a degree of coherence and a unity of interests that is not observed among technical experts or in speeches that refer to the authority of science. There is an extended image of science as a building founded upon consensus that does not mesh well with the fact that it is a community in which the disagreements about research strategies and the interpretation of results can be quite virulent. Scientific experts do not act as a group, specialized knowledge is not unified, and it does not seem there will be definitive consensus among experts in the future. Instead, the discovery of power and the simultaneous fragility of scientific knowledge ends up weakening the authority of the experts and creating skepticism about the idea that expert opinion is impartial and objective. Experience teaches that "technological controversies have the form of a competition between two plausible interpretations of a situation" (Barnes 1985, 106). Nothing further from the truth than the idea of a group of conspiratorial elites who submit peacefully to the objectivity of procedure and who find consensus in their single common objective against those who are not experts.

The thesis of a new class, of new forms of opposition between classes, of new political and economic conflicts (Galbraith 1967; Larson 1984) is very questionable. Believing it would mean assuming the experts can develop a sufficient coherence of interests, organization, and political solidarity, although that would still not suffice to form a class. The traditional concept of class does not seem to apply when science's expansion into current social relationships bears a particular fragility in the social structure that stands in the way of the formation of monopolies. Against this fiction, we can establish with some certainty that the experts are not in control of the knowledge society. This is not so much the result of the modesty of the experts or their aversion to power, but simply depends on the matters under consideration. The mobilization and application of these specialties lead to a paradoxical—and probably unintentional—decrease in the probability that this group of experts will assume a dominant social position. To the extent that knowledge means a capacity for action, for doing something, or putting something in motion, the clients of the experts always reduce their dependency to some degree, even if only because they can question the knowledge they received (Stehr 1994, 363).

Another of the criticisms that collapses when knowledge societies are analyzed is the threat of general homogenization. There is a plurality of local, regional or national identities that successfully tackle the universal process of homogenization for the same reasons previously cited for doubting that scientific knowledge will replace all other forms of knowledge. But what makes this universal leveling most improbable is the very nature of the knowledge that our societies manage and transmit: its interpretative and contextual character, the diverse possibilities for its application, its flexible availability. As Ralf Dahrendorf emphasizes, the limits of homogenization have to do with the fact that "all cultures have integrated the symbols of modernity into their own tradition; each culture makes those symbols into part of their life and only their life" (1980, 753). In other words, the extreme conception of homogenization makes the mistake of considering local social contexts as agencies that are exclusively passive in the face of exterior influences. Local situations not only offer resistance; they also have resources to actively "assimilate" imported cultural practices. Cultural practices and products do not determine the exact way they will be used and applied as distinct from the contexts of application.

We have gotten used to thinking of knowledge as an instrument to consolidate existing power relationships, as if scientific progress always supported the most powerful members of society, was easily monopolized by them, and successfully eliminated traditional forms of knowledge. I believe this idea of science as a particularly repressive instrument that favors the powerful is inaccurate. For this reason, one could say that "in the new global Alexandria of computerized information there is no ultimate perceptual security, no ultimate validation of a text back to an original text or authority. It is a culture based on a ceaselessly interpretative notion of knowledge" (Smith 1986, 162). Knowledge is a potential liberator for many individuals and groups. The difficulties and interpretative spaces that accompany knowledge open a series of opportunities for many people (Smith and Wynne 1989). The very necessity that knowledge should always be re-produced and that the actors should appropriate it afford the possibility in a manner of speaking—of imprinting a personal stamp on knowledge. The process of appropriation leaves a mark. In the course of the process of appropriation, agents take on new cognitive capabilities, hone those they already possess, and generally deal with knowledge in a more efficient manner. This then affords them the opportunity to develop a greater critical capacity for new knowledge and to discover new possibilities for action. The social distribution of knowledge is not a zero-sum game (Stehr 1994, 516–17).

3. The structure of knowledge societies

Our conception of social structure is still strongly connected to the theory of the industrial society. In that society, social hierarchies are built and legitimized through the production process and the consequences of their specific organization. In a very similar fashion, almost all the theorists of the postindustrial society assumed as a starting point that social, economic, and cultural realities would be determined by rationalization and planning and that the instruments of that control would be concentrated in the hands of state organisms. This thesis implied that it should have been easier to control individual behaviors administratively, subsuming any social movement within administrative protocol.

That being said, to the extent that the work is increasingly carried out by knowledge professions—he most politically active groups in society—the configuration of the political system must necessarily be modified. More importantly, the possibilities of reproducing traditional relationships of dependency will have to be changed. In a knowledge society, the possibilities for action by individuals and small groups of people have been considerably expanded, even though it should not be assumed that this expansion in operative capacity is valid for all levels of action and all actors. But in general terms, these changes lead to a more superficial and volatile state authority. In this sense at least, one can conclude that the growth of knowledge and its progressive social expansion create greater uncertainty and contingency; they do not allow for a more efficient control of central social institutions.

The fragility of social structures increases considerably in knowledge societies. The ability for a society to act upon itself is incomparably greater. But knowledge societies are politically fragile, not because they are liberal democracies (as many conservatives would like to maintain) but because they are knowledge societies. Knowledge societies increase the democratic character of liberal democracies. To the extent that there is an increase in the opportunities many people have to participate effectively, there is a decrease in the state's ability to impose its will. The "resistance" of circumstances has become much more significant, and the exercise of power more balanced than in the industrial societies of yore. The availability of reflexive knowledge reduces the ability of traditional control centers to demand and impose discipline and conformity. There has been a more than proportional increase in the ability to apply counter-pressure.

Scientific knowledge affords possibilities of action that are continuously growing and shifting. In contrast to the orthodox image of modern societies, we must emphasize the ability social agents have for conquered action, flexibility, heterogeneity, and the changeability of social structures, as well as the possibility that a greater number of individuals or groups can influence and reproduce those structures according to their own criteria. The ability of individuals to act in their own interest has also been strengthened. "Science becomes a component of politics because the scientific way of grasping reality is used to define the interest that political actors articulate and defend" (Haas 1990, 11). The imposition of political interests is largely based on conceptions of society as they are articulated by science. But we should not forget that a politics that rests on scientific knowledge can also be a politics of opposition and resistance. Given that modern scientific speech does not enjoy a monolithic position, it becomes a resource of political action for individuals, groups, and organizations that are pursuing very diverse interests and goals. Science is not only a harmonizing instrument, quieting conflicts and moderating tensions. Knowledge increases the range of actions that can be pursued by everyone, not only by the powerful.

In the majority of the analyses by social critics, it is assumed that modern society is a unit of civilization that tends toward homogenization of all aspects of life and forms of expression. Many observations of this type contain a crude determinism precisely because they do not understand that the type of knowledge configured by knowledge societies is not the exact and disciplined knowledge afforded by the positive sciences, but a more malleable and fragile knowledge from which it is not easy to establish a rigid social organization.

Therefore, the process of modernization should be understood in a less rigid and more flexible manner. Even the concepts of functional differentiation and rationalization of social reality that were seen as the motor of modern societies should give way to more open versions of social evolution. For example, the principle of the fragmentation of society, which leads society to lose its center and configure itself into a series of autonomous subsystems, should be corrected so as to also register movements in the opposite direction. Conceptions of a less deterministic society already discuss the processes of integration and *dedifferentiation* (Tilly 1984, 48) that can in turn modify the dominant tendency of modern societies toward greater variability, fragility, and contingency of social connections. The idea of a unique evolutionary tendency is therefore very questionable. It is noteworthy that many limits do not act as a barrier; there are now previously unknown possibilities of movement between supposedly impermeable boundaries. The process of modernization should not be understood as a series of strictly predetermined evolutionary states, but as an open, often even reversible, process, the expansion of social action. Modernization would then be a multiple, not a linear, process of extending operative possibilities.

The increase in the social control of knowledge is one of those phenomena that helps modify the status given to knowledge when technological and scientific civilizations are being criticized. The very existence of this control is indicative of how the sphere of knowledge is not absolutely autonomous and is susceptible to control from other social realms like law or politics.

At first, science and technology can be easily put to the service of any decision. Science's esoteric character, its inaccessibility for many people, converts the scientific system into a resource that symbolizes independence and objectivity. That is why science has frequently been hailed as an authority that can be employed for controversial decisions. But a degree of distrust has always accompanied the development of science and technology, even though it does not seem that the future will be any different. A curious coincidence occurs in contemporary society: the loss of fear and respect for authority figures and for governmental regulations is accompanied by a growing concern about the negative effects of technological and scientific progress. When we consider the problems of the environment, the consequences of using certain technological devices, the perception that not all social problems can be rationally controlled or avoided or resolved through planning, it is clear that science and technology no longer enjoy general and unquestioned trust. It seems as if our decrease in fear is being compensated by an increase in concern.

Meanwhile, the social control of both scientific and technological knowledge has increased considerably. In all the developed countries, there are complex rules and a large number of organizations that focus on registering, permitting, verifying, and supervising everything from pharmaceutical products, the use of high-risk technologies, research methodologies, patents or the control of foodstuffs. We are no longer living at a time of a completely autonomous scientific realm that rejected any exterior interventions. The application of scientific knowledge leads to knowledge becoming a part of an external, non-scientific social context. One consequence of this incorporation of scientific knowledge into a context that is external to the scientific system is that the existing control mechanisms influence knowledge. Knowledge cannot be freed from the processes of selectivity of those contexts. That is why the political supervision of knowledge is no longer bemoaned as an intolerable break from scientific norms. To the extent that knowledge becomes a constitutive component of societies, the production, reproduction, distribution, and fulfillment of knowledge cannot be separated from explicit political discussion and legal regulations. The production and distribution of knowledge have become characteristic issues to be considered when making political and economic decisions.

It is no longer the case in the knowledge society that a few actors control almost everything; instead, a lot of people control relatively small amounts. This knowledge is more available for everyone, which reduces the ability for traditional control measures to impose their will. The possibilities held by the individuals and diverse groups that configure civil society to influence, exercise resistance, and assert themselves have increased more than proportionally. Discovering these possibilities also opens the door to new ways of exercising freedom and the nightmare of subtle manipulation loses its force. The progress achieved by science has been accompanied by a decrease in our faith in science: its ability to impress us is short lived; it only lasts as long as it takes to banish the ghost that we thought was in the machine until we understood how it worked. Knowledge is knowing how precarious knowledge is, how scattered it is, its easy access, its vulnerability to criticism, its inability to combat the obstinacy of common sense and deep-seated habits. In short: knowledge is knowing that life is not very governable and that the final guarantee of personal liberty is the resistance that things have to being managed.

Bibliography

Barnes, Barry (1985), *About Science*, Oxford: Blackwell.
Bell, Daniel (1960), *The End of Ideology*, Glencoe: Free Press.
—(1973), *The Coming of Post-Industrial Society: A Venture in Social Forecasting*, New York: Basic Books.
Böhme, Gernot (1984), "The Knowledge-structure of Society," in Gunnar Bergendal (ed.), *Knowledge Policies and the Traditions of Higher Education*, Stockholm: Almquist & Wiksell, 5–17.
Bourdieu, Pierre (1990), *The Logic of Practice*, Stanford: Stanford University Press.
Brzezinski, Zbigniew (1970), *Between Two Ages: America's Role in the Technotronic Age*, New York: Viking Press.
Dahrendorf, Ralf (1980), "Im Entschwinden der Arbeitsgesellschaft: Wandlungen in der sozialen Konstruktion des menschlichen Lebens," *Merkur* 34, 749–60.

Durkheim, Emile ([1912] 1994), *Les formes élémentaires de la vie religeiuse*, Paris: PUF.
Foucault, Michel (1977), *Discipline and Punish: The Birth of the Prison*, New York: Pantheon Books.
Galbraith, John K. (1967), *The New Industrial State*, New York: Houghton Mifflin.
Gehlen, Arnold (1949), *Sozialpsychologische Probleme der industriellen Gesellschaft*, Tübingen: J. C. B. Mohr.
Giddens, Anthony (1990), *The Consequences of Modernity*, Stanford: Stanford University Press.
Haas, Ernst B. (1990), *When Knowledge is Power: Three Models of Change in International Organizations*, Berkeley: University of California Press.
Krohn, Wolfgang and Rammert, Werner (1985), "Technologieentwicklung: Autonomer Prozeß und industrielle Strategie," in Burkart Lutz (ed.), *Soziologie und gesellschaftliche Entwicklung: Verhandlungen des 22—Deutschen Soziologentages*, Frankfurt: Campus, 411–33.
Lane, Robert E. (1966), "The Decline of Politics and Ideology in a Knowledgeable Society," *American Sociological Review* 31, 649–62.
Larson, Magali Sarfatti (1984), "The Production of Expertise and the Constitution of Expert Authority," in Thomas L. Haskell (ed.), *The Authority of Experts*, Bloomington: Indiana University Press, 28–80.
Lieberman, Jethro K. (1970), *The Tyranny of Experts: How Professionals are Closing the Open Society*, New York: Walker.
Lübbe, Hermann (1987), "Der kulturelle Geltungsschwund der Wissenschaften," in Helmut de Ridder and Heinz Sahner (eds), *Wissenschaft und gesellschaftliche Verantwortung*, Berlin: Arno Pitz, 89–108.
Luckmann, Thomas (1981), "Vorüberlegungen zum Verhältnis von Alltagswissen und Wissenschaft," in Peter Janich (ed.), *Wissenschaftstheorie und Wissenschaftsforschung*, München: Beck, 39–51.
Marcuse, Herbert ([1964] 1989), *Der eindimensionale Mensch: Studien zur Ideologie der fortgeschrittenen Industriegesellschaft* en *Schriften* 7, Frankfurt: Suhrkamp.
McDermott, John (1969), "Technology: The Opiate of the Intellectuals," *New York Review of Books* 13 (2), 25–35.
Mumford, Lewis (1962), *Technics and Civilization*, New York: Harcourt Brace Jovanovich.
Ravetz, Jerome R. (1987), "Usable Knowledge, Usable Ignorance," *Knowledge* 9, 87–116.
Richta, Radovan (1972), *Technischer Fortschritt und industrielle Gesellschaft*, Frankfurt: Makol Verlag.
Salomon, Jean Jacques (1973), *Science and Politics*, Cambridge: Cambridge University Press.
Schelsky, Helmut (1961), *Der Mensch in der wissenschaftlichen Zivilisation*, Köln and Opladen: Westdeutscher Verlag.

—(1965), *Auf der Suche nach der Wirklichkeit: Gesammelte Aufsätze*, Düsseldorf: Diederichs.

Smith, Anthony (1986), "Technology, Identity and the Information Machine", *Daedalus* 115 (3), 155–69.

Smith, Roger and Wynne, Brian (1989), *Expert Evidence: Interpreting Science in the Law*, London: Routledge.

Stehr, Nico (1994), Arbeit, Eigentum und Wissen. Zur Theorie von Wissensgesellschaften, Frankfurt: Suhrkamp.

Tilly, Charles (1984), *Big Structures, Large Processes, Huge Comparisons*, New York: Russel Sage Foundation.

Touraine, Alain (1984), *Le retour de l'acteur: essai de sociologie*, Paris: Fayard.

5

The Dialogue between Knowledge and Power

The age-old question about the relationship between knowledge and power, which dates back to the Platonic theory of the philosopher king, has been depicted in recent times by two figures that represent the type of knowledge that should guide politics. In the right-wing version, we have the figure of the expert, while on the left, we have the intellectual. The expert embodies the superiority of science and advocates objectivity. The intellectual claims to assert moral superiority and, rather than objectivity, offers knowledge that is critical and engaged. The two figures are dual versions of the same model, and this convergence highlights their deepest anachronism: the model of "speaking truth to power" (Wildavsky 1979), as if experts and intellectuals were strangers to the uncertainty with which all other mortals, including politicians, live. Although I may be oversimplifying matters and glossing over certain nuances, this schematic approach can help us comprehend why the model of a body of knowledge that politics would merely have to obey must be relegated to the past since it does not reflect the complex relationships between knowledge and power that exist in contemporary societies. We must now think differently about the conditions under which political ideas can be realized through the political process.

It is a well-known fact that, within knowledge societies, knowledge is not only a support for economic productivity; it also plays an increasingly important role in the social legitimization of political decisions. Scientific reports, studies, and expert commissions are now part of our habitual political and social landscape. We must also continue to augment the amount of knowledge transferred between the social sciences and government institutions. Nevertheless, if we are to understand how knowledge and power are currently expressed, we must consider the fact that the status of knowledge has changed; it is no longer cloaked in the traditional signs of authority. Nowadays, then, 1) knowledge is not the exclusive product of experts, but is more often a social construct; and 2) knowledge is more aware of its own limitations and the growing body of non-knowledge that inevitably accompanies it. The knowledge that democratic governments need is found within this new context.

The conditions under which politics operates today can be summarized by saying that "facts are uncertain, values in dispute, stakes high and decisions urgent" (Ravetz 1999, 649). The problems generated by risk are redefining the boundaries between science, politics, and public opinion. Competing expert opinions, the questionable scientific assessment of risk, and the threatening potential of scientific innovations have led us to challenge the traditional image of science as an authority that provided reliable, objective knowledge with universal validity. Science increases knowledge, of course, but it also increases society's uncertainty and non-knowledge. We must therefore do away with the idea of using science to create an objective and indisputable foundation for politics.

The relationship between knowledge and power is largely paradoxical nowadays. We ask science to make relevant knowledge available in order to help us make important collective decisions. At the same time, there is less confidence in science or at least a restructuring of its traditional role as an indisputable provider of unquestionable knowledge. The Eurobarometer survey from 2005, "Social Values, Science and Technology," reveals that science is more trusted than other social institutions, but confidence in the objectivity of scientific experts is a thing of the past. To put it more controversially: "in a knowledge society, the significance of knowledge increases, but the relevance of science decreases" (Willke 2002, 12). A knowledge society is one in which knowledge, rather than science, is afforded great significance. We cannot fully understand a knowledge society without considering the fact that, in its functioning and its conflicts, it encompasses many different types of knowledge, some of them contradictory. That is why knowledge politics must become the politics of the diversity of knowledge (Rammert 2003, 501), and the processes of interpretation and negotiation must embrace a wide range of people and places.

At the same time, we can see what Jasanoff has called a "peripheral blindness" in modern states, privileging what is known at the expense of the unknown, relying too heavily on their image of reality, focusing on the short term, paying more attention to immediate risks than to indeterminate, synergistic, or long-term risks. From this point of view, we could say that our principal demands on politics can be summarized by a cognitive imperative that persists in spite of our understanding that the instruments used by politics to comprehend reality clearly leave room for improvement. Learning has become the true objective of civic deliberation. "The capacity to learn is constrained by limiting features of the frame within which institutions must act. Institutions see only what their discourses and practices permit them to see" (Jasanoff 2005, 386). If that is the case, the question of how to rethink the relationship between knowledge and power is a crucial issue for contemporary democracies.

Using this as my starting point, I intend to analyze how best to comprehend the politics of knowledge, the governance *of* knowledge *through* knowledge (Schuppert and Vosskuhle 2008). This study will, in other words, address the forms and processes in which the conflicts and risks caused by the knowledge and non-knowledge of science are socially defined, negotiated, and configured. Its setting is the public space, the hybrid agora where science and society, politics and the marketplace converge (Nowotny, Scott, and Gibbons 2004, 253). By examining this collective question, we can judge whether politicians and public institutions have at their disposal the knowledge they need in order to make decisions. It is important to remember that part of the legitimacy of their decision making stems from their promises to act rationally. In other words, they must know what they are doing when they prohibit smoking in public places, for example, or when they determine educational curricula or decide to introduce a particular vaccine. The development of the welfare state has made the need to base decisions on a systematic elaboration of knowledge even more urgent.

1. The power of knowledge and the knowledge of power

When we talk about the politics of knowledge, we are fundamentally referring to two things: governing knowledge and knowledge about governing, and how society's knowledge is governed and what the knowledge that governs society is like. These two central points lead to a series of questions of great importance to any democratic society, which must be comprised not only of legitimate decisions but also of adequate knowledge. Democratization refers to the production of knowledge, the availability of knowledge, access to experts or knowledge that guide governance. The democracy of knowledge requires, for example, an examination of how knowledge is distributed throughout a society, how authority and economic growth emerge from knowledge, the influence knowledge has over power relationships.

If knowledge is a central component in contemporary societies, its production, regulation, and distribution cannot be separated from explicit political confrontations. Knowledge's central role as a political battleground is revealed not only by the fact that politics and economics compete for knowledge, but also by the fact that ideological confrontations are sometimes presented as scientific disputes, as if knowledge were the cause of the disagreement, and the fact that everyone appeals to knowledge to justify their positions.

a) The politics of knowledge is, first and foremost, concerned with *governing knowledge*. The attempt to regulate knowledge politically is not new. This goal was carried out in a particularly perverse fashion during the totalitarian regimes of the last century, and it is still visible at times when diverse groups and institutions try to manipulate knowledge, through historical revisionism, for example, or the attempt to prohibit the teaching of evolutionary theories.

Clearly, the democratization of knowledge has nothing to do with the political control of knowledge, nor does it mean that questions of knowledge should now be decided by democratic vote. The growing interest in supervising knowledge (Stehr 2003) or in controlling the externalities of the application of technological and scientific knowledge reveal the new emphasis on the social legitimization of science. Innovation in terms of knowledge has become the principal source of economic value and social power; the way this knowledge is regulated is the best indicator of the civilized nature of a society and its institutions. Regulation does not have to imply prohibition; it can mean support for best practices, attempting various approaches, revealing options, and helping to put them into practice.

Governing knowledge refers, in the first place, to collective decisions we should adopt regarding knowledge and technological inventions that have controversial applications and social consequences. The development of a politics of knowledge is, to a large extent, a reaction to the extraordinary speed with which new knowledge and technological possibilities have been developed in today's societies. Collective fear about the consequences of scientific development has transported us to a new stage in the relationship between knowledge and society where people demand the supervision, regulation or governing of knowledge. From this point of view, the politics of knowledge is carried out in a context that is particularly difficult and controversial, where desires for innovation, the freedom to research, and divergent perceptions of the non-knowledge that is present in society must be balanced with future risks or hard to predict consequences.

With the politics of knowledge, criteria other than purely scientific factors attain relevance. For example, decisions to fund scientific research depend not only on criteria of scientific excellence but also on collective usefulness. Our ideological, political, and legal debates have begun to focus on anything that has to do with the supervision of knowledge in a knowledge society. These discussions revolve around the meaning, morality, responsibility, economic advantages or environmental costs of scientific and technological innovations. Society's control of knowledge has become one of the essential questions for the new democratic citizenry.

It makes sense nowadays to suspect that we may know too much or, to say it in a less provocative fashion, that our knowledge is not balanced by other criteria. It is not only a matter of accumulating data that is, in practice, trivial, unnecessary, and irrelevant, but that even certain innovations can lead to catastrophic consequences if we do not keep criteria of sustainability, equality or justice in mind. The politics of science make sense because we need to articulate a plurality of criteria to evaluate knowledge adequately. The fact that something is true is not sufficient; it must also, for example, be democratic, equitable, and respectful of the environment.

b) The second dimension of the politics of knowledge is *knowledge about governing*. Anyone who wants to act rationally needs specific knowledge to do so. The government has always tried to be a rational actor. As Norbert Elias (1977) explained so well, the rise of the modern state is associated with the configuration of key monopolies, particularly those government resources that were inherent to the beginnings of the modern era, like power, rights, and authority. The efficient use of knowledge is another of these key resources.

In this regard, we now find ourselves at a time when we must move from the knowledge that classic governments needed to the knowledge required to govern an advanced knowledge and innovation society. The production and availability of knowledge is a fundamental problem in the new political culture. New political tasks like risk prevention, regulation of the financial marketplace, bio-politics, or the environment are challenges to government competence that demand, from the start, the creation and availability of specific knowledge.

In the traditional formulation of the idea of government, there is a clear distinction between the subject and the object of governance. This assumption has been fading, and the state, understood as the sovereign control center, has started to recognize a plurality of actors and evolve toward a more collaborative conception of power (Mayntz 2006). Political authority is not facing a simple, passive society, but subsystems and political actors that are difficult to govern. In the end, the question comes down to who is controlling whom, with what tools and what degree of efficiency. The perspective of governance merely reaches the conclusions dictated by the fact that current social plurality, dynamism and the complexity of the tasks with which it is charged demand, not a central governmental subject, but the cooperation of governmental and non-governmental actors, at various levels and with differing methods and tools. For that reason, while classic theories of the state focus their attention on the governmental subject, theories of governance highlight regulatory structures.

From the point of view of government knowledge, what is needed is a new consideration of knowledge that is more conscious of its shared and provisional nature; if our experiences are provisional, we must develop a specific sensitivity for deviations and irregularities. If the concept of governance has any value, it is for putting in motion processes through which an established public space is observed from alternative vantage points. The subject of governance is not a sovereign actor, but a plurality of actors who wield indispensable knowledge. That is why governance should be understood as a process of reflexive co-ordination, as communication. The central problem when it comes to governing a knowledge society is how to organize the co-production of knowledge.

There is a need for procedures to take advantage of the social intelligence that tends to be specialized, disjointed, and fragmented. The problem with democratic societies is how to articulate that knowledge without neutralizing the wealth of ideas, experiences, perspectives, and innovations that arise in a knowledge society. "The quality of the collective shaping of public will depends on the quality of the collective shaping of knowledge" (Willke 2002, 174). At a time when the hierarchical decision-making structures have become decentralized and individualized, bureaucracy and state planning no longer monopolize expert knowledge, which has become a wide-spread social commodity.

If our societies have one requirement, it is to modify the rules that organize collective learning and to systematically elevate society's capacity for self-observation and learning. We must institutionalize a greater reflexivity of structures and procedures. It is a question of learning under conditions of great uncertainty, which is a difficult and controversial task. As a matter of fact, the deliberative theory of democracy points in that direction, conscious that, in the face of these collective challenges, the process of political discussion should generate knowledge, not merely tactics.

The primary function of government in a knowledge society consists precisely of establishing the conditions where collective intelligence is possible. If the primary role of the modern state was to prevent civil war or of the welfare state to fight poverty, the characteristic role of government in a knowledge society is to establish the best possible bases for taking optimal advantage of the "knowledge" resource. From the perspective of risks and danger prevention, one of its most important public tasks consists of developing procedures to confront ignorance wherever systemic risks threaten. And from the point of view of utilizing knowledge, it is a question of establishing the structural conditions that turn collective intelligence and innovation into society's primary function.

2. Expert knowledge and political advising

There was an intense debate in the 1960s about science and technology. One side denounced the illegitimate influence that science and technology had on politics while the other side expected a resulting end to all ideology. The technocratic right-wing and the anti-technology left-wing concurred in their positivist conception of scientific knowledge, granting it an objectivity that would render politics unnecessary. Accompanying this discussion was the simultaneous question about the role experts should play in the political process. Meanwhile, the aforementioned modification of the concept of knowledge also had major implications for the concept of political advising. In spite of the technocratic dream, the truth is that science is but one voice in the crowd. Political, ethical, and ideological considerations also demand their place as legitimate partners in the decision-making process. Science can proffer advice, but it is not a replacement for other players.

Knowledge societies are also advising societies (Schützeichel and Brüsemeister 2004). They are, in other words, societies in which the centrality of knowledge signifies that more and more areas of life require cognitive competence. People do not always possess this competence, but they can gain access to it: governments and organizations seek advice, but so do students, couples, and even souls. Contemporary societies have formed a dense advice-giving network;

they demand a high degree of reflexivity about their actions since there is an increased need for information and a heightened demand for justification. Decisions must be fortified by expert knowledge, but this knowledge, to the extent that it increases the reflexivity of decisions, also emphasizes decisions' contingent nature. Advice giving is as much the result as a cause of growing reflexivity in social life.

Politics is a field that can no longer be carried out without continuously resorting to expert knowledge. Expert knowledge is the main thing that bolsters politics when it is attempting to implement risky and controversial decisions. There is hardly any field of public administration that does not mobilize scientific knowledge in some way when it needs to inform and legitimize certain decisions. That being said, can we expect a rationalization of politics on the basis of scientific advising?

The current appeal to the need for political advising does not mean asserting an alleged objectivity to which politics must submit, in part because that conception is not supported by the enormous diversification of expert knowledge. Which expert should we obey when they are so ubiquitous and when they often hold opposing views? The pluralization of knowledge implies a weakening of its ability to command. The power of experts decreases when their number increases, and as the use of expert knowledge becomes more widespread, knowledge itself is also problematized. "Risk societies tend to be self-critical. Their experts are relativized or are dethroned by counter-experts" (Beck 1996, 32). The proliferation of expert knowledge, which is becoming increasingly generalized and diversified, means it is no longer the exclusive privilege of any particular state or government; instead, it is theoretically within the reach of any state or group in a civil society. Thus, in spite of the supposed technocracy of the experts, we are seeing an overall democratization of expert knowledge.

On the other hand, the relationship between power and knowledge is much more complex than assumed by the theory that power is subordinate to knowledge. At times, in fact, the exact opposite holds: expert knowledge is manipulated by those in power to justify previously adopted political decisions. In addition, the world of experts is not generally peaceful or uncontroversial. At times, political conflicts reproduce the disputes that are taking place within the heart of the scientific community. Science is rarely able to resolve political disputes; instead, scientific controversies frequently add fuel to political disputes. Every expert has a counter-expert, which helps deprive scientific knowledge of its alleged certainty. Scientific opinion, far from putting an end to debate, very often serves to increase the number of perspectives and consequences that must be taken into consideration. Thus begins the game with experts on either side, making it clear to the public that, in the case of complex issues with political and social repercussions, scientific precision in no way ensures rational decisions.

In recent years, a lot of progress was made in the democratization of expert knowledge, both in regard to the choice of experts and the production of and access to expert knowledge. The key issue is how to regulate control of the knowledge involved in the political advising process: the type of knowledge sought, the selection of advisers, the fields of knowledge they represent, their institutional affiliation, the manner in which they present their results (whether through recommendations or fact reports). The "democratization of expert knowledge" does not mean adding more players to an unchanging institutional and cognitive framework. Instead, and most importantly, it implies reflecting on and transforming the very framework itself, its perceptions and implicit goals, as well as its deliberative processes.

There are already many regulations in place to allow us to take advantage of expert knowledge while simultaneously preventing a true colonization of governments and parliaments by the experts' uncontrolled influence over democratically legitimized politics. Since it is true that, among other problems, political advising may lead public actors to become dependent on private experts, it can "departiamentize" decisions or postpone them indefinitely. It can also afford politicians immunity from political criticism. To avoid these dangers, regulations have been introduced on the selection of experts and their qualifications, control, transparency, and openness. The code of practice for political advisory committees formulated by the Chief Scientific Adviser of the United Kingdom has openness and transparency of the process as its primary goals. According to the White Paper on European Governance (2001), the Commission of the European Communities has also formulated guidelines regarding the use of expert advising. One recent measure is a newly created registry of lobby groups proposed by Commissioner Kallas in 2008. The aim of these and other measures is primarily to ensure the openness, plurality, and integrity of the expert knowledge that is employed in order to safeguard quality and trustworthiness.

The larger question that this poses can be formulated as follows: What procedures and protocols of scientific advising can both ensure the quality of expert knowledge and be effective in the context of political action? In any case, the belief in a direct translatability of scientific knowledge to policy decisions has now been rejected as simplistic. The traditional conception of advising approaches the question in a top-down manner in which "ready-to-use" results are transmitted. What both the decisionist approach (first politics, then the experts) and the technocratic model (first the experts, then political judgment) have in common is a strict separation between knowledge and decision making (Millstone 2005). Both view the transfer of knowledge as a linear model that suggests a temporal separation between a place where knowledge is produced and another where it is applied, as well as a clear distinction between facts (scientific) and values (political). In both the decisionist and technocratic models, the function of experts and politicians remains separate. Advising is carried out as a monologue: either science dictates solutions to politicians, or politicians determine what science must justify.

The constructivist model of political advising is quite different and has broken the links that proceed from the identification of the problem to expert advice and finally to political decision making. In contrast, the constructivist model opts for a process of argumentation. Advising is not meant to simply transfer information that is already known; it is a moment of self-reflection for both science and politics (Gill 1994). Political advising must be conceived, not as subordination, but as a communicative process. Jasanoff speaks of co-production between adviser and advisee (2005). Advising is a process of negotiation in which experts and decision-makers discuss the suitability of available knowledge to the particular problem they are attempting to decide. Advisers do not simply present facts related to a given problem; the knowledge communicated during advisory sessions is interpreted and assessed by all parties. Similarly, when it comes to risky decisions, the judgment of the experts should also clarify risks and uncertainties. Political problems should be translated into the language of science, but the scientists' answers, in turn, are not applicable to politics until they have been expressed in the format of political decisions. There is no immediate conversion of scientific judgments into political decisions; the knowledge offered by scientists must be weighed in part by political considerations. With this recursive model, we are shifting from a "speaking truth to power" approach to that of "making sense together" (Hoppe 1999).

Advising would then serve to enhance the image of reality held by the political class and would strengthen its capacity for reflection. The emphasis is not on transferring knowledge from science to the political domain, but rather the stimulation of politics through scientific knowledge (Martinsen 2006). This holds true because the problems that need to be resolved are not clearly defined. They need framing and negotiation, which is a multilateral process between politics, science, and any other involved party (Bijker, Bal, and Hendriks 2009).

Given the current debates about the uncertainty of knowledge, these ideas could be formulated as follows: Political advising is meant to provide more political options, but politics itself must make a final decision about what particular knowledge to recognize as most appropriate and politically relevant (Schützeichel 2008, 16). The great challenge of political advising is to link scientific knowledge, which is produced in accordance with the scientists' criteria of relevance, with the criteria of political relevance. The knowledge of advising is distinguished from other types of knowledge by the fact that it must be simultaneously scientifically correct and politically useful and feasible.

3. The new relationship between science and politics

The knowledge upon which modern political institutions were built was conceived as something reliable and progressive, so the axiom that "knowledge is power" (Bacon) made perfect sense. But that is no longer the case, and it makes no sense to hope that science will afford politics objective knowledge with which to support political decisions or proof with which to legitimize them. The fact is that the nature of knowledge, our conception of science, and the meaning of political advising have all undergone notable changes in recent years.

This, then, gives rise to the paradox that politics needs more than ever to resort to expert knowledge, but this guarantees neither legitimacy nor consensus. Knowledge can no longer be used to convert political decisions into irrefutable certainties. At the same time, science is forced to dialogue with the economy, politics, and civil society concerning the relevance of its research priorities, their application to politics, economic costs, and the inclusion of consumers and citizens in the process of defining problems. From this point of view, not only does science provide knowledge to society, but society can respond to science as well. This new intersection of discourses and ways of thinking has led to a real blurring of boundaries between science, politics, and society (Nowotny, Scott, and Gibbons 2004). This can be summarized in the phrase "society speaks back to science" (Nowotny 2005, 36); in this new reality, the public will not settle for simply being enlightened by science, but also increasingly articulates its expectations and demands for science.

The disappointment politicians experience when they are not provided with clear and certain counsel corresponds with scientists' disappointment when their advice is not heeded. Both of these failed expectations raise the question about how to organize advice so as to satisfy the double requirement that the advice be both true and viable, meeting the demands of objectivity and legitimization.

First of all, the classic division of labor between science and politics cannot be maintained when science operates in highly politicized fields such as the environment, genetic engineering or economic decisions. The new politics of knowledge must break from two dogmas: the strict separation between facts and values and the strict separation between science and politics (Latour 2001). The complexity of today's world demands a stronger connection between political institutions and scientific infrastructures.

Modern democracies, especially when understood as knowledge societies, are legitimated by the conjunction of democratic representation and scientific rationality (Weingart and Lentsch 2008, 7). The great dilemma of contemporary democracies is that decisions must be made in the light of available scientific knowledge, but they must also be democratically legitimized. In order to address this dilemma properly, they must first realize that these are two separate issues. In spite of all the expectations that scientific advice will alleviate the burden of political responsibility, science is still science, and politics, politics. Science and politics have different systemic rationalities. As Luhmann would say, science operates under the code of truth, and politics under the code of power. These distinct rationalities signify divergent expectations. We do not, for example, expect from politics the same objectivity and universality that must guide science; the criteria of compromise, feasibility or political opportunity are all foreign to scientific activity.

Neither science nor politics continue to be what they were fifty years ago; they do not encounter the same problems, nor do they act under the same conditions. Technocratic hopes have faded away. The belief that it would be possible to translate scientific knowledge directly into political decisions has been proven naïve. Political activity takes place in societies that are defined by the media, and politics must struggle, now more than ever, for popular legitimation through the media. Any proposed political decision must appear both rational and politically acceptable. It has, therefore, become part of the politician's job to combine objective solutions with subjective interests, and for that reason, political advising cannot ignore the interests and limitations of political actors. One of the central tasks of advising must be the assessment of the acceptability and feasibility of advice. Scientific knowledge is not "transported" to politics; politicians must simply do their jobs intelligently, according to the particular structures, processes, and rules of politics.

There is an initial stage when political judgment is indispensable: before even resorting to science, politics must take the responsibility for defining the problem properly. This is especially important when we face problems for which not only do we not know the solution but we are unsure of the specifics of the problem (Fischer 2000, 128). Democracy's deliberative space, its ability to generate not only a balance of interests but collective knowledge, plays a very important role in these cases of collective perplexity. Decision making is also particularly political, despite all the scientific coverage one can accumulate. The moment of decision making is recalled in Euripides' tragedy *Andromache*: "Again, when strong winds are drifting mariners, the divided counsel of the wise does not best avail for steering, and their collective wisdom has less weight than the inferior mind of the single man who has sole authority."

Thus, when we consider the relationship between knowledge and power, it is important to remember that neither of the two is all-powerful or all-knowing. They can each console the other for their loss of former privileges, sharing the same uncertainty in the form of theoretical perplexity on the one hand, and the anxiety of contingent decisions on the other. What privileges has power lost? The prerogative of not having to learn but simply command. What has knowledge lost? It has lost the certainty and proof that allowed it to dispense with any demands for legitimization; its social inaccuracies are now more visible. For this reason, the problem is not that we no longer know how to combine certain knowledge with sovereign power, but rather how to express both power and knowledge in order to compensate the weaknesses they each suffer so they can confront the increasing complexity of the world in tandem.

Bibliography

Beck, Ulrich (1996), "Risk Society and the Provident State," in Scott Lash, Bronislaw Szerszynski, and Brian Wynne (eds), *Risk, Environment and Modernity*, London: Sage, 27–43.

Bijker, Wiebe E., Bal, Roland, and Hendriks, Ruud (2009), *The Paradox of Scientific Authority: The Role of Scientific Advice in Democracies*, Cambridge, MA: The MIT Press.

van der Daele, Wolfgang (1993), "Zwanzig jahre politische Kritik an der Exporten," in Joseph Hubert and Georg Thurn (eds), *Wissenschaftsmileus: Wissenschaftkontroversen und soziokulturelle Konflikte*, Berlin: Sigma, 173–94.

Elias, Norbert (1977), *Über den Prozess der Zivilisation: Soziogenetische und psychogenetische Untersuchungen*, Frankfurt: Suhrkamp.

European Commission (2001), *White Paper on European Governance*.

Gill, Bernhard (1994), "Folgenerkenntnis: Science Assessment als Selbstreflexion der Wissenschaft," *Soziale Welt* 45, 430–53.

Hoppe, Robert (1999), "Policy Analysis, Science and Politics: From 'Speaking Truth to Power' to 'Making Sense Together,'" *Science and Public Policy* 26 (3), 201–10.

Jasanoff, Sheila (2005), "Technologies of Humility: Citizen Participation in Governing Science," in Alexander Bogner and Helge Torgersen (eds), *Wozu Experten? Ambivalenzen der Beziehung von Wissenschaft und Politik*. Wiesbaden: Verlag für Sozialwissenschaften, 370–89.

Latour, Bruno (2001), *Politiques de la nature*, Paris: Éditions La Découverte.

Martinsen, Renate (2006), "Partizipative Politikberatung: der Bürger als Experte," in S. Falk, D. Rehfeld, A. Römmele and M. Thunert, *Handbuch Politikberatung*, Wiesbaden: Verlag für Sozialwissenschaften, 138–51.

Mayntz, Renate (2006), "Governance-Theory als fortenwickelte Steuerungstheorie," in Gunnart Folke Schuppert (ed.), *Governance-Forschung: Vergewisserung über Stand und Entwicklungslinien*, Baden-Baden: Nomos, 11–20.

Millstone, Eric (2005), "Science-Based Policy-Making: An Analysis of Processes of Institutional Reform," in Alexander Bogner and Helge Torgersen (eds), *Wozu Exporten? Ambivalenzen der Beziehung von Wissenschaft und Politik*, Wiesbaden: Verlag für Sozialwissenschaften, 314–41.

Nowotny, Helga (2005), "Experten, Expertisen und imaginierte Laien," in Alexander Bogner and Helge Togersene (eds), *Wozu Experten? Ambivalenzen der Beziehung von Wissenschaft und Politik*, Wiesbaden: Verlag für Sozialwissenschaften, 33–44.

Nowotny, Helga, Scott, Peter, and Gibbons, Michael (2004), *Wissenschaft neu denken, Wissen und Öffentlichkeit in einem Zeitalter der Ungewissheit*, Weilerwist: Velbrück.

Rammert, Werner (2003), "Zwei Paradoxien einer innovationsorientierter Wissenspolitik: Die Verknüpfung heterogenen und die Verwertung impliziten Wissens," *Soziale Welt* 54, 483–508.

Ravetz, Jerome R. (1999), "What is Post-Normal Science," *Futures* 31 (7), 647–53.

Schuppert, Gunnart Folke and Vosskuhle, Andreas (2008), *Governance von und durch Wissen*, Baden: Nomos.

Schützeichel, Rainer (2008), "Beratung, Politikberatung, wissenschaftliche Politikberatung," in Bröchler and Rainer Schützeichel (eds), *Politikberatung*, Stuttgart: Lucius & Lucius, 5–33.

Schützeichel, Rainer and Brüsemeister, Thomas (2004), *Die beratene Gesellschaft: Zur gesellschaftlichen Bedeutung von Beratung*, Wiesbaden: VS.

Stehr, Nico (2003), *Wissenspolitik: Die Überwachung des Wissens*, Frankfurt: Suhrkamp.

Weingart, Peter and Lentsch, Justus (2008), *Wissen, Beraten, Entscheiden: Form und Funktion wissenschaftlicher Politikberatung in Deutschland*, Wieilerwist: Velbrück.

Wildavsky, Aaron (1979), *Speaking Truth to Power: The Art and the Kraft of Policy Analysis*, Boston: Little, Brown and Company.

Willke, Helmut (2002), *Dystopia. Studien zur Crisis des Wissens in der modernen Gesellschaft*, Frankfurt: Suhrkamp.

6

Scientific Citizenship

What we call a "knowledge society" can be understood, from a metaphorical point of view, as a *society of rumors*. By labeling it a metaphor, I am in no way attempting to reduce the conviction with which I define it or pointing out its acceptable imprecisions. We can accept the literality of the situation better if we examine what a rumor is. The two characteristics that best define a rumor are its hypothetical nature and the fact that the author is unknown. A rumor is a vague assumption with little evidential proof; it does not provide evidence nor is it formulated with arguments that establish unassailable truth. It is a mishmash of judgments and opinions that belong to the arena of what "people" say, but it is said either by no one in particular or by multiple and confused voices. So what does that have to do with the type of knowledge now available in our societies? Does this properly describe the role of science in today's world?

We want scientific principles and judgments about science to be cautious, hypothetical, provisional, and numerous. This description is reminiscent of a rumor. We live in a world in which opinions, judgments, assessments, journalistic reports and disclosures, the determination of facts, and political and legal principles form a somewhat chaotic chorus of rumors. None of these things wields guaranteed and indisputable facts, which would eliminate criticism and suspicion and strip other voices of legitimacy on principle. In an open society, untrustworthy opinions, controversial authority figures, doubtful data, and hopes and fears that cannot be expressed objectively have every right to circulate. Society is formed by rumors that struggle among themselves to marshal support, attract attention, foment or eliminate concern.

The knowledge society is not a society of exact, certain, indisputable knowledge that is dominated by uncontroversial science. An increase in situations and contexts has made knowledge more socially diffuse; the voices that are heard are very similar to rumors, in that they are multiple, controversial, open, uncertain assumptions that are not managed by an identifiable objectivity or completely free of self-interest. The world of clear and indisputable facts, which used to justify modern science and expert authority, has disappeared. Current diagnostics about the knowledge society frustrate the expectation that science will provide trustworthy knowledge, greater certainty, and more security. Instead, we are facing some return to doubt, uncertainty, and ambiguity. The knowledge society is a society of rumors, a society in which voices do not diminish or converge under one authority. Instead, they multiply and become weaker. That is why it makes sense to think of science as *rumorology*: a dispersion of knowledge that creates more voices and makes them less trustworthy.

The other side of the story is that demands for participation, protests or requirements for consensus have become more common in Western democracies even in fields, like science, that were once deemed inappropriate for these types of compromises. The idea of "citizen science" (Irwin 1995) or a "scientific citizenry" (Fischer 2000) refers precisely to the current challenges with introducing nonscientific agents into the decision-making process, taking local knowledge and experience into consideration, creating transparent communications about risk, and other similar demands for democratization.

Clearly, the democratization of science does not mean that all scientific questions should be decided by majority vote. It means something more subtle and finely calibrated regarding a series of demands for legitimacy on decisions that affect all of us, on the allocation of resources, or on controlling the fact that there are more and more actors and more forces intervening in matters that can no longer be considered a competition only open to the experts. In any case, the participatory turn should not make us think that by simply widening the circle of actors we improve corresponding decisions; this leads to cognitive problems, difficulties with coordination. At the same time, the concept of scientific citizenship includes rights and responsibilities: the right to be informed about science and technology, to deliberate and participate in decisions, but also, to an extent, the responsibility to be educated, to understand one's role as part of a collective, and to protect one's interests.

The relationship between science and society has suffered profound transformations. These changes could be summed up by considering the new complexity that stems from the weakening of the delimitations that guided traditional science. A whole set of circumstances is making us redefine the difference between facts and values, between experts and laypeople, between knowledge and non-knowledge. I am going to examine this new situation beginning with some of these distinctions, namely: 1) the distinction between the laboratory and the exterior world; 2) the distinction between science and other social systems which led to the establishment of classic scientific autonomy; 3) the distinction between scientists and everyone else or between experts and non-experts; and 4) the distinction between scientific truth and public opinion.

1. Experiments with ourselves

Some years back, a series of themes and problems that were unusual for the political agenda began appearing on the public stage: nature conservation, food security, the global climate, the genetic code, pollution, illnesses, health in general. Our greatest concerns currently stem from gas emissions, olive-residue oil, atmospheric temperatures, riverbeds and sea levels, genes or cattle; the protagonists are veterinarians, doctors, farmers, and firefighters. The governmental agencies that are related to science, nature or biology—which used to be considered less important—now stand on the forefront of public consciousness. There are political negotiations over issues that barely merited attention until now or, if they did, only technical specialists paid attention. Biological questions have become central to politics; one of the fundamental political issues these days is agreeing on a clear definition of what has come to be called nature politics or bio-politics.

These issues all reveal the increasing frequency with which society confronts the concerns, risks, and possible consequences of scientific knowledge and its technological implementation. What is unusual about these problems is that they ignore the divide between laboratories and the rest of the world. We are immersed in collective experiments that reject the relatively manageable limits of the lab. These social experiments are not performed inside a lab, and they lack established rules.

Traditionally, science has tried to avoid external interference as much as possible and detach itself from particular contexts. Many scientific techniques used to involve specific isolation; we can see this in the traditional idea of the laboratory. Traditional scientists worked with models and simulations that could be repeated, proved, and certified. It was possible to experiment first on animals, materials or software. Knowledge was produced at a concrete, specific location, with scientific controls, and from there it expanded—once sufficient time and other requirements had been met—to the rest of the world. The classic experiment based its success on the possibility of reducing and simplifying nature to a size that could be controlled in the laboratory. The practical application of knowledge obtained in this fashion was better when the conditions of the world more closely approached the reductions and simplifications that could be controlled inside the lab. Until the moment of its application, science was a private affair. The scientist's responsibility was relatively easily definable as long as there was a clear distinction between research and application, between what Graham called knowledge's "contexts of justification" and "contexts of relevance" (1981, 379). These two areas currently overlap to an extent that requires a reconsideration of our traditional way of thinking.

The separation between basic research and technical application is no longer valid (Schmoch 1996). Nowadays "knowledge is increasingly *produced* in the context of application" (Krohn 2003, 111). The distance between our theoretical knowledge and its possible practical applications decreases, and the uncertain consequences of its possibilities increase. When the amount of time between theoretical innovation and technical application is shortened (in some fields, this gap is almost non-existent), the relationship between research and practice becomes closer. Scientists are thus forced to anticipate the way their research can be applied. Science is now under greater pressure to justify itself since the determination of risks can only be proven through practice. The experiment and its practical application tend to go hand in hand. When we talk about nuclear energy, the financial configuration of the world, genetically modified organisms, or the use of certain chemical substances, we can barely separate the methodically controlled production of scientific knowledge and its application in open social and ecological contexts. To the extent that society and nature become laboratories, scientific autonomy is a principle that needs new legitimization.

While the laboratory works with a smaller model, current collective experiments are carried out on the original scale. We become concerned as we contemplate the complications of using the entire planet as our laboratory. Experiments are done on a one-to-one scale, in real time, with no possibility of repeating or minimizing the experiment or accumulating knowledge about the causes and consequences of our actions. There is no possible reduction of the collective experiment, nothing to replace it, which means it has to be carried out without sufficient certainty. Extending the laboratory in this way turns society into a general experiment. That is why it makes perfect sense to describe the knowledge society "as a laboratory" (Krohn and Weyer 1989, 349). That is also why scientific questions interest everyone now, generating concern and hope, or requiring participation.

The collective learning processes that have been called "true experiments" do not take place according to methodologically determined rules in a laboratory. Instead, they are carried out in an open environment in which social, technical, and ecological processes cross paths, incorporating the participation of many actors with different interests, values, and objectives (Weingart, Carrier, and Krohn 2007, 139). True experiments are carried out in an environment that cannot be completely reduced to theoretical models or isolated into an ideal research environment, in such a way that uncertainty is particularly intense and backtracking is practically impossible.

These difficulties are best perceived in the problem of side effects. If there were no side effects, if processes were reversible, science could count on absolution for its failed experiments. These parameters were assumed when scientific autonomy and freedom of research were configured. But the scientific system is ever more conscious of the fact that it has to anticipate its effects on a world from which it is no longer comfortably separated by the boundaries of the experimental arena. Science must remain cognizant of issues it cannot fully resolve. That is why it must develop its own way of managing uncertainty. One of its paradoxes is that the sooner the reflection about consequences begins, the greater the uncertainty about the knowledge of those consequences; the later the reflection, the greater the inefficiency when it comes to avoiding or correcting those consequences. The decision about whether or not to continue a scientific process is always made under uncertain assumptions. It is not possible, not even financially, to prove systematically and *ex ante* all the imaginable synergies that could lead to side effects. It seems as if we can only choose between decisions that are practically blind and a knowledge that comes so late that almost nothing can be changed. Many health norms, for example, arise from this paradigm of security and precaution that is not applicable to current problems. This explains the perplexity of government agencies or of public opinion about decisions that we might consider either precipitated or opportunistic, an abuse of power or an exercise in responsibility.

Current collective experiments cannot wait until absolute certainty is attained. Global warming, the configuration of the world economy, and food production are eloquent examples of this type of experimentation. The special concern or irritation these experiments produce is a result of their uncontrollable size, their lack of regulation, and the difficulties of backtracking. With these experiments, we cannot give ourselves time for a learning curve after we make mistakes because these are not simply preposterous hypotheses or practical failures; they are potentially fatal errors from which society must be properly protected. We have gone from a consistent manner of solving problems that arose from the development of science and technology to the reduction or prevention of unwanted consequences. The politics of knowledge cannot afford to act indifferently, limiting itself to *a posteriori* repairs. We can no longer put everything off for a later intervention.

For these experiments that we make with ourselves, there are no protocols. Protocols would have to come from the mediation between science and the desires of society, in those "hybrid forums" (Callon and Rip 1991) in which scientific and political controversies take place. Until now, we have lived with a clear distinction between science and politics. The unusualness of our situation consists of combining the precise and exact criteria that control scientific tasks with the space of politics where they attempt to generate confidence and make a choice (Latour 2001). The comfortable distinction between people and things, between facts and values, between the two cultures (the sciences and humanities) has been broken. The most interesting part of it is now found in connecting political realities with science and technology. We can affirm that the scientific fields where there are not too many exterior factors to be kept in mind are less creative, while those that are more "contextualized" are more relevant (Nowotny, Scott, and Gibbons 2004, 211). It is obvious that scientific objectivity is possible, but objectivity is greatest when the project is more abstract and holds less practical significance.

At the same time, although science has achieved a monopoly on the explanation of the natural world, it does not control all interpretations. Other types of knowledge continue circulating, making claims of validity. The desire for meaning, for example, cannot be satisfied just by science. This would lead to the paradox that science is more successful than common sense when it comes to the discovery and explanation of reality, but less so when it comes to interpreting what it all means. The greater the extent of meaning that resides in science, the greater the involvement of other social actors. Scientists are in charge of science, of course, but many other people intervene in its interpretation, which makes it, in the end and to varying degrees, a collective task.

2. Science as a task for everyone

The process by which the ideal of scientific autonomy was configured has been accompanied by a process that separates science from society. The *value* of autonomy corresponds with the *fact* of the differentiation of science. Although we can and should distinguish that value from this fact nowadays and redefine the relationships between science and society, there is an indisputable logic to that process. The sciences were formed at a certain distance from society. They allowed us to gain access to a new territory, and the rules that produced this new knowledge did not allow any type of external control. This distance regarding society is of a systematic nature, given in part the dynamic of differentiation inherent to science, that even affords it its own language and a preferential interior audience. This fully justifies its goal of autonomy, and the corresponding establishment of the radical difference between experts and laypeople. There is even a scientific "class" that Don Price (1965) compared to an estate, understood as societal groups that demanded financing but were not prepared to submit to any control of responsibility. This situation has changed radically in a democracy of knowledge, which demands rethinking the relationships between science and society in the context of new realities and new responsibilities.

What has recently made it necessary to come up with a new definition for the traditional relationship between science and society as well as the classic version of scientific autonomy? Essentially, there has been a complex process leading to a "dedifferentiation" of science and a certain reintegration of science into society, basically in the heart of the corresponding social and political responsibilities. Some people have discussed a "delimitation" of science or a loss of its institutional exclusivity, in other words, a reflexive questioning, so that the cognitive and institutional separation of science from other social environments, actors, and forms of knowledge is weakened (Krohn 2003, 111). The growth of the social relevance of science has been accompanied by society's growing intervention in science, something that demands revising the traditional ideal of self-regulation. Science is a social business, which influences and also depends on its social context. As an organization, it needs to be assigned resources; as a social institution, it requires legitimacy.

We can now say that the scientific "class" has lost the unlimited authority it originally enjoyed. For some time now, there have been a plethora of public controls over a social group that receives funding for an activity whose successes are often invisible and whose quality cannot be judged only internally.

"Self-regulating science" is, alongside the myth of the self-regulating economic system, the latest scandal of democratic society (Weingart 2005, 49). In fact, since the 1990s, science's social contract has been renegotiated. Social responsibility, the demand for accountability and public obligations are some of the concepts through which public institutional weight is given to controls, external assessment or competitive rankings. Everything indicates that this is the end of a particular scientific establishment and that there is a demand for the democratization of expert knowledge.

Debates about the conflicts attached to risk (and similar conflicts) have revealed that the influence science exercises over society has been considerably modified. With the technocratic theories of the 1960s and 1970s, the original assumption was that science would provide clear, singular direction for political and social action. Since then, it has been revealed that "scientification" is a more complex and tense process; it not only includes the influence of scientific knowledge on social relationships, but also the effects uncertainty and scientific non-knowledge have on society. The fact is that society is brought face to face both with "true" knowledge, which is scientifically certified, and with a fundamental uncertainty about the scope of that knowledge, its application in different contexts, and the presence of latent non-knowledge that is found within knowledge. Consciousness of this new knowledge constellation is what has made us move "from a culture of scientific autonomy to a culture of accountability" (Gibbons et al. 1994, 119).

Alongside all these processes, science has lost the monopoly of certain knowledge. Science cannot help but disappoint expectations of attaining trustworthy, certain knowledge that is free of risk. Other social systems end up compensating this type of social inaccuracy. Advances in science have expanded political territory to the extent that they have produced new demands for norms and regulations. The criteria to determine the quality and relevance of knowledge are no longer defined only by science but also by those who apply knowledge. These criteria arise in the context of the application of knowledge where social, political, and economic schools of thought are all powerful. The production, diffusion, and application of knowledge is reflexive and carries social debts; it is regulated by a series of social compromises in the face of some modified legitimacy requirements, making knowledge an eminently political question.

The perplexity with which we address these questions stems from the fact that there is now no validity in the traditional definition of a science that is only applied or a politics that is rational decision making as advised by the experts. Our collective experiments are enormously complicated by the fact that consensus and certainty are more difficult to achieve with them than with the regulated exercise of science inside a lab. The increase in public controversies about scientific issues shows that the traditional model of science or ideology barely meets our needs. The fact that there is always a compromise to balance political and scientific criteria means that knowledge is no longer irrefutable as an instrument of legitimization. Acting rationally in any field does not mean carrying out a preconceived plan but delving into the unforeseen consequences of a provisional and revisable project.

In a democracy of knowledge, there is now no use for the strict division of labor based on the assumption that no perspective wants the responsibility of taking other points of view into consideration. New challenges will require continuous attention to varied schools of thought that must be put into play in forums that can be rather tense. Social changes are not going to be produced through the initiative of a science to which society responds passively or by a social mandate directed at a science that is assigned specific tasks. Science has forced its way into society and society into science. Our primary concerns must be identified and managed during the scientification of society and the corresponding socialization of science.

In this way, society becomes a complex framework formed by actors with different resources, interests, and spaces for action. Society dramatizes the argument between diverse points of view to adopt the decisions of our collective experiments and thus configure our common world. We live in a world that demands that we be something like "specialists in contexts," capable of finding the relationship between different disciplines, comparing schools of thought, paying attention to unexpected causalities, contemplating risks and opportunities. The integration of diverse social systems, when it occurs, consists precisely in the interchange of points of view to compensate one's own blindness and find formulas that make different viewpoints compatible.

It would be a question of activating collective processes of reflection like those "hybrid forums" (Callon and Rip 1991) that work to register the modifications of the criteria with which knowledge is measured. They would also afford self-reflection and improved attention to social demands, or the idea of *agora* (Nowotny, Scott, and Gibbons 2004), which is not the bureaucratic world of the regulators but a space in which to realize a series of interactions between competing interests: diverse perspectives, economic limitations, global dynamics, political and legal regulations, budgetary priorities, etc.

Science, politics, and public opinion must find new and innovative paths to encourage science's social role and to manage the growing ignorance about science's consequences in a productive, transparent, and democratically legitimated fashion. Our choice is not between controlling science (as if there were an institution capable of doing so without destroying its innovative capacity) or giving it free rein and "naturalizing" existence (which would mean believing that processes such as climate change or global economic tendencies, for example, are inevitable realities that allow no intervention). The democracy of knowledge is affirmed as a key example of mediation within the maze of controversies, interested parties, and divergent cultures.

3. Science and people

Another distinction that is blurred within the current knowledge constellation is the clear differentiation between the expert and the layperson. The public presence of scientific ideas nowadays does not mean that scientific competition no longer makes sense, but that the distinction between those who are on the inside and those on the outside of the scientific disciplines has been softened. Previously, when there were experiments, they were always under scientists' control, while everyone else was relegated to the often-unwanted roles of spectators of something they could not judge. But we no longer live in a time period when experts would talk about indisputable data and use their knowledge to put an end to any controversy. In a knowledge society, people have more cognitive abilities. New organizations and interest groups appear and help weaken expert authority. What used to be an esoteric power of knowledge is now publically debated, controlled, and regulated. The democratization of science does not mean abolishing the difference between experts and non-experts, but politicizing that difference.

First off, the democratization of knowledge is tied to the fact that scientific authority is not indisputable. This is best seen in the value we assign to expert judgment, which is also submitted to democratic demands. I am not trying to formulate a political imperative but to assert a verifiable fact: the government, opposition parties, protest movements all have their own experts, and different experts have, of course, differing opinions. The legitimizing function of scientific knowledge has led to a paradoxical competition between experts. For this reason, we can say that the increase in knowledge in a given society does not necessarily mean greater consensus; instead, it reinforces dissent by providing reasons and the means for argumentation. The consequence is that political decisions are not adopted, as hoped, in a more rational, obvious, and consensual fashion, but in the midst of more intense controversies, with insufficient knowledge, and greater consciousness of risks.

The first condition for the democratization of expert knowledge and its social supervision consists of clearly establishing who is to be considered an expert, a question that can in no way be answered in advance. The closer a question gets to politics, the less important the distinction between layperson and expert. It is not that there are no experts, but that the distinction between their competencies must be legitimized. We must justify the reasons why the experts are the leaders of their respective scientific disciplines. Expert status may be conferred on "normal" citizens or laypeople (as we can see with juries, for example, or with the universal access to public positions afforded in a democracy) or those who are locally affected, who have been called "non-certified experts" (Collins and Evans 2002). What we would then have is a type of "extended peer communities": the circle of those who can and should evaluate the quality and usefulness of scientific knowledge for the resolution of certain problems is wider than the circle of experts in the corresponding field.

In fact, there are already many texts that emphasize that non-expert knowledge should be taken seriously in numerous situations (Wyne 1989). This does not mean that we should vote on the truth of scientific questions or that all opinions are equally valid, but that we would do well to listen to the non-experts, especially when expert authority is not always indisputable on every question and we have seen that laypeople sometimes know more than specialists. There are plenty of examples of the democratization of expert knowledge or citizen involvement with scientific questions. In Europe, there is a long history of the participatory governance of science and technology in the field that has been called "participatory technological assessment" (Joss and Bellucci 2002). The Danish "consensus conference" model is the one most cited. The European Union governance program, for example, tries to involve civil society in diverse stages of research, especially in the definition of financial priorities (Commission of the European Communities 2000, 8). Along the lines of the democratization of expert knowledge, we could mention a willingness to facilitate access to knowledge, limits imposed on administrative secrecy, the right to know who is assessing specific public decisions or how positions of relative scientific significance—such as professors, juries, expert commissions—are determined.

The discourse of the knowledge society used to be focused on the production of knowledge and, therefore, on the experts, while the account of the risk society, by emphasizing those who suffer that risk—consumers, voters, citizens—situates the distinction between experts and non-experts on a secondary plane. Laypeople lack specialized knowledge but may be affected by the decision being made or have first-hand experience with the matter being addressed, which sometimes allows them to have a broader perspective than politicians and experts. These non-experts can represent civil society, be competent when it comes to values, or have at their disposal "local knowledge," that "disparaged opinion" that Husserl tried to save. In any case, and also for epistemological reasons, it is important that science not discredit "outside" impulses or irritations as if they revealed ignorance or hysteria. Especially in those research fields that attract a lot of public attention, a "sociologically sensitive epistemology" (Nowotny, Scott, and Gibbons 2004) should not waste the opportunities for reflection and justification afforded by the non-knowledge produced by that very public attention.

Demands for democratization and participation attempt to integrate the perspective of non-experts and those who are directly affected in order to put processes of collective learning in place. This "cognitive politicization" (van den Daele and Neidhardt 1996) attempts to resolve the democratic contradiction suggested by a society of non-experts that is directed by an elitist group of experts. The objective of a democracy of knowledge is to treat everyone as citizens who bear equal responsibility for political decisions, without negating their differing degrees of competence. We are increasingly less able to use scientifically determinable facticity or the professional competence of experts to determine what knowledge and what normative criteria are relevant to resolve many of our principal controversies because they themselves are subject to social controversies and negotiation. Participation is important when decisions have to be made in the midst of great uncertainty and when expert counsel is insufficient.

All technical–scientific innovation holds risks that stem from non-knowledge, and that is why the decision about whether a society wants to expose itself to those risks is a political decision in which normative considerations also intervene. They must be considered expressly as political decisions and not defined as risk assessments derived from a scientific verification of facts. This carries at least two consequences. First, non-cognitive arguments and criteria—such as social utility, opportunity, economic costs or the consideration of other alternatives—can and should be involved in political decisions. Another consequence is that we are dealing with matters that need to be negotiated politically and are not predetermined by the objective criteria of experts. The political conclusions that are deduced from expert advice are very rarely irrefutable.

Because of this, our biggest problem consists of how to carry out a social reintegration of science when we know that the questions at stake are too important to leave in the hands of specialists. In our collective experiments, it will not work to have the expert play the role of mediator between the production of knowledge and society. In the new knowledge society, experts are replaced by what Michel Callon has called "co-investigators." No one in this society is satisfied simply to apply innovations without knowing their origins. The time when the application of scientific knowledge was unquestioned and necessarily useful is now gone. In a knowledge society, there is an increase in the number of organizations that are intelligent and investigative and that cannot limit themselves to being "consumers" but rather "producers" of knowledge. That is why there is nothing strange about citizens having increasing aspirations to be heard and to participate in collective experiments. Of course, it is not an attempt to establish a type of customer mentality to science as if we had a right to comfortable truths; science in a democratic society still has the obligation to speak truth to power, in other words, to public opinion. In any case, the politics of science and democracies of knowledge are central concerns of the new citizenship.

4. Scientific truth and public opinion

If scientific knowledge can legitimize distinct positions and political decisions, then it is not easy to maintain the idea that knowledge describes a hard, objective, visible, and one-dimensional truth. Scientific knowledge cannot be as clearly separated from value judgments as the technocratic and decisionist model would have preferred. The relationship between knowledge and decision making is more complex. It presents many questions about how it formulates problems, its trustworthiness, its range of interpretations, the number of answers it allows, and the relationship that knowledge has with social values and political interests—in other words, with its context of meaning. The final distinction we will need to retrace assumes that scientific truth and public opinion are two absolutely different things.

In a democracy, the application of knowledge is a "public" affair, in other words, it needs collective approval. That is why the observations that the means of communication make about science are very important in the knowledge society. Science has become a matter of public concern since the media observes and informs on it, discussing its ethical implications or the risks of research. The media is a social institution that intervenes in the configuration of knowledge and its collective legitimacy. Of course, the means of communication, like any social system, have a unilateral view of reality, which must be balanced with other points of view. But its role, particularly its emphasis on the legitimacy of knowledge, is irreplaceable in a knowledge society. It has acquired an importance explained by the very development of democratic societies.

The relationship between science and the media should not be understood as the traditional popularity of some forms of knowledge understood hierarchically. According to that model, the scientific system produced truths that were revealed to public opinion, generally in a simplified and popularized form. The "Enlightenment model" was still being influenced by the pre-democratic forms of public opinion. The public was generally passive and undifferentiated, unable to judge the knowledge it received. The communicative process only ran in one direction. Because of this asymmetry, mediation was not given any specific function. Many popular science programs were meant to attract attention through specific events or entertainment; they imagined a generalized and badly structured public. Allowing "the people" to return to science means something more than providing them with a closer, more humane, or more communicative image, even when that is very important. It is not a true democracy of knowledge if science is presented as a collection of facts whose origin either remains in darkness or is attributed to a few famous thinkers.

In contrast to this elitist vision of science, we have begun accepting the idea that knowledge is everybody's business, a task that is supported, not only by scientists in the strict sense, but also by every citizen. Little by little, we have begun recognizing the ability of all human beings to participate in research, inventing and doing science, or at least judging some of its conclusions. At the beginning of the 1990s, organizations like the American Association for the Advancement of Science (AAAS) and UNESCO popularized the slogan "Science for all," summarized in the following principle: "not only science in the service of everyone, but science *by* everyone." There is no democracy of knowledge if we do not recognize the principle that everyone has the ability to participate actively in science, understood as a collective task.

This is the context in which the current "mediatization of science" should be considered: science's focus on the means of communication has increased considerably because of the importance that the media has acquired in shaping public consciousness, political opinion, and, in the end, world perception. There is also the fact that there is a large competition both within the sciences and between the sciences and other social systems for scarce resources and public attention. In the space between science and politics, the media have the task of transmitting themes that confer legitimacy. The means of communication can no longer simply be faithful transmitters of scientific knowledge or of any other event. By their very nature, they tend to question science's legitimacy, relevance, opportunity, and compatibility with other social demands. The means of communication have not replaced the criteria of validation for science, but they have complemented them with a particular perspective that a democratic society cannot do without.

Democracy nowadays demands a certain recuperation of sovereignty over natural things and processes under current complex conditions. It must try to resist the preconception that there is no alternative (in other words, politics) because the world is unanswerable and is defined by privileged people. Hans Magnus Enzensberger (2001) recently claimed that our laboratories contain "coup supporters": scientists who want absolute power and do not want to submit their decisions to the processes of public deliberation. In spite of their not-infrequent contradictions, environmentalists or anti-globalization movements respond to this demand for participation with a reasoning that is very similar to the battle that was unleashed in the past against absolute monarchies: they want to stop being subjects and start co-defining the common world. What has changed the least is that we find ourselves immersed in the same struggle to reduce authoritarian voices into the democratic conversation of rumors.

Bibliography

Beck, Ulrich and Bonß, Wolfgang (eds) (2001), *Die Modernisierung der Moderne*, Frankfurt: Suhrkamp.

Callon, Michel and Rip, Arie (1991), "Forums hybrides et négotiations des normes socio-tecniques dans le domaine de l'environnement," *Environnement, Science et Politique: Cahier du GERMES*, 227–38.

Collins, H. M. and Evans, R. (2002), "The Third Wave of Science Studies: Studies of Expertise and Experience", *Social Studies of Science* 32, 235–96.

Commission of the European Communities, Working Document: *Science, Society and the Citizen in Europe*, 14 November 2000.

Daele, Wolfgan van den and Neidhardt, Friedhelm (eds) (1996), *Kommunikation und Entscheidung: Politische Funktionen öffentlicher Meinungsbildung und diskursive Verfahren*, Berlin: Edition Sigma.

Descola, Philippe (1996), "Constructing Natures: Symbolic Ecology and Social Practice," in Philippe Descola and Gisli Palsson (eds), *Nature and Society: Anthropological Perspectives*, London: Routledge, 82–102.

Enzensberger, Hans Magnus (2001), "Putschisten im Labor: Über die neueste Revolution in den Wissenschaften", *Der Spiegel* 23/2001, 2 June 2001, 216–22.

Fischer, Frank (2000), *Citizens, Experts, and Environment: The Politics of Local Knowledge*, Durham, NC and London: Duke University Press.

Galison, Peter and Stump, David (eds) (1996), *La Disunity of Science: Boundaries, Contexts, and Power*, Palo Alto: Stanford University Press.

Gibbons, Michael, Limoges, Camille, Nowotny, Helga, Schwartzmann, Simon, Scott, Peter, and Trow, Martin (1994), *The New Production of Knowledge: The Dynamics of Science and Research in Contemporary Societies*, London: Sage.

Graham, Loren (1981), *Between Science and Values*, New York: Columbia University Press.

Irwin, Alan (1995), *Citizen Science: A Study of People, Expertise and Sustainable Government*, London: Routledge.

Joss, Simon and Bellucci, Sergio (eds) (2002), *Participatory Technology Assessment: European Perspectives*, London: University of Westminster Press.

Krohn, Wolfgang (2003), "Das Risiko des (Nicht-)Wissens: Zum Funktionswandel der Wissenschaft in der Wissensgesellschaft," in Stefan Böschen and Ingo Schulz-Saeffer (eds), *Wissenschaft in der Wissensgesellschaft*, Wiesbaden: Westdeutscher Verlag, 97–118.

Krohn, Wolfgang and Weyer, Johannes (1989), "Gesellschaft als Labor: Die Erzeugung sozialer Risiken durch experimentelle Forschung," *Soziale Welt* 40 (1989), 349–73.

Latour, Bruno (2001), *Politiques de la nature*, Paris: éditions La Découverte.

Nowotny, Helga, Scott, Peter, and Gibbons, Michael (2004), *Wissenschaft neu denken: Wissen und Öffentlichkeit in einem Zeitalter der Ungewissheit*, Weilerswist: Velbrück.

Price, Don K. (1965), *The Scientific Estate*, Cambridge, MA and Boston: Harvard University Press.

Schmoch, Ulrich (1996), "Die Rolle der akademische Forschung in der Technikgenese," *Soziale Welt* 47 (1996), 250–65.

Weingart, Peter (2001), *Die Stunde der Wahrheit? Zum Verhältnis der Wissenschaft zu Politik, Wirtschaft und Medien in der Wissensgesellschaft*, Weilerwist: Velbrück.

—(2005), *Die Wissenschaft der Öffentlichkeit: Essays zum Verhältnis von Wissenschaft, Medien und Öffentlichkeit*, Weilerswist: Velbrück.

Weingart, Peter, Carrier, Martin, and Krohn, Wolfgang (2007), *Nachrichten aus der Wissensgesellschaft: Analysen zur Veränderung der Wissenschaft*, Weilerswist: Velbrück.

Part Three

The Cognitive Challenge of the Economy

7

The Intelligence of the Economic Crisis

When there are economic crises, the demands to which humanity is exposed increase to maximum levels. The first demand is to gain a good understanding of the crisis and confront it intelligently. If we want to govern ourselves according to criteria of rationality and justice, the intelligence developed by our societies must be synthesized around a series of principles required by the current world: foresight, confidence, responsibility, and cooperation. Some of the proposed solutions to the crisis are doomed to failure from the start. These include ideas that posit a world with no risk or no need for confidence. They also include solutions that propose a unilateral or protectionist solution to the crisis or conceive of responsibility in a way that fails to do justice to the complexity of today's society. What we need, instead, is the capacity to anticipate collective risks, build confidence, clarify responsibility, and achieve cooperative intelligence.

1. A political crisis

Crisis situations are not the best time to test the concepts with which we try to interpret a crisis. Truisms appear to become more firmly entrenched during crisis situations. One of the maxims that seems to have taken hold blames the economic crisis on a market failure and happily announces a return of the state. The budgetary and monetary measures adopted by many states, particularly the financial bailouts adopted since September 2008, have probably helped strengthen the impression of a return to classical Keynesianism. Of course, the crisis can only be explained as an aggregate of failures, but the accusation against the marketplace has become so thoroughly monolithic that, in order to fully understand the crisis, I believe we must emphasize that it is, more than anything, a crisis of politics—in other words, a crisis of the state. (States are, of course, the primary political actors of the day.)

Appearances suggest that the excesses of the marketplace are responsible for the current crisis: the banks have forgotten sensible rules, investors have risked too much, credit rating agencies have misled us about the appreciation of risks … The marketplace made many mistakes, and sanctioning it is logical. Nevertheless, anyone who claims that the marketplace is the only guilty party has not fully understood the corresponding failure of political institutions. This is important because a faulty diagnosis of the problem does not bode well when it comes to searching for solutions.

One of the less-fortunate approaches to understanding the economic crisis has been to analyze it within the debate between neoliberalism and social democracy, as if this were truly the ideological playground in which possible solutions need to be unleashed. This approach fails to acknowledge that this duality no longer has any legs when it comes to addressing global crises. The crisis, logically enough, has done more damage to the neoliberal than the social democratic point of view, but that is no cause for celebration among those who predict a return to the state and cannot clarify what that return might mean. What needs to be explained and should be confronted is that the state that is emerging from the crisis is a much less powerful state, given the global nature of the crisis and the limited efficacy of the traditional instruments of economic politics.

In the last few years, states have made huge mistakes in monetary and budgetary policy. The increase in the leverage effect on the world economy is more attributable to the failure of macro-economic policy than to a failure of the markets, whose only mistake has been reacting in predictable ways to political incentives. It was the state that urged the banks in the United States to develop subprime mortgages, beginning with the Clinton administration in 1999, which was pressured by associations that denounced the discriminatory nature of mortgages. A few weeks before the beginning of the crisis, members of both the right and left wings of the French parliament were discussing a proposed law to grant universal access to credit. This is worth emphasizing because we must remember that political decisions, not only the decisions of the marketplace, are dictated by short-term electoral agendas and are in serious danger of quickly becoming incoherent.

It is frequently said that the crisis was caused by insufficient financial regulation, but we forget that bad regulations are as pernicious as a lack of regulation. We cannot lose sight of the fact that banks have moved toward securitization because they were encouraged to do so by regulations that did not place any demands for capital on this type of credit, no matter its quality, while credits registered on bank balance sheets weighed heavily on capital, especially poorer-quality credits like subprime mortgages. Regulators seem not to have thought enough about the fact that an increase in external balance risks can affect the banking system as much as an increase in internal balance risks, once the increase exceeds a certain size and becomes systemic. Banking regulations have revealed the ineffectiveness of their microprudential nature, meaning that they consider risks caused by the insolvency of a particular bank, but not the insolvency of the banking system in general.

This, in my opinion, is the political system's principal failure when facing a crisis of a global nature: the biggest mistake the states made was ignoring their responsibility to respond to systemic risks. The political system, consumed by the most immediate social risks, failed to carry out its responsibilities regarding the supervision and prevention of systemic risks. At times, the political system delegated that task to entities that are not responsible for it, such as the marketplace or independent authorities.

We are probably reaching the end of the era of the welfare state, understood as a state whose only source of legitimacy was redistribution. We are entering a new era in which the prevention of systemic risks is at least as important. The crisis is making us realize that protecting against systemic risks is as decisive as the fight against social inequalities and that the struggle for equality is only possible if we are protected from systemic risks. Neither the neoliberal plan to dissolve the state nor classic social democratic interventionism will assist us in this new task. We are now faced with trying to save one of the most important examples of the shaping of political will, but within a global context that demands other strategies.

The crisis pushes us toward a reconfiguration that includes completely renovating the role of the states in order to give them back the room for maneuvering they have lost. The debate between supporters and dissenters distracts us from the fundamental problem: it is not a question of more or less state or even of reforming the state, but of redefining its mission in a global knowledge society, in other words, in a world where sovereignty leads to powerlessness and where the authorities have no more knowledge than the actors they must regulate. If we do not reflect anew on the purpose of politics—for which the state is nothing more than a means to an end—we will continue to prevent the state from fulfilling tasks for which it is responsible.

2. Being more intelligent than the crisis

We have discussed the knowledge society and the knowledge economy extensively, but we may not have realized that in order to meet their challenges we need to be more clever, in a manner of speaking, than the problems they create. The profound truth of these labels—knowledge society and knowledge economy—is none other than the warning that the root cause of our problems is a cognitive failure and the best way to overcome it is to learn from them, developing the corresponding knowledge.

In a knowledge society, we need forms of government that manage knowledge properly. We have focused a good deal of attention on the importance that knowledge has in our societies, but we have not focused as much on the ambivalent consequences of the production of knowledge, for example, in the global financial system when it comes to managing economic risks.

This is the context for the current crisis, which responds to an imbalance between the innovative capacity of the financial markets and our collective ability to configure them intelligently. While the financial markets have grown spectacularly for the last three decades, social expectations regarding public regulation of those markets has experimented very little progress. Financial innovation is always at least one step ahead of regulation. There is an asymmetry between private and public knowledge. The acceleration of the production of knowledge in global finances contrasts with the minimal capacity of the regulating institutions.

Financial innovations have been driven by two forces. On the one hand, there is the extremely competitive environment, in which every financial institution tries to gain an advantage, even if it is temporary, over its competitors. The second force stems from modifications to domestic and international regulatory environments. At times, even before new regulations were put into place, financial institutions were already searching for ways to avoid them or creating new products to get around them. All of this has created a consistent "regulatory dialectic" in which the authorities have tried to gain control and those who were regulated have tried to escape it. In addition, the asymmetrical nature of information has placed regulators at a constant state of disadvantage. Regulators have barely been able to keep up with new tendencies and have had to resign themselves to simply organizing the changes that had already taken place.

Politics and the law are not only incapable of offsetting the deterritorialization of the markets through the development and implementation of globally binding laws; they are also losing "cognitive competency" (Nonet and Selznick 1978, 112) that would help balance the playing field with economic innovation. One example of this can be found in the ambivalence of financial regulation. Various empirical studies have warned that some political and legal measures have exacerbated problems. This is the case with the Basel Accords, whose pro-cyclical nature is now evident. Their arrangements regarding funds lead to the expansion of credit in favorable periods and its restriction when times are bad. These regulations not only encouraged an increase in the type of derivatives that led to the current crisis but also made the credit market more instable. In fact, various voices have already warned that, considering the current economic situation, these arrangements should be reconsidered.

The 1988 Basel Accords were the first to establish international principles for the supervision of banks. The nucleus of the agreement was to have banks insure their loan risks with a sufficient capital of their own. The goal was to prevent possible crises that would arise because of a lack of confidence between banks. The response to this loss of confidence was to create the criteria of "adequate capital." This "capital requirements directive" was based on the finding that financial institutions were undercapitalized if we included the risks of liquidity, credit, and operations that are exposed to an increasingly more globalized financial system. Although this accord successfully unified international norms, it quickly became clear that its risk calculation was too static. The global system reacted to this imposition with a series of financial innovations. New financial instruments and methods such as derivatives were not taken into account in this model. There were regulations for the credit operations of banks, but there were no effective methods to calculate so-called "market risks" that came about particularly from derivatives.

By definition, any financial crisis leads to the confirmation that affected institutions had insufficient capital. But it is misleading to think that demands for capital can provide effective protection against systemic crises. No financial institution is in a position to provide sufficient capital to confront a systemic crisis. The search for less risk at any price, whether by removing the banks' balance risks (with securitization and derivatives) or through demands for ever greater amounts of capital, have uncontrollable side effects on the financial system, where risks are irresponsibly exported. None of this does anything but reveal the intrinsically systemic character of the risks that the banking institutions confronts, risks that must be dealt with in another fashion.

The 2004 Basel II Accord was an attempt to replace that static and quantitative control with a more flexible institutional agreement through the principle of a "dynamic provision system" that would help counterbalance pro-cyclical effects on the calculation of the sufficiency of funds. It was created out of the experience that, in the end, regulation is not effective if there is not intense cooperation with those who are regulated. The current economic crisis has revealed the inadequacy of these arrangements, but it has allowed us to continue completing the framework that is required for an intelligent regulation of the financial system. It is difficult to guess how and when a new agreement will be produced, but there is no doubt that it should constitute an exercise in adaptive intelligence and be carried out in the spirit of cooperation.

It is no exaggeration, therefore, to say that one of the causes of the crisis is a cognitive failure. Why does the financial system appear more intelligent and dynamic than the world of law and politics? It is fundamentally because the economy has a cognitive attitude, flexibility, and an enormous capacity for learning, while politics and the law are accustomed to a style based on norms, which means they have a tendency to give orders in areas where they should be learning. Law and politics tend to react to disappointments normatively, while the structure of expectations that controls the workings of the economy in general, and the financial system in particular, is characterized by a predominance of cognitive, adaptive expectations and a willingness to learn. That is why the economy and the financial system are in the forefront when it comes to defining problems and coming up with ways to confront them.

The complexity and velocity of financial innovation has placed banks and insurance companies into a position of cognitive leadership. The weakening of state authority regarding financial questions is well known: "where states were once the masters of markets, now it is the markets which, on many crucial issues, are the masters over the governments of states" (Strange 1996). Public authorities have fallen behind regarding technical capabilities and expert knowledge. If the regulators and supervisors cannot keep up with innovations, they will not be able to regulate them effectively (Steinherr 1998).

This is the reason that we can affirm that there will be no true solution to the crisis until public actors are capable of generating the necessary knowledge. Until now, the emphasis on the role of the states and the hierarchy as a means of control has prevented us from paying attention to the cognitive and cooperative aspects of governance. We cannot wield supervisory and regulatory responsibilities if we do not have access to the corresponding knowledge, which allows us to understand new financial instruments and warn operators about specific risks. In order to have a healthy financial system, supervisory agencies and investors must have information that allows them to correctly assess risks, something they have been unable to do during the current crisis.

It is not a question of prohibiting financial innovation, because innovation is legitimate and can be of great use to many sectors of the economy. Financial instruments did not cause the crisis, but the way they were used did. It is a question of avoiding abuse and demanding transparency, which will clearly not be easy given that we do not know what the innovations of the coming years will look like. The objective should be to correct dangerous and unacceptable practices without suppressing innovations that are useful for the community. This is particularly difficult because certain types of risk that cannot be managed with traditional economic and political instruments have been acquiring great significance in recent years.

In order to understand the problems the global financial market is currently having with governance, we must consider the characteristics and consequences of the production of knowledge in the financial system and the relevance of knowledge to politics. These new situations present us with questions to answer, and the old solutions that were associated either with the primacy of the market or with the direct and unilateral intervention of the state are of scant use. If solutions must be innovative, it is because the problems are unprecedented. What new forms of governance correspond to the growing deterritorialization and autonomy of financial transactions? Which institutions and regulatory systems will be most appropriate for a world of financial innovation and globalization? How do we overcome political difficulties when it comes to configuring global governance and intervening effectively in the processes of globalization? Politics has to decide, definitively, if it wants to carry out that function or if it is going to settle for playing the victim.

3. The economic construction of confidence

The current economic crisis reveals a vision of a systemic loss of confidence that exposes the degree to which the structure of confidence is fragile in the knowledge economy. The fact is that confidence is essential to the economy, especially to the stock market. Investors trust that balance sheets are correct, that analysts inform, and that the supervising authorities are competent. Small investors trust big investors, although they generally do not know how they manage funds. It is assumed that the system has enough controls and that they function independently of the interests or personal preferences of those who apply them. It is expected that credit rating agencies and auditors not only assess but are especially attentive to any relevant problem in the system; they should sound an alarm when creditors are going bankrupt or when businesses present inaccurate data on their balance sheets. That is why the failure of the credit rating agencies is one of the most unsettling aspects of this crisis.

The current lack of confidence can be interpreted as the reaction of investors to an opaque financial system that is so large they cannot completely grasp it:

> The mathematical complexity of financial innovation and transactions has been running ahead not only of the ability of regulators to follow (much less to control *a priori*) but also of the ability of many firms and financial firms to understand. (Cerny 1994, 331)

The economy is certainly not a simple reality, but when inevitable complexity is transformed into suspicious opacity, actors are blocked and markets stop functioning.

The crisis of confidence is averted by employing political and legal measures that can reestablish consumer and investor confidence. Nevertheless, while government intervention has helped avoid a panic spiral, the behavior of economic actors continues to be negative, and there is still a lack of confidence that is blocking the credit market. What this all reveals is that the difficulty of controlling processes is one of the government's fundamental problems in a global knowledge society.

Why is confidence necessary and inevitable in a complex society? First off, because in an advanced economy, confidence in the stability of the value of money is not based on people's knowledge. It is confidence in the system, which is indispensable for economic action in an uncertain future. To the extent that money is invested in countries where one has not travelled or lent to companies whose people and products one does not know, there is an increased economic need for systemic certainties. All the knowledge of the investors and the banks is not sufficient to assess the possibilities of credit based only on personal observation. The needs for knowledge from an outside observer explains why credit institutions resort to external observations. Risk no longer refers only to the individual components of a system, which are also understood as mechanical and in which a perfect division of labor prevails; it refers to the operating mode of the system as a whole, in which specific concrete risks, because of their interconnectedness, can result in systemic destabilization (Willke 2001, 9).

It is now routine to affirm that contemporary societies are characterized by an increase in both their spaces of possibility as well as their risks. The risks are such that they do not allow any choice between risk and non-risk. Most economic decisions have consequences that exceed the range of the predictable. Economic interdependence and complexity make it especially difficult to calculate the consequences of decisions and risks. Market dynamics force us to make decisions about a non-transparent future (Nassehi 1997, 339). Prevention has its risks as well, especially when it is redundant (Wildavsky 1988). It makes it difficult to react appropriately to new risks since it reduces the learning opportunities of dealing with them. Thinking preventatively is in conflict with innovation. If prevention is the attempt to avoid as many mistakes as possible, innovation means continually experimenting with new possibilities. Innovation is a process that reads mistakes as learning opportunities.

In this context, traditional mechanisms of assessment and control are unable to absorb uncertainty, or can only do so in a very limited fashion. The knowledge economy reveals the extent to which we depend on other people's knowledge and the reasons why confidence is a resource we cannot do without, even though it can fail. This is why we pay increasing attention to the phenomenon of confidence. The boundlessness of society turns confidence into a resource that is as rare as it is important. Confidence becomes very relevant when there is an increase in the amount of non-knowledge we must confront. Here we can reiterate Luhmann's idea that confidence is a mechanism for reducing social complexity (1989). Confidence allows us to accept greater complexity and uncertainty; it responds to the need for mechanisms to produce security that will compensate the absence of certain, rational calculations when weighing risks.

For this reason, organizations that structure uncertainties and assist in decision making are ever more important. Credit rating agencies respond to this very demand for building confidence, to those "infrastructures of security" (Hammer 1995) that provide confidence, calculability, and protection. Credit rating agencies provide assessments about the trustworthiness of debtors, thus allowing greater risk premiums. That is why they have been defined as "guardians of trust" (Shapiro 1987, 645) and even as "quasi regulatory-institutions" (Sinclair 1999, 159). They respond to the growing demand for mechanisms based on knowledge that allow them to face the risks of the global financial system. As Michael Power (1997, 123) affirms, contemporary society is only lacking confidence superficially. The economy not only demands a greater need for confidence, it also needs examples of a "lack of confidence that generates confidence." In this way, audits and the corresponding certificates contribute to shaping confidence and facilitate the adoption of economic decisions.

Credit rating agencies transform indeterminate contingency into structured and manageable complexity. With their advice about the probability of non-payment, agencies rate indeterminacy and translate it into a combination of letters that can be easily understood. In any case, we should not forget that, just as regulation inevitably produces its own risks, credit rating agencies, by facilitating the management of economic insecurities, also increase the speed of financial transactions.

In any case, it is clear that we should improve models for determining risk. In a global knowledge economy, future events cannot be controlled with mechanisms that are static and quantitative. Traditional instruments like the balance sheet, which used to provide rationality, calculation, and credibility, have lost a good deal of their effectiveness; institutions that have been carrying out control functions are barely in any condition to provide certain knowledge that can be put to the service of regulation. The question of the rationality of risk continues to be one of our principal challenges—in other words, the problem of recognizing the cognitive and operative instruments of the banks, credit rating agencies, and supervising authorities when it comes to managing current risks in the financial system.

We need to improve the instruments for weighing values and risks now that, from the objective point of view, our supervisory capabilities have diminished in recent years because of the increase in products not subject to balance sheets. These are the "knowledge assets," like patents, software, strategic alliances, etc. (Boisot 1999; Litan and Wallison 2000). It is increasingly important to quantify intangible goods whose indeterminacy places the validity of current valuations into question. From a temporal point of view, our starting point is the complication that accelerating the production of knowledge "defuturizes" accounting and makes it less valuable. It is increasingly difficult to use the past to reach conclusions about the future, especially in fields like information technology or financial services. Competency not only requires a permanent revision of products and services but also means that expert knowledge is valid for a shorter period of time.

4. The principle of responsibility

The idea of an interconnected world, which has served as a commonplace to denote the reality of globalization, implies, in principle, a world of little or diffuse responsibility or open irresponsibility. We cannot establish control over this world, and no one is in charge. The interconnectedness means, on the one hand, mutual balance and restraint, but it also alludes to contagion, the cascade effect, and the augmentation of disasters, as is the case with the current financial crisis. The interconnected world is also that "runaway world" that Giddens discussed when describing the less-pleasing aspects of globalization (2002).

The current economic crisis is, in the end, a crisis of responsibility, and the procedure that best represents it has been the spread of financial products like securitization, which translated the desire to postpone risks indefinitely, in other words, to accept risks without wanting to assume the consequences. This is what I have called "risks without risks." This has led to a true perversion of the function of credit, which is the most essential role carried out by the banks. They have constituted lines of products and combinations of values and proposed them to investors who were increasingly anxious for profit. Looking at things from the comfort of hindsight, the get-rich engine was running and no one knew how to stop it. In this way, the crisis has shown that financial globalization is much more fragile than commercial globalization.

Securitization functioned as a global mechanism of irresponsibilization that both disseminated and concealed risks, making markets opaque. These and other financial products let us clear or neutralize the risks of lending operations by transferring the charge to speculative markets. The opacity of the markets prevented control and permitted excessive risks, opaque securities with risks no one was able to assess. The lack of transparency was helped along by the development of new and exotic non-liquid financial instruments, greater numbers of increasingly complex derivatives, the fact that many financial institutions are opaque or not very regulated. This opacity has destroyed investor confidence. The difficulty of assessing prices, risks, or toxicity has led to general uncertainty.

None of this would have happened if, at the same time, the states, central banks, and global financial institutions had not neglected their responsibilities. Economic and financial directors committed the error of placing absolute trust in the self-regulatory capacity of financial markets and accepting the irresponsibility of credit markets, subject to the same model of behavior with which the stock markets function. They then provided bailouts that, while they may have been inevitable, will not promote responsible behavior. Economic actors who can assume excessive risks without having to suffer the consequences because their bankruptcy could produce a series of catastrophes throughout the economy have benefitted from these measures.

The crisis demands that we construct a new financial responsibility, something that will be carried out more through control and supervision than through normative regulation. Our leaders should understand that it falls to them to make the great economic and financial actors face up to their responsibilities: the responsibility of lenders to limit securitization, in other words, limiting the opaqueness of risks in the derivatives market so that debts are not used as instruments of speculation; the responsibility of shareholders to limit the right to vote to those who make a stable commitment to the company so a true strategy can be implemented; the responsibility of states to understand a system of stable parities, thus preventing violent oscillations of foreign currencies, which are disconcerting for economic agents.

We need to construct new agreements for responsibility without losing sight of the fact that these compromises must be achieved in the midst of an ever-thicker network of dependencies, where obligations lose visibility and clarity. At the same time, a world of growing interdependencies also decreases our ability to pinpoint responsibilities for actions. We should not let ourselves be seduced by the temptation of simplifying reality and personifying responsibility excessively. The current crisis is not attributable either to fiscal paradises or administrative remuneration, contrary to the crisis in 2001–3, in which these remunerations did play a decisive role in the creation of the dot-com bubble. Even though the crisis allowed us to discover the excessiveness of certain remunerations, we should not conclude that that excess is the cause of the crisis. The fact that states can limit remunerations in companies they save from bankruptcy should not make us think that the previous level of these remunerations caused the companies' difficulties and that from now on, thanks to this simple step, it will never happen again.

This and similar combinations of circumstances justify classifying our societies with an "organized irresponsibility" (Beck 1988) label. It is worth asking whether there might not be a lack of organization instead, whether our inability to organize responsibility in a social fashion stems from the fact that some of these dynamics clearly contradict many of our rights and responsibilities. The weakness of the sense of responsibility is not a question that can only be attributed to politicians or to citizen indifference; it comes from this mix of institutional weakness and fatalism that characterizes our democratic commitments. Many things can be organized to identify responsibility and transform blind dynamics into governable processes.

The difficulty stems, in the end, from changes in the way we thought about and exercised social responsibility. We now have the task of conceiving and articulating a complex form of responsibility (Innerarity 2009, 69). The problem lies in how to represent that responsibility at a time when the relationship between my individual behavior (as a lender, consumer, shareholder, voter, or client) and global results is no longer clear. The illustration of this new relationship between private and public will only be achieved if we develop a concept of responsibility that does justice to current social complexities and matches our reasonable expectations of achieving a world that can be governed and over which we take responsibility.

5. Cooperative intelligence

The best form of social intelligence, the one made most necessary by today's principal challenges (not only economic, but also our ecological threats, security issues, or social disturbances), is, without a doubt, cooperative intelligence. This cooperation is especially important at a time when the financial system has almost completely lost its territorial reference and has, therefore, been freed from state frameworks of regulation and control (O'Brian 1992). One of the principal difficulties of financial governance stems precisely from the fact that neither the legal nor the political system follows the rhythm of the global financial system, since law and politics are barely imagined beyond the limits of the nation-state. States are only capable of conceiving of entering into globalization as a zero sum game, conflictive by definition, and only acceptable in a strictly interstate picture. But the interstate framework is incapable of responding effectively to a global crisis because it does not have the resources. It is, more generally, incapable of preventing global economic and financial instabilities. The states' interim responses to the crisis are one thing, but the articulation of a new economic order that is just and intelligent is another. The states' reference framework is clearly insufficient to achieve this second goal. If we want to point in the direction of this ambitious objective, we have no choice but to overcome the lack of proportion between the global size of problems and the helpless provinciality of solutions, between the global character of the financial markets and the domestic character of the central banks and supervisory agencies.

Any solution depends on correctly interpreting the global character of the current crisis and reaching the corresponding conclusions: securitization and derivatives markets have collapsed throughout the world, in the same way and for the same reasons; the financial crisis has followed the economic crisis in the same fashion in almost all countries; the most critical financial innovations have been very globalized conglomerates when it comes to geographic setting, financial strategy, and management. The current crisis is not an American crisis that quickly became international because of economic and financial ties between the United States and the rest of the world. It is a global crisis, in the strong sense of the term, perhaps the first truly global crisis. This fact is verified when we see that globality contributed to the seriousness of the crisis. Normally, economic and financial relationships tend to play a moderating role in national crises. International movements of capital and exchange rate variations allow us to minimize the initial impact by partially diverting it onto the "rest of the world." But in the case of a global crisis, in contrast, there is no "rest of the world" that can carry out this moderating function, and the crisis cannot help but follow its internal logic to the end. In fact, it has already been noted that internationally synchronized crises are stronger and more economically costly than other crises. This is even more true for global crises, to the extent that we are not equipped with institutions capable of managing globalization and its risks.

Our failure to understand the meaning of the globalization of the economy and the global nature of the crisis explains a lot of our previous and subsequent errors. A lack of cooperation was one of the factors that led to the crisis. More serious than the failure of financial supervision in the United States or Europe is the absence of a structure of international coordination. The accumulated imbalance caused by AIG or Lehman Brothers reached such large proportions because the auditors were incapable of exchanging a minimal amount of information. Even more surprising and disturbing is the fact that this lack of collaboration is not limited to relationships between countries on opposite sides of the Atlantic but also affects relationships between auditors from the European Union and between insurance and banking auditors in the same country.

The responses to the crisis have not substantially improved this lack of cooperation. Until recently, states were responding to the crisis with measures that did not take their impact on other countries into consideration. When they refuse to recognize the global nature of the crisis and the necessity for a global response, states assume a good deal of the responsibility for the prolongation of the crisis. Meetings of the IMF, the G20, and the European Union have not managed to overcome our addiction to national politics, leaving the crisis without a global response. We must not lose sight of the fact that uncooperative policies do nothing but further weaken the global economy. To fight the temptation of protectionism or unilateral solutions, we must remember that the market was not what failed in the 1929 crisis; it was the states and their lack of collaboration. The reform of financial norms and of their surveillance should be carried out on an international level. Even though the idea of a global financial regulator is not very realistic at the current time (and may not even be desirable), the solution to the crisis requires greater coordination of the policies of financial regulation and supervision.

In the last analysis, the challenge we are given is to carry out intelligent governance of the financial economy. This means we must fully reexamine the function of politics in the knowledge society so it acquires the capacity to govern events, supervisory authority, a comprehension of complexity, a vision of the whole, systemic intelligence, strategic competence, and foresight. The true goal of politics would be to put forms of "cognitive cooperation" in motion, in other words, creating conditions for best combining heterogeneous functionalities, structures of governance, and knowledge resources, thus promoting collective learning. Only in this way can we make it so that appropriate complaints lead to effective solutions.

We need to develop a new paradigm for regulation and supervision that cannot be exclusively about control and sanctions. Intelligent supervision, in agreement with the current process of an ever more heterarchical and innovative world, cannot be carried out through traditional instruments of hierarchical authority. Regulation understood as order and control, the type of regulation that assigned an essential function to the states, is being progressively displaced by the rules of global accounting. GAAP and IFRS agreements reveal that global regulation can no longer be understood as something states carry out. Neither the hierarchical forms of control, like the iron fist of the state, nor the anarchic invisible hand of the marketplace are adequate to understand the complex interactions between different actors who are implicated in the regulatory space. A concept of regulation open to heterarchical forms of coordination and cooperation would be better prepared to articulate the relationship between mutually interdependent actors.

Forms of regulation based on norms are insufficient to govern the dynamics of the financial system that was established in the global knowledge society. Legal regulations are permanently confronting innovations that were not only not foreseen but that are unknown. Political and legal systems must change because the financial system constantly avoids regulation by building new instruments and products. Mechanisms of social coordination like the regulation of financial system risks have lost their effectiveness. This means that a solution to this problem cannot be found with *more* regulation to reform content but with *better* regulation, with procedures such as allowing affected parties to participate. The economic crisis is going to put our cooperative intelligence to the test, both regarding local pacts as well as the global capacity for cooperation between states or the interaction between banks and supervisors with the goal of achieving an innovative model of banking supervision.

Cooperation has become a new paradigm to resolve crises and conflicts at a time when the limits of the market and the state have been revealed. These limits can be seen both in aspirations for a spontaneous, deregulated evolution of the economy that would develop according to a satisfactory rationality as well as the dreams of those who entrusted the increase in rationality to a hierarchical and controlling direction over the markets. I would attempt to formulate it in this way: the new discussion will not set neoliberals against social democrats or the market against the state; instead, it must search for the type of cooperation that is most appropriate to resolve the problems we will be confronting.

We are probably very far from finding a balance between the two extremes; perhaps the way to articulate these two possibilities will vary throughout history and will sometimes require the liberation of initiatives, while at other times we will need to strengthen regulation. What is certain is that none of that can be successfully realized except within the context of what we could call cooperative rationality, in other words, through procedures of governance that articulate foresight, confidence, and responsibility. This is something that can only be done to the extent we strengthen our sense of what is public and common, ranging from domestic spaces to global dimensions of our common humanity.

The economic and financial crisis has once again revealed that the state alone (even the most powerful state) does not embody the critical dimension in the age of globalization, that the current logic of international competitiveness between states is incompatible with dealing with global problems, and that, for these reasons, we must move toward a model of cooperation. This is a profound paradigm shift, since we are accustomed to thinking about a multipolar world—a world made up of non-cooperative relationships of force.

We live in a world that cannot be abandoned to its luck, to simple evolution, if we do not want to pay the enormous price that that presumes in terms of injustice, destruction of the environment, and lack of security. Neither can the world be managed hierarchically, in a unilateral fashion, or based on trust in a control that has been revealed to be ineffective. The true response is building cooperative intelligence at all levels, at a time when we have challenges that no one can resolve on their own, not the market or the state, not the supervisors or those who are supervised, not one state without all the others, not short-term protectionism. For that reason, I will conclude by stating that intelligence and the will for cooperation has never been as necessary as it is now.

Bibliography

Beck, Ulrich (1988), *Gegengifte: Die organisierte Unverantwortlichkeit*, Frankfurt: Suhrkamp.
Boisot, Max H. (1999), *Knowledge Assets: Securing Competitive Advantage in the Information Economy*, Oxford: Oxford University Press.
Cerny, Philip G. (1994), "The Dynamics of Financial Globalization: Technology, Market Structure and Policy Response," *Policy Sciences* 27, 319–42.
Giddens, Anthony (2002), *Runaway World: How Globalisation Is Reshaping Our Lives*, New York: Routledge.
Hammer, Volker (ed.) (1995), *Sicherungsinfraestruturen: Gestaltungsvorschläge für Technik, Organization und Recht*, Berlin: Springer.
Innerarity, Daniel (2009), *The Future and its Enemies: In Defense of Political Hope*, Sandra Kingery (trans.), Stanford, CA: Stanford University Press.
Litan, Robert E. and Wallison, Peter J. (2000), *The GAAP Gap: Corporate Disclosure in the Internet Age*, Washington, DC: AECI Press.
Luhmann, Niklas (1989), *Vertrauen: Ein Mechanismus der Reduktion sozialer Komplexität*, Stuttgart: Enke.
Nassehi, Arnim (1997), "Das Problem der Optionsteigerung: Überlegungen zur Risikoestruktur der Moderne," *Berliner Journal für Soziologie* 7, 21–36.
Nonet, Philippe and Selznick, Philip (1978), *Law and Society in Transition: Towards Responsive Law*, New York: Harper & Row.
O'Brian, Richard (1992), *Global Financial Integration: The End of Geography*, London: The Royal Institute of International Affairs.
Power, Michael (1997), *The Audit Society: Rituals of Verification*, Oxford: Oxford University Press.

Shapiro, Susan (1987), "The Social Control of Impersonal Trust," *American Journal of Sociology* 93, 623–58.

Sinclair, Timothy J. (1999), "Bond-Rating Agencies and Coordination in the Global Political Economy," in A. Claire Cutler, V. Haufler, and T. Porter (eds), *Private Authority and International Affairs*, New York: State University of New York Press, 153–67.

Steinherr, Alfred (1998), *Derivatives: The Wild Beast of Finance*, Chichester: John Wiley & Sons.

Strange, Susan (1996), *The Retreat of the State: The Diffusion of Power in the World Economy*, Cambridge: Cambridge University Press.

Wildavsky, Aaron (1988), *Searching for Safety*, New Brunswick and Oxford: Transaction Books.

Willke, Helmut (2001), *Atopia: Studien zur Krisis der Ordnung moderner Gesellschaften*, Frankfurt: Suhrkamp.

8

An Economy for an Incalculable World

Politics is an inaccurate activity because it refers to the government as a social totality. Many political decisions are adopted based on the success of their proponents or their theoretical models even though their calculations are socially inaccurate. Decisions that have to do with ecological or financial risks, for example, require an overarching vision that can only be obtained, in the best of cases, from a political perspective. Of course, the deliberative process should include expert judgment and attention to individual interests, but the decision cannot be anything but political, because politics is what we do when we have stopped calculating and it is still not clear what to do.

One of the failures that explains the current economic crisis is the weakness of the political system when it comes to establishing regulations about the potential risks of financial innovation. There has been no political counterbalance to the financial system's faith in its own accuracy. The very fact of presenting financial matters as excessively technical and complex has facilitated a transfer of authority to the supposed experts and devalued the authority of the government. This has depoliticized these issues and removed relevant decisions from public discussion. This depoliticization of global finances has had important consequences on the type of priorities suggested by political agents, including the promotion of efficiency over social equality, justice, or democratic responsibility.

The states have wanted to imagine that a system open to innovation, such as the market economy, could be developed without risking a systemic crisis. This type of crisis dwells within an open system even if only because of the intrinsic possibility of individual and collective errors. The crisis reminds us of the persistence of those risks and the limits of financial culture over the last thirty years: it is as if the economy were unable to take note of these limits unless there is a crisis. But these risks can only be anticipated (and only in a rather limited fashion) by accepting that economics is a human science—all too human.

To what can we attribute this collective failure? I believe our difficulty when it comes to thinking about economic realities depends fundamentally on the weakness of our prudential and cognitive anticipatory instruments. We are witnessing the way the economy's anthropological, social, and political factors are ignored and the failure of the illusion of accuracy that has presided over the mathemetization of the economy.

1. The illusion of accuracy

The first demand whose failure to be met led to the current crisis was the knowledge, measuring, and foresight of collective risks. Looking specifically at the most recent financial crisis, irresponsibility began with a lack of foresight. Warning and risk prevention systems functioned very poorly. Relevant authorities did not perceive the seriousness of the crisis. This lack of foresight does not reveal a moral or political problem, but a serious cognitive failure. It is hard to understand why a history full of speculative bubbles with disastrous consequences did not lead to the logical conclusions. The crisis of the "New Economy" is very recent, and we have still not learned the lesson that, at that time, we were heralding the dawn of a very promising economic era. When financial euphoria is upon us, hypotheses about crises seem distant and unable to provoke the reactions that prudence would advise. In contrast to what is widely believed, the banking sector frequently errs on the side of excessive optimism. The enormous profitability of certain products encourages them to underestimate or even ignore risks.

The first anthropological explanation for this carelessness is that no one ever welcomes the bearers of bad news. But there is also an ideological explanation: those who defend the theory of financial efficiency have spent recent years saying that the market is never wrong. They celebrate the self-regulation of operators and "the wisdom of crowds" (Surowiecki 2005) with nearly magical confidence in market discipline. This discourages the creation of regulatory instruments.

I do not know if it is a lack of financial memory, as some people have said, or blindness in the face of disaster. In any case, it is clear that we are very bad at anticipating catastrophic developments even though we have no lack of sophisticated mathematical calculations. We did not have a precise roadmap of the risks that would have allowed us to foresee the irrational chain of events.

Some of the risks were dispersed throughout the marketplace in such a way that financial institutions could barely measure them and estimate their future impact. When the temporal horizon shortens and only the most immediate interests are kept in mind, it is very difficult to avoid catastrophic developments. Investment banks were working with hypotheses and statistical models to "package" complex products and evaluate their safety. But these statistics relied upon short historical series, rejecting extreme cases and the accumulative effects of a sharp drop in real estate prices in a given area. From the perspective of both information and control, self-regulatory mechanisms have revealed their inadequacies. All of this makes it clear that we still do not know how to detect, manage, and communicate global risks.

A worrisome question: how is it possible that improved risk analysis models did not help us foresee catastrophic results? We might think that the cause of our failure to foresee the crisis stemmed from an incorrect calculation of future risks. But what if it were exactly the opposite? What if one of the causes of the crisis was the illusion of accuracy, the belief that mathematical calculations have no limits when it comes to establishing future risks? If this were the case, then we could conclude that the crisis was caused less by an unlimited desire for profits and more by our failure to recognize the intrinsic limits of mathematical methods. These methods are especially inaccurate when it comes to measuring the risks of specific financial products. The economic crisis emerged out of calculations and measurements that presumed a degree of accuracy that they cannot provide (Charolles 2008; Beauvallet 2009).

Improved mathematical models would not have to seduce us with the mirage of suppressing all uncertainty. In fact, there are increasing numbers of voices that warn about the limits inherent to any modeling. They question the supposedly absolute trustworthiness of measuring systems and the accuracy of forecasts. Current debates revolve around this question, reconsidering certain accounting principles and the accuracy of statistics and modeling or common models for measuring progress. These models are excessively dependent on measurements that are simplified, such as the GDP. We should not forget the nature of mathematics; it is always a simplifying tool. The numbers always reference estimates and change with them. Taking measurements means making choices, and the political meaning of those choices is of primary importance. This inaccuracy is even more pronounced in the financial market, which rests on probabilities and foresight into the future. In this case, it can be rightfully affirmed that the models with which we calculate risks are, at the same time, risky. Janet Tavakoli in her book on credit derivatives talked about the "limitations of trying to apply mathematical models to define unknowable unknowns" (Tavakoli 2001, 2).

We need a true epistemological revolution to abandon the illusion that we can live in a world that is calculable if we fully apply the scientific model that we inherited from the natural sciences to social realities. This model owes its accuracy to measuring objective realities, which are external to the subjects of study, but it is very limited when it comes to calculating human behaviors such as the actions of the financial system. The financial system is not external to society and cannot be controlled by knowledge and technology; it is, instead, a social reality that comes from the sum of our actions. Calculations of probability are very problematic when related to human behaviors or the financial markets, since markets reflect human opinions, expectations, and fears, which cannot be treated as objective measures. That is why economic science must be considered human science, a science in which there is no separation between the subject and the object of research, which is why it is not an exact science.

We have analyzed risks without giving full value to the importance that significance or meaning has for them. Credit rating is not a technical process, as it tends to be understood. It is, instead, extremely inconclusive, qualitative, a judgment call. The rating is more than anything and principally an interpretation of the world and the routine production of judgments based on that interpretation (Sinclair 2005). It is an error to handle this type of measurement as if it were a physical reality, ignoring the fact that subjectivity filters into all the social relationships of agents. This epistemological perspective is extremely important. The modeling of risks is not just any type of modeling. It is not a typical case of applied mathematics with the discretization of finite elements. In this case, interpretations and meanings are what transform the numbers.

The majority of risks have an interpretative component that depends on an interpretation of the economy. Trusting the "common knowledge" estimate of risks (as we do when risks are introduced into the marketplace) is a logical error, since the majority of the actors who intervene in the market base their decisions on the mathemetization made by credit rating agencies and, therefore, they afford nothing new to our already inadequate understanding. In other words: in the liberal market economy, there is no rationality in risk material except for perfectly calibrated and statistically determined situations. The crisis has revealed the error of extrapolating certain beliefs of free exchange to abstract goods that include an interpretation of the future. The market is not good at interpreting doubtful cases.

Regarding finances, the limits of probabilistic modeling are ever more obvious. The mathemetization of financial risks is an attempt to create models for all possible interpretations of a situation. But as long as there are so many observers making unexpected readings of economic phenomena, risks cannot be quantified. In a world that is as dense as ours, the idea of causality has progressively lost its capacity for resolving problems. The growing relevance of "ambiguous uncertainties" (Bonss 1995) marks the transition from linear constructions to complex constructions of risk. Given that derivatives, for example, are based on other financial instruments and often combine various additional risks, the potential for losses cannot be fully measured. It is impossible to relate all relevant risk elements to each other, which makes it extremely difficult to give advice about operational risks. Furthermore, the idea of systemic risk in the global financial system reveals that the dynamic of innovation in global finances forms a chain of risk that may increase general risk through unknown influences and combinatorial effects.

Mathematical calculations, in spite of methodological precautions, have a tendency we could label innate for concealing ignorance. We are in no condition to truthfully quantify the risks connected to the market, to liquidity, much less the risks that stem from human error or a regulatory modification. Mathemetization is only accurate for processes in which interpretation plays a minimal role, which is not the case in the financial market. For that reason, the qualifications made by credit rating agencies summarize risk, omitting their interpretative nature. This is why giving agencies more independence would change nothing until we modify our conception of the true nature of financial risks.

The illusion that we could measure risks accurately also fostered the dream that we were capable of minimizing risks. The idea of a "risk without risk" is the ideology supported by financial mathematics that is at the heart of the current crisis. The financial crisis is to a large extent the result of a series of financial instruments that were developed to provide new forms of security, instruments that supposedly rested on calculations of safe risk. What has now become clear is that these calculations and prognoses are not only inaccurate, but at times also dangerous (Beck 2007, 43).

Previous societies were never as dependent as we are now on the methods used to calculate risk, and the fragility of those calculations has never been so obvious. The sophistication of mathematical models coincides with the evidence that the complexity of social systems cannot be completely reduced by any model. It is a fantasy to think that risk, including financial risk, can be fully eliminated. While banks are not casinos, as certain demagogues tend to say, both institutions do accept the role of chance in their operations. The transactions of the global financial system are based on extremely uncertain prognoses; the market is accustomed to volatilities whose dimensions cannot be foreseen or eliminated.

The current crisis has revealed one of contemporary society's basic properties: the specific risks (which are, increasingly, global risks) generated within them sometimes become collective crises. Unlike earthquakes or other natural catastrophes, these crises do not emerge from outside of our societies; instead, they stem from the failure of technology and social institutions. One of the reflections that is surely going to keep us busy in coming years is the question of how to confront the challenges this all creates for us. We need a more profound analysis of the concept of risk and the procedures to manage risk collectively according to democratic procedures and available knowledge.

A fundamental requirement for adequate risk management is realizing that risks are not objective. They depend on the reading of the situation made by the person trying to prevent risks or make the best possible decision. Any assessment of collective risk is fundamentally political. It is impossible to judge the advantages and disadvantages of a certain technology objectively given that such assessments depend on political values. This makes sense since risk assessment is based on the future that is desired or feared, which is a profoundly political question (Douglas and Wildavsky 1982, 10).

How can we evaluate risk when its very existence is uncertain? What decisions should be made when there is a weak or non-quantifiable risk with very serious consequences? Our collective appraisal of acceptable risk is what should take precedence. Risks must be measured and managed with social and political criteria. Regarding the coverage of financial, health, or ecological risks, only public debate resulting in universally accepted rules will be able to provide a frame of reference. Not even the mathematicians can eliminate the need for that debate.

2. Another economic science

The economic crisis has also affected the instruments that should describe it, the intellectual and conceptual framework that supports our comprehension of economic realities. The loss of confidence in financial mechanisms has led to an age of more general uncertainty toward dominant economic science. We imagine that economic science is tied down by an excessively narrow conception of human behavior, based only on the maximization of profits with a very simple mechanistic model, insensitive to the systemic and social aspects of economic reality. Could it be that the crisis, which expresses an unavoidable disconnect between economic and social factors, was preceded by an economic science that systematically ignored that interaction? No one can question the right of any scientist to elaborate models and abstract theories, but when it comes to recommending collective decisions, theoretical digressions must face public scrutiny about its effects on society.

Many analysts have noted that the roots of the recent financial crisis are found in the evolution of economic science since 1970. The causes that are habitually cited to explain the current crisis are all true, but we should not fail to mention epistemological or scientific causes. Theories are not always harmless; there are times when what one thinks affects what happens. There has been, of course, unlimited greed, contamination effects, and failures of regulation, but none of that would have been possible if the road had not been paved by a particular school of economic thought. In recent years, economics has constructed a very abstract representation of the market as an almost perfect self-regulating mechanism. The rationality of agents, the efficiency of markets, and a focus on economic affairs that is completely detached from social realities have been established as incontestable truths.

The crisis gives all of us particular areas of responsibility. It affords economists the chance to take an open-minded look at their profession, remembering that some of their principle sources of confusion come from the inertia of an epistemological framework that gives their practice a strong structure. This is especially true since economics has succumbed to the temptation of claiming the status of a science, which guarantees specialization and accuracy.

We could summarize this situation, from the epistemological point of view, by affirming that economic science's goal of becoming a precise, hyper-specialized body of knowledge has meant a loss of the necessary ability to understand the social complexity of economic realities. Economics has lost its critical capacity, as well as its nature as a social, ethical, and political science. The mathemetization of economics confers a false precision to a field that is filled with arguable premises, excessively simplistic models, and the ideological taking of sides.

The infancy of economics as a discipline is marked by the ambition to resemble a science as much as possible. At the end of the eighteenth and beginnings of the nineteenth century, when economic knowledge as such was being constituted, physics was the dominant science. The quest to resemble physics, to become something akin to the physics of economic realities, meant understanding that the objectivity of economic predictions demanded a rejection of all subjectivity, of those anthropological and social aspects that prevented accurate judgments. The history of economics as an objective science is the construction of an edifice that excludes everything that could undermine its status as an exact science. Political economics became mathematical analysis and was then converted into economic mathematics, econometrics, a pure data analysis technique that could be applied to any object and any society. While financial economics was a part of the field of economic theory until the 1970s, it is now fundamentally in the hands of statisticians; the discipline has been automatized to the point that it is almost unrelated to traditional financial macroeconomics. In a certain sense, the current crisis is the crisis of the division of labor between economists.

Seduced by the goal of accuracy, economics seems to have forgotten its nature as a social construct. Markets are not supply curves that coincide with demand curves on paper, but social and historical constructs, human institutions, social networks, and loci of power. Prices are states of opinion, psychological dispositions, social conventions. Economic values do not have the intrinsically objective consistency that economic theory has wanted to grant them. This is evidenced by the way they drop when there is a decline in social confidence. Even the models with which we try to understand economic behaviors are social constructs. The observer or theoretician exercises a powerful effect on the reality that is being studied. Economics cannot presume accuracy if it is incapable of measuring the impact its own theories have on the object under study. No one has made a model, for example, of the way in which models themselves can be used to give the financial sector a false sense of security.

When we ignore its social dimension, economic abstraction becomes a true distraction. The hunger for accuracy gives way to enormous social inaccuracy. This is why abstract economic science is bad at formalizing the social and political aspects of a market economy. The efficiency of the division of labor in economic research means we fail to comprehend the interdependencies that act on all economic processes, which are, as we should remember, a societal event. Here we encounter the first contradiction demanding critical examination.

Economics sees itself as a hard, specialized science, but this is not compatible with its previous goal of offering a general discourse on social order, human government, and national destiny. Or is it that the accuracy afforded by specialization has no price?

The price could not be very different from what is paid by any excessive amount of attention: the loss of an overarching vision and its ability to manage that which, because of its very nature, does not fit well into a model of mathematical accuracy. Economists have achieved the precision of their models at the cost of the probability of their forecasts. This would not be particularly serious if they had not tried to convince us that the achievement of accuracy meant we did not need to pay attention to less precise variables. The failure of economists when it comes to anticipating the crisis is explained by the specialization and fragmentation of their diverse specializations, more specifically, by the illusion of calculability that this specialization provided. That is the reason behind the curious paradox that the best economic experts were incapable of detecting a bubble while, as an American economist noted, every taxi driver in Miami could tell his or her clients the exact characteristics of the real estate bubble that began developing in the first decade of the twenty-first century. For this reason, economics now finds itself in a paradoxical situation: at a time when it appears to be best prepared to explain economic and social phenomena, it finds itself defenseless and perplexed by a financial crisis it was unable to foresee.

The myth of accuracy begins with an unjustified extrapolation. The microeconomic environment is where economic theory is most empirically verifiable. However, its transposition to more complex economic spaces or to the global economy has enormous limitations. There are a whole series of non-linear elements and unforeseen reactions that are in play on a macroeconomic level that microeconomic theories cannot anticipate. The limits to models that they would like to extrapolate to global processes are primarily due to the fact that we are not well versed in the laws of probability for extreme and infrequent events. Economics is incapable, for example, of explaining how the guarantee of a risk that is optimal at a microeconomic level can lead to a systemic crisis. Neoclassic theory disguises the immensity of poorly understood or unstable situations. An event that any theory might struggle to explain is incomprehensible for reductionist models: how can it be possible that the addition of individual behaviors—that were rational in the sense of economic theory—could lead to overwhelmingly irrational results?

The fact that accounting norms have abandoned their photographic neutrality in recent years also contradicts this simplistic vision of accuracy. For some time now, we have not really known exactly what our measuring models measure. The Enron case made us more aware of the limits of accounting principles that have retained a view of economic cycles stemming from the industrial revolution.

Similarly, doubts have been raised about our indicators for economic measurement. We are more and more conscious that economic measurements are not neutral acts; they imply a series of preferences. A social reading of economic data is imposed so growth indicators do not mask other questions about their distribution in society.

The whole debate about new wealth indicators revolves around this question. The fact that we value environmental quality, security, cultural dynamism, or the gratifying feeling of living in a just society reveals that our subjective wellbeing depends on goods that are not exactly inside the marketplace. The use value of these resources, products, or services can be correctly reflected by exchange values. This conceptual change has been the objective of France's "Stiglitz–Sen–Fitoussi Commission" concerning economic development and social progress (Stiglitz, Sen, and Fitoussi 2009). By proposing a modification of the way we calculate GDP, by questioning how to take wellbeing into account or how to deal with environmental questions through statistical data, it attempted to guide the economy toward a measure of wellbeing that surpasses growth dogma and the strict mercantile framework. This is a goal that should engage us beyond the occasional moments when we are "escaping the crisis" or having a ritual discussion about "another economic model." It would be an attempt to measure wealth more precisely without focusing on a measurement that makes the extremes seem insignificant.

Economic theories about strict compliance tend to ignore the other social sciences or subject them to their own structure. Economic science has tried to bracket off the profoundly subjective nature of economic behaviors in order to achieve its goal of being an exact science and favor increasing its mathemetization. We should revise the idea of science that we have inherited from the natural sciences, their mechanistic model, statistical abstractions, the reductionist conception of causality, or the idea that there is only one possible solution.

The crisis seems to have suggested the possibility of other courses of action such as what we could call the return to *an economy of passions*. We can observe a desire to recuperate an integral vision of the economy as an anthropological and social reality, articulated with human and social sciences, which takes into consideration human passions and social repercussions, beyond the abstract models that are currently employed. The return to passion in economic vocabulary is a return to the origins of economic thought that has, since Adam Smith, placed the economy in an anthropological context. One part of this approach is seen in Amartya Sen's attempt to expand the reach of economic rationality to "abilities." He criticized Arrow's idea of the "rational idiot," which has served as the foundation for dominant economic theory. There are many other contemporary examples, such as Sen 1999; Latour and Lépinay 2008; Cohen 2009; and Akerlof and Shiller 2009.

It does not seem coincidental that the economists who have erred the least regarding the crisis are those who approach this science with more appreciation toward other related sciences. There are many examples, but I would highlight Stiglitz or Akerlof, who questioned the neoclassical hypothesis that market participants have perfect information. They also emphasized the importance of considering herd psychology when explaining economic phenomena. The crisis of economic reason calls for the activation of other types of rationalization that involve symbolic and cognitive resources, fundamentally the governance of social goods and the institutions that structure the social field.

The self-sufficiency of economics as an academic discipline feeds into a very naive interpretation of the economic field. There are no economic relationships without institutions, without states, without regulations, without language or culture. Economics must become a social and historical science again; it must reconnect to social and political philosophy and not use mathematical modeling more than as an accessory or aid. If the economists who are closest to politics or sociology made fewer mistakes about the crisis, it is primarily for this reason. Given that the economic crisis stems from a divide between the economic and social spheres, we now need an economic perspective that understands the connection between both dimensions of human activity.

Economics is a social science, and the long period during which it was separated from other social sciences, claiming full autonomy, was not satisfactory for economics or the other social sciences. The growing complexity of economic matters justifies technical specialization, in economics as in any other science. But specialization should not imply losing sight of the place economics holds among the instruments used to explain human realities, especially the relationship between economics and politics. It is time to return to those who have always considered economics a social science and not an exact science. Applying theories to the real world requires knowing a great deal about politics, history, and the local context. That is how Smith, Marx, and Keynes understood it. They all thought of the economy as a system of relationships and not as a simple collection of juxtaposed markets. We could also mention the importance granted to economic sociology in the rich tradition of Weber, Durkheim, and Polanyi. The interdisciplinary or multidimensional nature of economic activities should lead it to practice what Richard Bronk calls "disciplined eclecticism" (2009, 282). It would have to solicit the collaboration of all knowledge, freeing itself from one-note explanations, and privileging reflections founded on interactivity, uncertainty, and complexity. In short, economics should step outside of the economy if it wants to understand the contemporary phenomena we are confronting.

There is such a contrast between current economic esotericism and the simplicity of Alfred Marshall, who was a great mathematician as well as a great economist. He advised one of his students to do everything possible to "prevent people from using Mathematics in cases in which the English language is as short as the Mathematical" (Marshall 1996, 130).

All the encouragement to construct "another world," the impulse that upholds the ethical criticism of capitalism, are signs that alterglobalization concedes too much reality to the model it is fighting. If we must move toward another world, we end up saying, it is because this one is beyond repair, and our explanation is monopolized by "realists." However, it is not at all clear that the "realism" that economic science claims for itself is as consistent as is generally assumed. If there is anything economics has been lacking—we can say this now with the perspective granted by recent history—it is realism.

There is also a perverse effect of this criticism: ethics is not enough to modify the economy, and it can even act as a counterweight to commercial logic. The people who monopolize economic realism feel quite comfortable if their critics confront their values rather than their description of reality. The criticism of contemporaneous capitalism, if we want to be more radical than moralistic, should focus on combating the supposed realism of dominant economic science.

We cannot continue thinking, as Popper affirmed, that we need only choose between astronomy and astrology, that our choice comes down to selecting either that which is accurate or that which is irrational. Most of the reasonable lessons economics affords us are neither; they are not irrefutable because of their accuracy or worthless because of their total lack of rigor. Like almost everything that is human, they generally exist in the range of probable certainties, neither precise enough to declare any discrepancy irrational nor baseless enough that they cannot be employed to make coherent decisions.

What is most revolutionary today is a good economic theory. The question is not to imagine another world but to elaborate another economics to describe this one and be able to improve it. We do not need a different world, but different economic theories.

3. Nostalgia for calm passions

When the financial crisis began, greed was used as a recurring explanation of what was going on: the greed of bankers, irresponsible speculation, excessive ambitions, unsustainable consumption, etc. Of course, there has been a lot of frivolity, blind optimism, opportunism, and herd behaviors in the financial realm that have given way to a gigantic collective stupidity. It is also true that the greed of investors, bankers, consumers, and business owners played an important role in the creation of the crisis.

In spite of all that, the idea that greed is the cause of the economic crisis is not very useful for understanding what is going on because it explains both too little and too much at the same time. Of course, human beings are always looking out for their own advantage; we are much more capable than other animals of perceiving the opportunities we are afforded. But such a basic human characteristic does not explain why the crisis happened. We need to ask about the interaction between actors and institutional conditions.

Anyone who focuses unilaterally on greed is stuck in the old way of thinking according to which only individuals fail, never the system as such. In the same way, calls for greater responsibility, while politically correct and morally indisputable, are mistaken, since they seem to presume that the issues to which one should respond are self-evident. If we want to give the concept of responsibility any value, we must do so by considering processes of collective decision making. Responsibility must be reformulated for a complex society.

In addition, calling greed "excessively human" serves to conceal systemic causes of the disaster in the financial markets, in the same way as understanding it as an addiction removes responsibility from the actors. The cause of the financial crisis would not exactly be a lack of regulations for the financial marketplace but a supposedly inevitable passion. Blaming the crisis on greed is, indirectly, a general exoneration. Since all human beings are greedy, bankers have done nothing we would not all have done in their place.

The crisis cannot be explained on the basis of greed, among other things because greed is an individual property, while the crisis is a systemic result that no one individual sought or produced and that no one individual could have prevented. The crisis should be understood as the systemic, non-intentional result of many individual actions. Systemic results do not come from individual motives or bad intentions, but from systemic imperatives from which the individual can only distance him or herself at the cost of economic ruin. We must search for the cause in an institutional order whose failures have been revealed through the economic crisis. These failures incited certain irrational behaviors, like low capital demands for banks or mistaken perceptions of the risks that were being assumed. It is similar to what has happened with corruption, which is primordially an organizational problem and only secondarily a problem of individual morality. In other words, it is a problem of the conditions that allow it or do not disallow it structurally.

Referring insistently to greed in order to explain the financial crisis actually informs us about the emotional state of financial capitalism: the emotional life that characterized modern capitalism has been significantly transformed. The explanation for all of this demands a revision of the way liberalism classifies passion and self-interest.

Max Weber described the origins of capitalism as the history of the separation of rationality and emotion, of interest and passion. Modern capitalism is not characterized by greed but by moderation. Passions are strong emotions, almost impossible to control, and they can swing from constructive to destructive at any time. Passions are outside of rational control and encourage people to exceed all limits. The "passive" aspect of passion is the incontrollable impulse of satisfaction claimed at any cost. Passions prevent us from achieving any reflexive distance. That is why Weber found it inconceivable for an unleashed passion such as greed to be the motor of modern capitalism. It would be just the opposite: capitalism means the fundamental domination of irrational impulses (Weber 1988 [1920], 4).

Albert Hirschman holds a conflicting opinion; he tried to show that the contrast between passion and self-interest was not part of the idea capitalism had of itself. Seventeenth-century capitalism understood greed as a useful passion that could provide the strength both to maintain the will to earn and to limit self-destructive passions (1984, 50). Economic self-interest would be a hybrid of passion and reason, a mediator between greed and calculability (Pixley 2004).

This concept of the economic usefulness of passion is the basis for the idea of the transformation of private vices into public virtues as expressed in the fable of the bees written by Mandeville in 1705. The pleasure of greed is the only thing capable of providing a sufficiently persistent will to earn beyond the comfortable satisfaction of material needs. When greed is linked to economic self-interest and its potential to excite is limited, it is finally transformed into what David Hume called a "calm passion" of clear economic and social utility.

While the founders of liberalism were familiar with the depths of passion, in twentieth-century economic science, greed has been primarily understood as the harmless self-interest of rational utility. The irrational side of the desire for profits has disappeared completely. This is a world of rational economic subjects, free of lies and trickery, free of opportunism and inauthenticity, just pure instrumental rationality without emotion. Greed was understood as a desire to earn, free of any destructive dimension. That is why some contemporary sociologists write defenses of greed: they view it as equivalent to the harmless self-interest of economic progress.

But do things really work like this in the current financialized economy? Does this economy contain a motor of calm passions that result in general usefulness or is there a type of greed that is less individually owned and more characteristic of the system as a whole? Let us look for a moment at how unlimited desire works and how it interacts with the possibilities of money and financial markets.

Since Democritus, greed has been understood as limitless desire, desire that cannot be satisfied because it is not related to any object. This contrasts with the desire that pursues something specific and is calmed after achieving it. With excessive greed, pleasure is in the attempt, not the attainment; expectation increases excitement more than actual experience does. If the passion of greed cannot be satisfied, it is because pleasure is not in the object but in the expectation of it. That is why greed has the oft-criticized property of being insatiable and unlimited.

The greatest greed awakens a desire that is objectless. This tendency is excessive, without any specific or limited application; it enjoys infinite possibilities. In Georg Simmel's view, this is what creates the greed for money in modern culture. Given that money becomes an "absolute medium" (Simmel 1999 [1900], 312), it ends up generating pathology on top of any utility. For the greedy, any transitory satisfaction is less exciting than the expectation was.

The more abstract and indeterminate the expected means of pleasure, the more powerful the ambition stirred up by unlimited possibilities. That is why money is the ideal object of greed, since "every point reached is no more than a passing phase" (303).

Does the structure of pure passion have anything to do with current financial markets? We can affirm without exaggeration that greed has never been less capable of exercising the useful function assigned to it by classic liberalism as it is within financial organizations and business models. Why is that the case?

Financial markets are specifically characterized by controlling not goods but expectations that are focused on the future valuation of capital investments. Even when financial markets speculate with goods, such as prime materials, the corresponding bets refer to expectations in relation to other speculators' expectations of price fluctuations.

Financial markets have allowed our expectations of greater and riskier profits to be continuously stimulated. The greater the willingness to run risks, the greater the potential profits and the lesser the sense of responsibility. This is fundamentally true for businesses in the financial arena, but it also occurs in the investment department of banks, which want to assume the same risks and achieve the same profits. Banks can hardly place systemic limits on financial markets in a manner that does not limit the increase in profits for speculative investments.

To the extent that banks operate in the realm of credit, in the financing of businesses or the administration of private holdings, what we have are economic activities that, in their objective dimension, hold particular goals and objectives; in their temporal dimension, they span a long period of time and do not depend on events or decisions; in their social dimension, these economic activities are linked to lasting social relationships, which are in turn the foundation of stability and confidence.

However, everything is very different when the banks' principal business is to speculate in financial markets. In this case, there are no investments, but only bets that are unattached to the objects on which they are placed; they are purely self-referential. Speculators do not try to avoid these moments of uncertainty that every investor with his or her own capital tries to eliminate as much as possible. They do not do so because these moments of uncertainty are precisely what they want to enjoy with their economic gambles; they experience them as excitement that they would like to repeat continuously.

The temporal dimensions of financial markets contribute to the emotional turbulences that follow the rapid sequence of expectations and disappointment, euphoria and depression, fear and greed. The extremely short temporal horizon in which brokers and money managers act are, on the one hand, technologically conditioned. The frequency of transactions in real time is now possible because of extremely rapid computer systems in which the expression "money never sleeps" is literally fulfilled. This creates the expectation of larger profits in ever shorter periods of time. An objective explanation for these behaviors is found in the fact that some funds gave larger profit margins than had previously been earned anywhere except in drug trafficking.

Pixley successfully summarized the crux of the question when she affirmed that "greed is merely a byproduct of the trust (through distrust) necessary to imagine a controllable future" (Pixley 2004, 159). The rhythms of the financial markets, which have an extremely short cadence, presume a generalized distrust of our ability to control the future, an excessive exploitation of the present, an economization of the smallest units of time, and, finally, a ruinous competition around the "last minute," which gives the decisive advantage to those who compete for the largest profits. The greed of investment banks is not a quality that should be attributed to people but to a structural principle of their way of acting. Greed necessarily accompanies a type of competition in which the dominant criterion is never to waste the opportunity for an even greater return. In this way, some months before the crisis broke out, our situation was similar to one of those car races where you drive toward a wall as fast as you can, and the last person to brake wins. No one is prepared to brake because the next car over will simply brake a little bit later, so in the end, everyone ends up crashing into the wall. The risk of harmful passions is revealed in this collective "forward escape" (Neckel 2008), imitative and stupid.

In the financial crisis of 2008, the belief that risks could be calculated, secured, and sold to other people led to the assumption of more risks (Arnoldi 2009, 64). At the same time, various groups helped produce the illusion that things were under control: financial mathematics suggested the risks were calculable, and dominant economic science, with its "efficient market theory," claimed it could demonstrate the complete rationality of price setting in the financial marketplace (Fox 2009). The presumed protection against risks promised by these situations and mechanisms institutionalized the addictive power of greed throughout the financial market.

We have instituted procedures for financial markets and banks that do exactly the opposite of the procedures classic liberalism tried to put into place to neutralize harmful passions. In some ways, we have also proven the limits of the transformation of passions into interests as described by Hirschman. If the calculation of economic interests is revealed to be an illusion, then there cannot be mediation between passion and reason in the financial marketplace. Greed cannot become a calm passion until we reduce the excitement potential of the "fancy finance" of investment banks and derivatives and until being a banker is once again—as Paul Krugman recommended—a boring affair. Capitalism cannot renounce the profit motive, which is as old as money, but we should be able to reduce the gratification that greed enjoys in the financial marketplace of emotional capitalism. The function of what we call global financial governance should be a definitive return to calm emotions, which we long for in the current financial whirlwind of destructive passions.

Bibliography

Akerlof, George and Shiller, Robert J. (2009), *Animal Spirits: How Human Psychology Drives the Economy and Why it Matters for Global Capitalism*, Princeton, NJ: Princeton University Press.

Arnoldi, Jakob (2009), *Alles Geld verdampf: Finanzkrise in der Weltrisikogesellschaft*, Frankfurt: Suhrkamp.

Beauvallet, Maya (2009), *Les stratégies absurdes: Comment faire pire en croyant faire mieux*, Paris: Seuil.

Beck, Ulrich (2007), *Weltrisikogesellschaft*, Frankfurt: Suhrkamp.

Bonss, Wolfgang (1995), *Vom Risiko: Unsicherheit und Ungewissheit in der Moderne*, Hamburg: Hamburger Edition.

Bronk, Richard (2009), *The Romantic Economist: Imagination in Economics*, Cambridge: Cambridge University Press.

Charolles, Valérie (2008), *Croissance, inflation, chômage, crise financière ... Et si les chiffres disaent pas toute la vérité: Chroniques économico-philosophiques*, Paris: Fayard.

Cohen, Daniel (2009), *La prospetité du vice: Une introduction (inquiète) à l'économie*, Paris: Albin Michel.

Douglas, Mary and Wildavsky, Aaron (1982), *Risk and Culture: An Essay on the Selection of Technological and Environmental Dangers*, Berkeley: University of California Press.

Fox, Justin (2009), *The Myth of the Rational Market*, New York: Harper.

Hirschman, Albert (1984), *Leidenschaften und Interessen: Politische Begründungen des Kapitalismus vor seinem Sieg*, Frankfurt: Suhrkamp.

Latour, Bruno and Lépinay, Vincent-Antonin (2008), *L'Économie, science des intérêts passionés,* Paris: La Découverte.
Marshall, Alfred (1996), *The Correspondence of Alfred Marshall,* Vol. 3, J. K. Whitaker (ed.), Cambridge: Cambridge University Press.
Neckel, Sighard (2008), *Flucht nach vorn: Die Erfolgskultur der Marktgesellschaft,* Frankfurt: Suhrkamp.
Pixley, Jocelyn (2004), *Emotions in Finance: Distrust and Uncertainty in Global Markets,* Cambridge: Cambridge University Press.
Sen, Amartya (1999), *Development as Freedom,* New York: Knopf.
Simmel, Georg (1999 [1900]), *Philosophie des Geldes: Gesammelte Werke 6,* Frankfurt: Suhrkamp.
Sinclair, Timothy (2005), *The New Master of Capital: American Bond Rating Agencies and the Politics of Creditworthiness,* Ithaca and London: Cornell University Press.
Stiglitz, Joseph, Sen, Amartya, and Fitoussi, Jean-Paul (2009), *Vers de nouveaux systèmes de mesures: Performances économiques et progrès social,* Paris: Odile Jacob.
Surowiecki, James (2005), *The Wisdom of Crowds: Why the Many are Smarter than the Few,* London: Abacus.
Tavakoli, Janet (2001), *Credit Derivatives & Synthetic Structures: A Guide to Instruments and Structures,* New York: John Wiley & Sons.
Weber, Max (1988 [1920]), *Gesammelte Aufsätze zur Religionsoziologie,* t. 1, Tübingen: Mohr.

Part Four

Geography of Creativity

9

The Value of Creativity

What a fearsome exhibition this is! What a dire battle! ... Whatever your area of expertise, argue upon it, attack with it, spread out for us the old and the new ... it's about time someone said something subtle, something wise!
Aristophanes, *The Frogs*, Intervention of the Chorus of Initiates, 1099–109.

Creativity is one of those things everyone talks about yet no one knows. As always when speaking about difficult concepts, we are more capable of comprehending it in a negative fashion, imagining what we would lose if it did not exist. Without creativity, there would be no competitiveness in the marketplace or new attractions in the area of culture; without creativity, we would have nothing but boredom in our private lives. In spite of this first negative liminal distinction, the unfinished business of the positive description of creativity continues to concern us. What assumptions support creativity, how can it be encouraged and organized? It is hard in principle to answer this question because we can neither determine the unexpected nor prescribe novelty. There are no recipes for freeing creativity. So much has been said about innovation that it is hard to discuss in a novel fashion. The only thing we can do is examine some approaches that falsify creativity, note its not-infrequent paradoxes, and indicate some conditions for it to emerge, knowing they do not guarantee something that cannot be guaranteed since we are dealing with a matter as unpredictable as the emergence of the new into history.

1. Rhetoric of innovation

Innovation has become an omnipresent rhetorical presence. We live in a world that celebrates novelty and privileges its manifestations, in a present that is lived and described as essentially innovative. This epiphany of beginnings can be interpreted as a compensatory phenomenon; it takes place in a culture where, in spite of the frenzy for innovation, what reigns is the secondary, the non-immediate. We buy what we have not produced, we sell what we have not invented, we eat what we have not hunted, we are tourists in places we have not explored, we use instruments we have not designed. Almost no one experiences the world directly: we work on assembly lines or use devices whose workings are unknown to us. Everything is, deep down, elaborated and preserved, second hand. Nostalgia for that which is immediate can only appear with this much intensity in a society that misses first-hand experiences. This is reflected in a science fiction novel by Jean Claude Dunyach that describes a world library that is so inundated that its director focuses on removing any text that does not express an original idea, grinding up that which is useless, and terrorizing writers to dissuade them from writing. The culture has an air of redundancy, and we occasionally rebel against it, when the weight of repetition strikes us as unbearable.

The rhetoric of innovation is unfolding at a time when utopia is in crisis. There was never a society as profoundly convinced that there is nothing new under the sun. We insist on the impossibility of creating anything truly new; everything is intertextual, a mixture of references, interpretation, recontextualization, modifications of already existing material. Society is convened for the future, but seems, at the same time, to trust very little in it. This lack of confidence is revealed in our subtle orientation toward past innovations in the area of fashion, the return of certain styles, trends recuperating things from the past, predictions of the return of something (e.g. the 1970s, Marxism, the gothic novel, conservatism, etc.). It seems as if the new for which we are always searching so insistently is nothing but the old on its cyclical return. Innovation increasingly responds to the spirit of nostalgia.

On the other extreme, we have what Hermann Lübbe called "the paradox of the vanguard" (1992, 94): the programmatic desire for the new, the establishment of an orientation toward the future as the cultural norm. This actually strengthens museumification and classicism. The inevitable destiny of the whole vanguard refers not only to the arts, but also to the accelerated cycles of production, fashion, and the "spirits of the times." There are few things that are more yesterday than the things of today, few more docile than criticism, less transformative than unrest, more ancient than the modern, more outdated than the present, more depressing than euphoria. This is what happens when novelty is conceived of emphatically, with the expectation that something will emerge after which nothing new will be able to emerge in the future. In this way, definitive novelty dominates the entire future. The future, then, would be understood as a mere continuation of the conquered present, in the same way that in the traditional world, the present was understood as a mere prolongation of the past. This is what Boris Groys has called "conservatism of the future": the future is understood in the same way traditional societies thought about the past, in other words, as something harmonic, definitive, and immutable. That is why some innovative ideologies adopted extremely conservative positions as soon as they reached power: because they understood that nothing new was any longer possible.

The lack of future in the emphatic sense results in a dynamic of innovation without novelty, the agitated inertia of a movement without anticipated future. Humanity seems to direct itself toward a future that does not promise a new beginning, seeing it, instead, as an increase to the familiar dynamic. Innovation denotes a generic preference for something new, but it frequently refers to a replacement in fashion or a mercantile substitution. In spite of what dominant discourses can lead us to believe, we can affirm that the new has truly diminished experimental space. While it is true that the new offers a great deal of fascination, we would also like to be free of undesirable surprises and control the unknown that could threaten us. That is why the age of innovation is also the age of benchmarking, monitoring, and the observation of best practices that are always yesterday's best practices (Hackett 2000). The rhetoric of the new, which makes us believe that everything will be different in the future, prevents us from recognizing that which does not change and does nothing but repeat itself while claiming to be new. The habitual is, instead, repetition and routine, practices to which we could apply the characterization of power Foucault gave us: "poor in resources, sparing of its methods, monotonous in the tactics it utilizes, incapable of invention, and seemingly doomed always to repeat itself" (1978, 85).

2. The paradoxes of creativity

All people want to be creative—at work, in their free time, in love—and this label extends like a command, unaware of its paradoxes. But to understand what novelty is and what our real chances of producing it are, we must reflect on the paradoxes of creativity. They can be summarized as follows:

a) *the paradox of producing it*: creativity is generally only achieved when it is sought, but it is not the result of an intentional action. Invoking the new does not simply turn it into an effective reality. Innovation continues to be an imponderable event. The Silicon Valley phenomenon was more a historic accident than the result of a specific political decision. There are no strategies that assure creativity. If something is truly new, it cannot, by definition, be produced intentionally. It is possible to reconstruct the social or cultural conditions that contributed to increasing creativity *a posteriori*, but it is not possible to reduce them to laws that would explain why something new emerges. Innovation is not in the hands of the institutions we design for these purposes. Innovation is not the privilege of a specific scientific or cultural elite. Every institution that promotes the new discovers the same dilemma: it wants to produce the unforeseeable and have it under control at the same time. It would like to make unheard-of uses possible and minimize their risks.

But planned or expected novelty is not true novelty. All the designs to provoke innovation conflict with the hazardous nature of inventiveness. We can establish the conditions for the emergence of innovation, but it is impossible to say what takes place at an innovative moment and when it is going to occur. It is possible to do many things to favor innovative conditions, but if innovation occurs, it always strikes us as surprising. An innovative idea can be recognized by the fact that it surprises. That which is truly new will differ from what we would have imagined as new.

When we talk about radical creativity, not merely variations or modifications, there is always a decisive factor of chance. "In contrast with epigenesis and tautology, which constitute the worlds of replication, there is the whole realm of creativity, art, learning, and evolution, in which the ongoing processes of change feed on the random" (Bateson 1988, 49). For that reason, Luhmann sees chance as the system's ability to make use of events that cannot be produced or governed by the system. Environmental irritants are indispensable resources for the evolution of systems (1994, 138). If one is attempting to encourage the arrival of the new, then greater modesty is imposed: we cannot determine with any certainty that investments in training, knowledge, and research necessarily lead to greater creativity. Creativity is not a sleeping resource that simply needs to be awoken with appropriate measures. Innovation cannot be organized. In any case, what we can do is provide the framework of conditions that would be necessary for a mobilization of creative forces, which is better than nothing, but still not sufficient. This would be the reason why, when dealing with creativity, it is easier and more logical to wonder what might be preventing it.

b) *the paradox of labeling it*: creativity belongs to individuals, but labeling something as creative depends upon its being recognized as such by everyone else. Creativity is a social and communicative matter. Cultural logic teaches that no one can predetermine the way a novelty will be received, interpreted, or valued. We cannot even predict if it is going to be considered a novelty. The meaning and value of the novelty is not something that anyone can impose in isolation; it must be decided in society's cultural sphere. The creative will of an artist, a politician, a jurist, or a thinker does not have absolute power over its reception.

This original uncertainty is one of the reasons we never find out beforehand if we are discovering something new or repeating the obvious, if we are inventing or reiterating. If something is a true novelty, then it is by definition something that cannot be previously known. Curiosity and work prepare us for something new, but we do not know exactly what form the novelty will take. The less predictable the new thing, the more it challenges our ability to perceive and describe. That is why the new, to the extent it cannot be explained based on something previous, has always appeared as an irritating provocation.

The criteria to establish something as creative cannot come from the subjective feeling of its author because people who produce banal or senseless things consider themselves creative as well. The criteria must be intersubjective, without forgetting that this approbation is not infallible either. The only thing we know for certain is that human beings must have overlooked a large number of truly new things, while we celebrate others as new when they are nothing more than comfortable continuities.

c) *the paradox of desubjectivization*: creativity is a fringe benefit of subjectivity, but it is only achieved by fighting against its own subjectivity. Creativity presupposes an intelligence that depends on its own non-knowledge; it permanently mobilizes suspicion of itself, rather than of others. Creativity would demand we avoid a narrow vision, limited by our own logic. We must observe the world doubly, with two gazes, our own and someone else's; one must see and imagine how he or she is seen.

At the same time, creativity presupposes collective forms of learning, even if only because of the fact that there is no intelligence that is not shared and sharable. Creative intelligence does not appear under conditions of voluntary or involuntary solipsism; it requires exchange and relationship instead. Innovations do not arise from mere aggregation but from coordination and cooperation between subjects who conspire around specific objectives. One's own intelligence is empowered with collective intelligence when various places are combined in an intelligent fashion.

We tend to associate creativity with an exuberant subjectivity, and this prevents us from understanding the role that intersubjectivity plays in it. The irrational, eccentric genius conception of creativity is present in clichés of romanticism, revolts, or management. But declared originality tends to be highly tedious, in the same way that transgression generally stems from poor creativity and tends to be standardized. There have been repeated attempts to achieve change throughout history, and they are followed by nothing that is unpredictable. True innovation is a difficult task. It does not arise automatically from forgetting the previous culture or by interrupting what is currently in place.

Novelty is always temporary and scarce, because it is very difficult to break with normality. It is not an exaggeration to affirm that banality is the normal state of human existence (Groys 1999, 47). The appearance of a true novelty is exceptional and random. We prepare ourselves with effort for an unpredictable event. There are many expressions that allude to the paradox that our aspirations for creativity are effectively fulfilled by chance. We say: inspiration exists, but it has to catch you working. Nietzsche said we must be worthy of chance, and Pasteur said chance favors only the prepared mind. These expressions avoid accepting the final verdict of coincidence as an excuse for laziness, which some romantic stereotypes presume to be more creative than the office or the workshop.

d) *the paradox of novelty*: if something is extremely novel, the culture does not have the means to recognize it as such. If it is easily recognized, then it is not so very novel. The fact that the new presupposes the old, even if only as a means of contrast, presents a pointed paradox. The "absolutely new" is inconceivable because we would not be able to use any known property to characterize something entirely new in every aspect. We would not even be in any condition to perceive it as new. In this sense, Heidegger was right when he claimed that a novelty, in order to be recognized as such, should be situated within a particular tradition, even if only to be contrasted or measured against it. In Luhmann's words: "the new always presupposes redundancies against which it can be recognized as a variation" (1998, 1008).

Novelty is paradoxical regarding the past, but also the future since true creativity, instead of exhausting the sources of innovation, always configures new starting points for later innovations. Innovation always presupposes the inauguration of new possibilities that go beyond acceptable routines. It is defined by its capacity for opening new spaces of action, whether in technical products, new markets, forms of organization, or other social achievements. This is why any theory of innovation must immediately account for the spread of innovations. In this sense, we can understand what Kierkegaard meant when he affirmed that "repetition is the reality and seriousness of life" (1980, 5). This means that a subject or an identity is only possible within the seriousness of life, beyond mere originality or the instantaneous event. Only when repetition is an experienced possibility does it make sense to talk about identity, and the subject knows that he or she is one and the same. Beyond the aura of the first time, the possibility of a second time is what gives the decision meaning and weight. In this sense, the fruitfulness of all creative action proves its worth by giving more of itself and offering many possibilities to others.

3. The learning of creativity

The knowledge society challenges human beings to be creative or capable of innovation. To fulfill this goal, organizations—whether enterprises, universities, political parties, or parliaments—are called upon to create knowledge and configure themselves as communities of learning. What does this mean in the context we are considering?

Let us begin with a distinction that is needed to differentiate between two types of learning or two corresponding levels of required creativity and innovation. The first refers to adaptation or improvement within a given framework, the mere expansion of knowledge or the simple modification of behavior within the normal repertoire. It is simply one more step in the course of a historical series, the continuation or the addition of a sign within a realm of established representation, in the archive, the museum, or library. This degree of innovation does not cause problems. At the most, arguments are sparked between the people who accept this novelty and want to provide it a place in the archives and those ones who consider it unworthy of that location. Both positions are defined in the context of a common history; they appeal to common criteria comparing the old and the new. Here we could situate the science from which, according to Nietzsche, we need not expect any disorder

(1988, 351). It later received the name: "normal science." Its discussion can be sharp at times, but it does not question the general framework of representation.

The second level consists of an expansion of the range of possibilities by transforming concepts and structures. This demands a qualitative leap. We can call them "second-level lessons" or reflexives. These are transformations that question criteria, paradigms, and frameworks, although not necessarily all at the same time. People who say, for example, that we must write a history of the unconscious instead of a history of consciousness (or about private life, women, and victims, instead of about public events, men, and victors), do not want to add a sign to an already existing archive, but to destroy the old archive and replace it with a new one. In this new archive, the new is not the only thing that would be valued. The old would also be valued, using completely different criteria. New criteria of assessment lead automatically to a new consideration of the past. New assessments that are carried out in the same archive can coincide because, even when there is disagreement in the assessment of novelties, the archive as such and the past that the archive contains is tacitly accepted. But different archives, which confront each other in radical innovation, have no narrative in common.

Once we question the conditions needed in order to be innovative and discuss ways to educate for creativity, we must introduce a distinction that is comparable to the previous one: the difference between skill and education. Skill turns us into robots that respond to stimuli in a predictable fashion; education makes us modify the questions being asked. On the one hand, someone acquires the skill to search for adequate solutions to identified problems presented to him or her; on the other hand, the problems themselves must be managed. They must be labeled, formulated, or reconsidered.

Creative intelligence is a property that cannot be completely described with traditional criteria of rationality. When one's most pressing desire is to have new experiences, not to simply trace acquired continuities, then intelligence would mean not optimizing the results but the ability to overcome errors, transforming disappointments into learning. Intelligence in its most creative dimension is the ability to cope in contexts where one is not fully in control.

When we talk about profound changes, about the reformulation of problems, about authentic creativity or radical innovation, we must know that we are inviting a type of life that lacks the convenient certainties in which we typically install ourselves. If people want to be creative, the first thing they need to learn is to live with instability, with change (Senge 1999). The creation of new knowledge requires an ability to handle the uncertainty that new options entail. We can only learn if we assume the risks of that uncertainty. In any case, it is comforting to know that "no risk is the highest risk of all" (Wildavsky 1979), that the greatest risk is trying to prevent any risks, in the same way that the worst mistake comes from systematically avoiding any mistakes, whether committed by oneself or by others. If a person's goal is to avoid mistakes at all costs, that person has already made a mistake; in this way, one manages to be mistaken from the very start.

In contexts of objective or desired change, when things lose the validity they previously enjoyed or when we want to submit them to intentional review, we suspect that everything learned is provisional, only conditionally valid, lacking in solidity. It is at times like these when we can understand the logic behind the expression: learning consists of unlearning; there is no innovation if known material is not abandoned. Wisdom, learning, and experience are not fixed installations but attitudes toward the new. Adorno summarized it with the idea that true experience presupposes a rebellion against the idea of experience as possession (1958, 117). If learning is closely linked with invention and innovation, that means that learning is re-learning. It consists of modifying the known, correcting expectations. Those who see in everything the opportunity to confirm what is already known do not learn anything. Neither do people who do not struggle against the "art of ignoring" (Luhmann 2000) that people and organizations typically cultivate.

Unlearning is especially costly in the case of people and organizations that have a successful past or a great tradition behind them and see no reason to think the future will be any different. In any case, it is good to know that a system, especially when things are going well, has a large capacity to establish "defensive routines." Some of them are very ostentatious and anyone can detect them, but there are also defensive strategies to avoid more subtle mistakes. There is, for example what Argyris and Schön have called the "learning paradox": a strategy where "the actions we take to promote organizational learning actually inhibit deeper learning" (1996, 281). It is a question of learning something new to shirk a deeper learning process, changing something so as to not change anything. This is seen in companies, organizations, institutions, or agendas for change that allow learning in "discussable domains," in safe and low risk environments, zealously preventing it in other areas where the modification of old rules is taboo. There is also unproductive learning: creating solutions that strengthen the problem (generally by eliminating symptoms and leaving the underlying reality intact), apparent solutions, opportunistic compromises, hidden contradictions, routines that let us disregard reality tests.

What type of learning allows us to have new experiences? It is fundamentally a question of maintaining a disposition toward reality that takes cognitive advantage of disappointments. The only people who learn are those who, after a disappointment of their expectations (of what they hoped, desired, or feared), do not insist on them but absorb these disappointments and modify their expectations. To do that, they must practice dealing with disorientation, the disposition of not being sure about everything. Luhmann expressed it by affirming that the acquisition of new knowledge demands the ability to be surprised, surpassing the "threshold of improbability." In other words, overcoming the fact that "the experience of novelty presupposes an observer who is capable of realizing that expectations are modified" (1994, 216).

This disposition toward learning presumes a struggle against the tendency we have as human beings to make a judgment before having all the information and to then look for proof that matches our judgment. Leaders get their supporters to advise them; doctors prescribe therapies without making a diagnosis; we select from reality only those things that confirm our preconceptions ...After disappointments, we can react in two ways: adapting the expectation to the disappointment or insisting that others change their expectations. As long as observers do not take responsibility for their expectations cognitively, but normatively or in an indeterminate fashion, this deviation will bother them and make them retreat and search for the way back to a normal situation. That is why creativity is only possible when the expectations that are cognitive and open to learning are not smothered by predictions; there must be a continuous comparison between what was expected and what really took place so we can react to deviations correctively. In the end, that is what learning is all about: putting oneself in the situation of having surprising experiences and modifying one's conduct in accordance with those discoveries.

For that, we need cognitive mobility that will strengthen our ability to maintain structural concerns that search out unexpected disruptions and unforeseen modifications. Systems learn when they are capable of increasing their structural concern: that is why subjects and social systems must pay permanent attention to unexpected discontinuities. Organisms and organizations owe their survival to their ability and willingness to establish a series of permanent verification checks. Knowledge is not produced when stable contents are appropriated, but it is produced to the extent that their structures of observation and expectations are continually repaired. Systems owe the sensitivity that is at the heart of their reflexive activities to this permanent concern. In other words: psychic and social systems are only stabilized through change. In some ways, this is how we verify one of the most surprising paradoxes of creative action; it serves to ensure survival to the extent that it entails a certain subversion of the need for stability that systems have.

When someone in an organization presents alternatives, it introduces the uncertainty that is necessary to once again observe forgotten or unattended aspects of reality. That is why one of the questions that an organization should consider is how to avoid a lack of dissent. Dissent is often undervalued. This is probably in part because of the preeminence of the theory of communicative action, in which Habermas submits communicative processes to an imminent teleology that points toward perfect agreement. For Habermas, there would be a "life-world" that consists of a reserve of inarticulate consensus to which we should recur when we attempt to transform controversies into rational discourses. But we can also imagine the "life-world" as a place teaming with disagreements. If Habermas were right, then we should ask ourselves why we continue communicating, how it is that communication has not stopped. Creativity does not traverse common understanding, but generally the opposite. At least in innovative organizations, a lack of dissent is a more serious problem than a lack of consensus. Creativity does not reside in the advance toward understanding, but in the evolutionary—and, for that reason, necessarily conflictive—character of communication.

4. An elegy for inaccuracy

This may be a much less creative time than we tend to think. The rhetoric of creativity is one the and another its effective reality. This situation is best expressed in the myth of accuracy, in other words, in the belief that the only good solutions are accurate ones, and that any problem can be reduced to its quantitative aspect based on the enormous amount of data we have at our disposition. We celebrate originality and the value of decisions, but we also live at a time of benchmarking, the search for quantification, "governing by numbers," which is nothing but a way of making decisions such that it seems no decision is being made (Porter 1995, 8; Miller 2001): indicators, rankings, data, and measurements. Of course, one cannot govern without observing what others do or without measuring the effects of our own decisions. But the data and numbers should be subject to a process of reflection that will interpret them suitably and favor collective learning. It would primarily be a question of avoiding the automatisms that are one of the great impediments to creativity when it comes to understanding and interpreting reality as well as making decisions.

Data analysis has been progressively acquiring primacy over other forms of knowledge. A neo-positivist cognitive model based on data management has been established. The availability of data is the distinctive sign of our time. The belief is that correctly interpreted data will afford us a mirror in which, for the first time in the history of humanity, we can know ourselves completely. To this way of understanding reality, both perception and also an essential part of conceptual analysis is considered superfluous.

All of this is inscribed in a tendency according to which the development of knowledge and the construction of meaning would not come from confronting reality with a theory but simply through the commutations and permutations carried out on enormous quantities of data. These statistical permutations are fundamentally agnostic, and the discovery process is understood on the basis of inductive reasoning. No theory is necessary: the model, if it exists, emerges from the bottom-up process of the statistical manipulation of data. There are even those who predict the end of theory and science in the habitual sense of conceptual development based on empirical proofs. They claim that knowledge will end up being derived exclusively by correlations extracted from large quantities of data; the age when data without a theory was no more than noise will be overcome (Anderson 2006). In this neo-positivist context, conceptual analysis becomes a useless activity. "Reality" would arise after the cognitive "precipitation" of computational particles.

This way of thinking is induced by numerous technological and cultural factors, among which the massive circulation of available cognitive elements in the form of computer data should be highlighted. The statistical treatment of that data is used to construct meanings and practical orientations. This possibility is not limited to scientific knowledge; it extends through the social fabric with an infrastructure of increasingly dense information, which allows data to be configured and transmitted. A furtive but crucial change is carried out in this process. It does not only affect the way researchers understand existence but also the way we all construct it. We tend to define life situations as cognitive problems whose nature is computational or is read in terms of navigation (what to see or do, how to find a movie and also a friend or a partner). Life situations can be resolved through complex automatized calculations, based on data and information that modern technologies and the modes of life associated with them provide.

We often think that what computers process is already information, but this is not true except in a very rudimentary way. What we as humans understand by "information" is not data on its own, but data with a particular meaning. Information only exists through the interaction between people and machines. Computers only process data or potential information. Strictly speaking, there is no information if the data have not been processed and interpreted, if it has not been inscribed into a context of meaning.

Of course, there is no sense competing with computers in speed, precision, or completeness. But there are at least two dimensions to our intelligence that machines lack: analogical abilities and the assessment of the whole. We can offer creative competence by thinking inaccurately. This occurs, for example, with the improper use of language we call metaphors. Creative inaccuracy is the heuristic force of all possible forms of analogy. Strengthening inaccurate thought means expanding our ability to calculate with intuitive and even non-rational abilities. The second specificity of human creativity is the ability to consider the results of all types of calculation, assessing and interpreting them. In this way, we prevent their unthinking application and remove errors in accuracy. Metaphoric thought, analogical ability, and deliberation are capabilities that all include the ability to navigate in the space that separates knowledge from non-knowledge. We could call this the management of ignorance. Creativity would then be something like knowledge about non-knowledge. Anyone who is interested in creativity simply pays more attention than normal to the area of ignorance that others ignore without the slightest concern.

In a very similar fashion, there is another area in which human creativity is revealed: the discovery and formulation of problems. The perspective of creativity teaches us that problems are more important than solutions and "problem discovery" is more important than "problem solving." For the same reason, questions require more intelligence than answers. We frequently reduce creativity to the solution of recognized problems, but the most necessary creativity is the one that identifies problems that were previously unknown. The most difficult and important activities are the ones that identify problems and the way they should be handled. Furthermore, the most skilled professions are those that are dedicated not to finding known solutions for known problems but unknown problems for possible solutions.

The resolution of problems does not form part of the most difficult creative activities. In "creative problem solving," problems that are relatively well structured are resolved. In these cases, more than creativity, what is needed is organized thinking. On the other hand, more complex problems are not structured at all. They are often not even recognized as problems, much less defined. In these cases, creativity is not required to find new solutions to known problems, but to discover new configurations or developments as potential problems. That is where creativity is manifested as the management of ignorance.

What sometimes happens is that a particular problem that is occupying our attention is concealing another very different problem. We have all experienced personal, familiar, or social circumstances in which we cannot resolve a particular problem without help. The difficulty is often that we have solutions for non-existent or modified problems, while no one has shed enough light on new problems to find appropriate solutions. There are communication roadblocks and conflicts that are consolidated as conflicts not because we lack solutions but because we have not managed to define the terms of the problem properly. They are "wicked problems" for which we not only do not know the solution but are not even very sure of the problem. In these cases, both the cognitive foundations and the criteria of norms and decision making are uncertain and controversial (Fischer 2001). The creativity that is then required is not very related to the solution but is needed to discover the true problem.

That is why creativity always implies a certain degree of sabotage against the established division of labor, against specialization and the division of knowledge, against the accuracy of habitual solutions. It presumes a review of competencies and expectations, a strong disposition to learn beyond knowledge and established practices.

5. A society of interpreters

We have gotten used to understanding the world as something immediate, available, and easily accessible. The typical discourse about the knowledge and information society understands society in terms of the circulation of goods and data, whose appropriation is not problematic. The dominant ideology is reproductive and communicative transparency, as if the correct reading of data simply required a corresponding code. This way of thinking tends to underestimate the moment of interpretation that exists with all knowledge. It favors immediate economic profitability and knowledge that is scientific and easily translatable to technological devices. It undervalues other types of knowledge such as artistic, intuitive, practical, or relational knowledge. This is a question worth examining because it entails gambling not only the future of the humanities, but the destiny of our political communities.

The failed connection between the sciences and the arts—to use a contrast that may be outdated but that we all understand—could result in a confrontation between data-driven economic sciences and interpretation-driven political arts (Citton 2010). In contrast to reducing communication to a mere elaboration of information or understanding the digital revolution as a mere investment in technology or the information society as a society of machines, the emphasis placed on interpretation underscores the active and complex nature of all knowledge. This is the true challenge of our time: interpreting data to obtain experiences and discourses to acquire meaning. This is where human and social sciences stand out as specialists of meaning, as types of knowledge that produce and evaluate meaning.

There is an axiom that places all expectations of collective progress on the development of knowledge understood through the model of scientific accuracy and technological practicality. But the truth is that most of our current debates do not revolve around data and information but around their meaning and relevance. In other words, the question is how we should interpret them and what is desirable, just, legitimate, or convenient. When we admit that what is in play in these conflicts is less objective knowledge and more interpretation, it means we must "de-neutralize" knowledge and give it all the political weight that knowledge has when we are valuing its human meaning. To say it with terminology that is familiar to us: beyond the material infrastructure of the knowledge society, there is a whole symbolic superstructure where the true questions of individual and collective existence play out.

Trying to prophesize, Ray Kurzweil (2005) claimed that in 2048 our inbox will receive a million e-mails every day, but a virtual assistant will manage them without us having to worry about it. It would even be possible for nano receptor transmitters to connect our synapses directly to some super-machine that would make us capable of thinking a million times faster. The problem is what "thinking" means under such conditions. In contrast to reducing intelligence to a reading of data or the acceptance of predefined forms, we must emphasize that knowledge requires not only free access to information, but also the ability to eliminate the "noise" of the insignificant. Storing data is not decisive in the way interpreting information is. The problem is not the availability but the assessment of information (its degree of reliability, relevance, meaning, the use that can be made of it).

The art of interpreting is by definition inaccurate, concrete, and attentive to irregularities. Humanistic disciplines are rather undisciplined, to the extent that they interrogate, criticize, assess, or contextualize. Interpretation is a cognitive operation that must improvise without implicit codes, decide in irregular environments, anticipate what we do not know. It all has to do with that reference to concreteness that characterizes the arts and puts into play an "economics of singularities" (Karpik 2007), in place of an economics of scale, the division of labor, and mass production.

Knowledge that confines itself to the concrete rather than the general has a strong intuitive dimension. From the imperialism of the universal sciences, interpretative intuition has been presented as a lesser form of knowledge, when not as completely irrational. But experience shows us that it is not wise to do without these forms of knowledge, especially in contexts of great complexity. If we think about things like the crisis provoked largely by the mathematization of the economy or the ecological imbalances that certain technologies invoke, what we have is a very contradictory picture: pretensions of accuracy have given way to irrational decisions. The only way we have been able to correct this social inaccuracy is through cultures of interpretation (those critical environments in which we question the insertion of technologies into society, we argue about their social applications, we assert ethical and political criteria). The interpretative intuition practiced by the humanities has an enormous epistemological, heuristic, and prudential value in spaces of great uncertainty (as found in societies today).

When certainties are scarce, getting a general idea is more important than the accumulation of data or the detailed examination of one sector of reality. Generalist interpretations position us better than specialized knowledge. This is the reason why foresight into the future is in such demand. The most unsettling questions that we face have to do with the way things might evolve (When will we get out of the crisis? How will terrorism change? What will voters do?). The most useful knowledge is not the knowledge that refers to an immediate or sectorial utilization but the knowledge that lets us gain a general idea about what is going to take place. This affords us the opportunity to put in motion operations that are as important as anticipating, foreseeing, favoring, or ensuring future eventualities. Prophetic activities—from meteorological forecasts to perspectives for economic growth, passing through opinion polls, risk measurement, and strategic bets—are in well-deserved disrepute, but at the same time, they are more necessary than ever. To satisfy this growing demand for foreknowledge, we do not need data as much as interpretive abilities about available information. It was never as necessary as now to develop the art of the reasonable prediction, which also includes interpreting the trustworthiness of prophecies and prophets.

Interpretation also has a special value in contexts dominated by rapidity and automatism. We live in societies in which communicative flows are continuously passing through us. Fluctuation societies require filters to avoid being crushed by information without meaning or banal clichés. True epistemological sovereignty comes from interrupting, not from reacting mechanically: not responding to e-mails immediately, resisting acceleration, escaping from a stimulus-response model, not contributing to panic or euphoria, establishing distance and delay, postponing responses, and even making something new and unpredictable possible. Subjective intelligence and freedom need to be established, especially nowadays, as centers of indetermination and unpredictability.

We have always connected the idea of education with authenticity, with the ability to think for oneself. Does this ideal still make sense in a knowledge and information society? It probably does, but only if it is understood with a new nuance that would connect true innovation with error or naïveté, distancing it, in other words, from those forms of thought and action in which it is not possible to make a mistake. To say it in a more provocative manner: we need fools who make mistakes, who think for themselves, beyond truisms, about what is said or about information accepted as such. Botho Strauss stated it particularly emphatically:

> there is an enormous loss of genuine foolishness or, stated in a more positive fashion, an enormous loss of naïveté. We no longer meet human beings but interlocutors through whom everything that is said flows. They let themselves be crossed by everything that moves through the communication channels. There is no longer clear discrimination or any form of naïveté; it is covered by the varnish of exterior intelligence. (Strauss, 2000)

Does all of this have any particular political value? How do we represent the interpretation culture politically? In what sense can we affirm, as Martha Nussbaum does (2010), that democracy needs the humanities? We can understand this contribution precisely through the political value of interpretation.

Our collective destiny is intimately connected to the capacity for interpreting our daily habits and our necessities; it depends more on a good interpretation of what makes a life truly human than on handling observable data. The political value of interpretative cultures consists of placing citizens at the center of social transformations. It requires a citizenship that interprets, in other words, a citizenship that discusses, deliberates, and decides. A society of interpreters is a society that reflects on itself, discusses, and is capable of taking responsibility for the novelty that emerges in social processes.

If we conceive of our democratic societies as societies that interpret themselves, then we have greater possibilities for escaping the dominant paradigm that understands the knowledge society as the vertical encounter between experts and the masses. Democracy can be understood as the political system that begins with the assumption that we are all interpreters. Society is the fragile and conflict-filled idea-sharing session of our interpretations, somewhat more democratizing than the submission to some supposedly objective data.

Against the automatism of readers, the idea of a society of interpreters is more discontinuous, complex, and unstable. A society understood in this manner does not fit with politics understood through a model of simple management. A politics of interpretation presumes to always abandon commonplaces, reconsidering our priorities, describing things in another way, formulating other questions, etc. In the face of this democratic indetermination, all would-be realists have always called on the data to prevent the exploration of possibilities. But we know that this is nothing but a subtle form of power that consists of insisting on the data without questioning the hegemonic practices through which precisely that data and no other is obtained. We have learned this critical dimension of interpretation in the cultivation of what we call the humanities, which is, of course, the greatest education for citizens.

Bibliography

Adorno, Theodor W. (1958), *Philosophie der neuen Musik*, Frankfurt: Europäische Verlagsanstalt.
Anderson, Chris (2006), *The Long Tail: Why the Future of Business is Selling Less of More*, New York: Hyperion.
Argyris, Chris and Schön, Donald (1996), *Organizational Learning II: Theory, Method, and Practice*, Reading, MA: Addison-Wesley.

Bateson, Gregory (1988), *Mind and Nature: A Necessary Unity*, Alfonso Montuori (trans.), New York: Bantom Books.

Citton, Yves (2010), *L'avenir des humanités: Économie de la connaissance ou cultures de l'interprétation*, Paris: La Découverte.

Fischer, Frank (2001), *Citizens, Experts and the Environment: The Politics of Local Knowledge*, Durham, NC and London: Duke University Press.

Foucault, Michel (1978), *The History of Sexuality: An Introduction: 1*, Robert Hurley (trans.), New York: Pantheon.

Groys, Boris (1999), *Über das Neue: Versuch einer Kulturökonomie*, Frankfurt: Fischer.

Hackett, Brian (2000), *Beyond Knowledge Management: New Ways to Work and Learn*, New York: The Conference Board.

Karpik, Lucien (2007), *L'Économie des singularités*, Paris: Gallimard.

Kierkegaard, Søren (1980), *Die Wiederholung*, Gütersloh: Siebenstern.

Kurzweil, Ray (2005), *The Singularity Is Near: When Humans Transcend Biology*, New York: Penguin.

Lübbe, Hermann (1992), *Im Zug der Zeit*, Berlin and Heidelberg: Springer.

Luhmann, Niklas (1994), *Die Wissenschaft der Gesellschaft*, Frankfurt: Suhrkamp.

—(1998), *Soziale Systeme: Grundriss einer allgemeinen Theorie*, Frankfurt: Suhrkamp.

—(2000), *Organisation und Entscheidung*, Opladen: Westdeutscher Verlag.

Miller, Peter (2001), "Governing by Numbers: Why Calculative Practices Matter," *Social Research* 68 (2), 379-96.

Nietzsche, Friedrich (1988), *Schopenhauer als Erzieher*, in *Kritische Studiensausgaben*, G. Colli and M. Montinari (eds), t.1, Berlin and New York: de Gruyter.

Nussbaum, Martha (2010), *Not for Profit: Why Democracy Needs the Humanities?* Princeton, NJ: Princeton University Press.

Porter, Theodore M. (1995), *Trust in Numbers: The Pursuit of Objectivity in Science and Public Life*, Princeton, NJ: Princeton University Press.

Senge, Peter (1999), *The Dance of Change: The Challenge of Sustaining Momentum in Learning Organisations*, London: Nicholas Brealey.

Strauss, Botho (2000), "Ulrich Greiner spricht mit Botho Strauss," *Die Zeit* 23.

Wildavsky, Aaron (1979), "No Risk Is the Highest Risk of All" *American Scientist* 67, 32-7.

10

On the Concept of Social Innovation

We lack an adequate concept of social innovation because we do not have a theory of the innovation society that explains the connection between the two concepts. This chapter attempts to help alleviate this conceptual shortfall. Its starting point is a criticism of (1) the idea that society can exist without innovation or with innovation that is limited to the technological–economic domain; and of (2) the effects caused throughout society by the lack of social integration of what could be called society-less innovations. The second, more proactive section explains (3) why no innovation comes about without society, or, in other words, why innovation is a social matter; and (4) why no society comes without innovation, at least no modern society in the way we understand the term.

1. A society without innovation

The dominant discourse about innovation seems to be characterized by a restriction that reduces innovation to a process of technical acquisitions aimed at strengthening competitiveness in a globalized market. This narrow vision of innovation can be seen in the definition presented by the OECD, the Organization for Economic Co-operation and Development. The determinism of the social conceptions of Marx, Schumpeter, or Taylor has been transformed into a rhetoric of innovation that makes social prosperity depend only on technological-economic acquisitions. Research into innovation, even when it attempts to explain society's structural changes, often has a focus that is very technicist. There is no theory that properly balances innovation and society. We could summarize this disconnect by saying that those who focus on innovation are not very interested in society and those who emphasize society do not seem to have grasped the central role innovation plays when it comes to understanding societies. In the end, society is seen as an innovation-less space; in other words, innovation is restricted and does not affect society's make-up.

Typical explanations of innovation are rendered inadequate by their determinism. The clearest example of this is Kondratieff's Wave Theory, subsequently reworked by Schumpeter (Kondratieff 1935 [1926]; Schumpeter 1939). According to this theory, basic technological and economic innovations unleash long cycles of economic and social development. Their weakness stems from the fact that the implicit relationship established between technological, economic, and social development is not sufficiently complex. Growth must not only be explained economically but through the interdependencies between socioeconomic and political–institutional processes. This theory of innovation ignores the dynamics, interdependence, and also the indifference of social subsystems that results from social differentiation.

Even the most recent theories about information and knowledge societies depend much more on social than technological factors. The relationship between innovation, technological development, and processes of social change is resolved in favor of one of these elements. The knowledge that is viewed as a source of innovation and social change achieves that role because of a combination of social networks and new information technologies. As with the "long cycles" theory, Castells also sees technology as the basis for change, although innovation is specifically found in the way information and knowledge is managed (Castells 2011 [1996]). Fundamental conceptions of the knowledge society recognize the importance of innovation for social change, but implicit causalities remain unexplained. By making social factors dependent on technological factors and by linking technology and innovation, we assume what should actually be explained. The relationship between technological development and social change should be explained in all its complexity if we want to adequately understand the relationship between innovation and society.

There are certainly reasons that seem to justify the technological and economic restriction of the concept of innovation, as well as the "high-tech" obsession of the policies of innovation: new technologies are more visible than institutional reforms; economic success is more calculable than social cohesion; social innovations can rarely be patented or sold. But the reasons explaining this restriction do not justify it. We must open the world of innovation to social and political realities, innovating the concept of innovation in a post-Schumpeterian sense. Problems like massive unemployment, the weakening of social protection systems, or ecological risks cannot be resolved without the introduction of significant social innovations.

Although the expression "social innovation" was recently formulated by Ernst Zapf (1989), its origin can be traced to the theory of social change William Ogburn articulated in 1922. According to this American sociologist, social change would take place in the interaction between two complementary cultures: the material culture (technological devices and projects) and non-material culture (rules and practices that characterize our relationship with technology). Based on this distinction, Ogburn formulated his oft-cited description of "cultural lag": the differential that arises between two cultures given their differing speeds of development. The example provided to illustrate this idea is the way forests were used in the United States. At the time of the first European settlements, forest clearing was considered a logical survival technique. Non-material culture remained in balance with the natural replacement rate of the forests as long as the demand for wood was not too high. But as the population grew, the cutting of the natural resource surpassed its replacement speed and threatened survival conditions. The social innovation of ecological consciousness is precisely what later made it possible to overcome the "cultural lag" between material and non-material cultures, thus favoring social progress. In any case, for Ogburn, it is clear that technological innovation is the main driver of social processes.

Mumford defends a radical modification of Ogburn's thesis when he asserts that the beginning of civilization did not depend on mechanical inventions but on "a radically new type of social organization" (1967, 11). There are other examples of how social or cultural innovations have preceded technological progress, in the case of electrification (David 1990) or the phone (Rammert 1993). It is now accepted that technological progress is only successful when it is prepared and accompanied by social learning processes (Hauff and Scharpf 1975). Technological innovation should be considered part of the social construction of reality (Rammert 1993).

In any case, it is commonly accepted that technological and economic innovations are not choices; they each require the other. Some people even claim that the interaction between technological and economic innovations will be even closer in the future (Freeman 1996; Meyer-Krahmer 1998). There is, in fact, already an increase in the importance of the social components or the "soft factors" of innovation such as qualifications, communication, or styles of behavior. According to Meyer-Krahmer, innovation's newest stage will be measured with the "complex innovation system," e.g. packaged products and services or new applications for information technologies, in which technological novelties and changes of behavior are intertwined.

Another moment in the history of social innovation stems from the same economic theory. When we want to understand the innovative process in all its social and political complexity, then its technological and economic version seems somewhat insufficient. The attempt to expand the concept of innovation socially was carried out by the evolutionary economy of institutions that criticized two aspects of the classic theory of innovation: its abstract conception of market behavior and its simplistic idea of companies. In classic economic theory, the market was understood as something natural, independent of all social considerations. The market would determine whether a technological innovation would succeed or fail based on objective laws. But in deregulated markets, social forces determine or influence innovations. The market is not independent; it is an institution with diverse interests. The development of many innovations, like nuclear or alternative energy, would be unthinkable without political interventions. Many markets for innovative products would not exist without public investment.

The other culminating moment in the criticism of the technological narrowing of innovation took place during the 1990s when the social consequences of technology were being addressed (Simonis 1993; Sauer and Lang 1999). In contrast to previous determinisms, they went so far as to assert the opposite way of thinking: the social was seen as a condition of possibility for technological innovations (North 1990). Innovations require certain social conditions that are not explained exclusively through technological innovations. As a result of these debates, emphasis was placed on the social assumptions of technological and economic innovations (both desired and non-desired), inserting these innovations into society, and the role of social institutions when it comes to implementing innovations. Focusing on the social aspect of innovation also emphasizes the social conception of technology. While the sociology of technology has tended to view it as a controlled, intentional, and repeatable mechanism, a sociology of innovation would stress the uncontrollable, non-intentional, and distinguishing aspects of technology instead. The emphasis would be on the fundamental uncertainty that social action produces and must simultaneously confront, overcoming an instrumental and mechanical conception of technology in this way.

At the same time, the social is now considered an area of innovation as well. Innovation appears not only in the natural sciences, technology, or the business world, but in other social spaces like politics, education, the health care system, or the administration, which are equally capable of discovery, novelty, progress, and invention. They also occasionally give rise to what William Ogburn called "social inventions": social achievements such as the introduction of women's suffrage, unemployment insurance, or peace accords that help improve group life conditions and promote social change.

To what extent do societies innovate, beyond their systems of technological, scientific, productive, and economic innovation? We effectively live in an unbalanced society: between technological-scientific euphoria and the illiteracy of civic values, between technological innovation and social redundancy, between critical culture in the scientific or economic world and a political and social space where there is little innovation or ability to articulate the balance between consensus and dissent, to channel conflicts and design models of coexistence.

At the same time, we must think seriously about the ability that politics (understood in its broadest sense) has for social innovation. There is nearly universal concern that the ability politics has to shape society is lost when it comes into competition with its own goals and the public function assigned to it. This weakness contrasts with the dynamism of other social systems. In our societies, innovation in the financial, technological, scientific, and cultural realms coexists with a sluggish and marginalized political system. The retreat of politics in the face of the vigor of the economy or the pluralism of the cultural realm should be considered a starting point in any reflection about the role of politics at the current time. Innovations have not emerged from the political realm for some time now; they develop out of the inventiveness that is more acute in other social spaces. We make changes, rather than coming up with something new, because of a chronic incapacity to understand social changes, anticipate future scenarios, and formulate projects to achieve an intelligent and intelligible social order.

Some people understand social innovations as a mere compensatory contrast to technological innovations, as a "complement of technical innovation" (Gillwald 2000, 36). But thinking of it that way ignores the fact that technological innovation already often includes social innovation. The best sociology of technology recognizes that technological devices are inscribed in a political and social order (Winner 1980). Social innovations are not compensation for technological innovations, but a part of them. This theory of social innovation as compensation is grounded in a dualism between the material and the spiritual where the technological is linked to the material and the social with the symbolic. Reducing technology to material artifact means ignoring all the explicit and implicit knowledge that is necessary for developing and utilizing technological innovation. Technology contains both material artifact and symbolically codified knowledge. The material–spiritual dichotomy is disastrous for social innovation since any social innovation, if it is to last, requires material stabilization.

There is no sense contrasting the technological with the symbolic; the fundamental question today is how to articulate symbolic and communicative innovations with technological and material innovations. The idea of social innovation forces us to think outside of the dualism between sciences and humanities, skill and values, identity and citizenship, global and local. The greatest innovations are going to be produced precisely in the renewed encounter between the areas that have, until now, been seen and experienced as opposites. The monopoly of innovation was assigned to one of two sides, while the other was charged with outdated repetition or historic delay. It was not a question of swinging back to the other extreme, but of questioning the contrast and looking for new redefinitions of these basic tensions.

We must overcome false contradictions between the economic and the social or between the technological and the social. Back in 1944, Polanyi was already defending the thesis that industrialization and growth were driven less by technologies based on capital than by the organizational sciences. In other words, the primary catalyst for the industrial revolution came from discoveries in the sociological realm, not technological inventions. With the reduction of the technological to a singular artifact, we must emphasize its insertion into social practices. Cultural and social considerations determine how the new emerges in the world more than an object's technological potential does.

How, then, should we understand the nature of social innovation? According to Zapf,

> social innovations are new ways for achieving goals, especially new forms of organization, new regulations, new lifestyles, that modify the direction of social change, solving problems better than previous practices did and thus deserving of imitation and institutionalization. (Zapf 1989, 177)

They may also elevate the adaptive abilities of society. For Gillwald, we can understand social innovation as "socially successful regulations of activities and procedures that deviate from the ways of thinking generally in place until that point" (Gillwald 2000, 1). But if it is a true innovation, the language of adaptation or deviation is inadequate. A collective debate would not be worth as much if we could not ask what should adapt to what (this question is often hidden by the banality of commonplaces in the cliché version of the innovation for competitiveness). And what if true innovation (not merely social innovation) was less involved in the invention of solutions for already existing problems than in the discovery of new problems, previously unnoticed or repressed? In a well-organized society, efficient solutions cannot completely resolve problems of legitimization. Democratic societies need a critical space where innovations that attempt to overcome or ban dominant criteria can be discussed.

This was what those who addressed the concept of political innovation in the 1980s claimed (Polsby 1984; White 1982). Noteworthy among these theories was Polsby's assertion that, unlike reform, which moves through official political channels, political innovations make use of social processes that break with institutional routines. There is always an implacable tension between creative action and the functional demands of adaptation. As the Future Commission of the Friedrich Ebert Foundation recently concluded in Germany, we cannot resolve problems such as financial crises, ecological risks, or the sustainability of social services without social innovations (Future Commission 1998). Finally, in view of the current financial and economic crisis, we can see that social innovations will be key to modifying our social practices of the economy and consumption, which will determine the type of world that future generations will inhabit.

To fully understand what social innovation can entail, we must rethink the relationship between technological development, innovation, and social change. It is a good opportunity to do full justice to the complexity of contemporary society and understand innovation in a new way that suppresses neither its tension nor its richness nor its ambivalence.

2. Innovation without society

Most problems in contemporary society do not stem from an excess or a lack of innovation as much as from the imbalance between different speeds of innovation. Innovation takes place without a society to shelter and integrate it in a balanced manner. The conceptual and practical weakness of social innovation encourages us to continue trusting that technological–economic innovations are going to guarantee the improvement of all living conditions. But the fact is that society-less innovations produce socially undesirable effects, and understanding and governing the social effects of innovation remains a completely open question.

The world advances at different speeds, so there are constant gaps between different innovative dynamics. These disparities or fault lines receive diverse names: *décalage*, gap, divide, shock, etc. All these terms reveal that temporal realities are different, incompatible, and even antagonistic, and that some of them have a very strong tendency to try to impose themselves on others.

Some *heterochronies* are revealed through the conflicts between individuals and groups (young people's time versus old people's time, the lack of equilibrium between generations, inequality in general) or a lack of synchronicity between diverse social systems (technological innovations versus the slowness of the law, the time of consumption versus the time of resources, media time versus scientific time). Social subsystems have also developed their own logic from the point of view of innovation and their dynamics, acceleration, rhythm, and speed are largely independent: the time of fashion does not coincide with the time of religion, nor does technological time coincide with legal time, nor economic with political time, nor the time of the ecosystem with the time of consumption. These dysynchronizations are proof that progress is not achieved in a united front, that progress in science and of technology, for example, does not correspond to social progress. The rather deterministic assumption that economic innovation and political development necessarily go hand in hand has been dispelled.

The large-scale lack of synchronicity that characterizes the world today materializes in the contrast between global time and local time, between global synchronizations (financial or communicative) and global desynchronizations (inequalities, tensions and disputes, Third World peoples, fundamentalisms, etc.). The imbalance is readily apparent and explains the background forces operating in global spheres: migratory movements, a lack of legal cohesion, distinct responsibilities regarding the environment, the hegemonic power that resists involvement in the realities of post-autonomous synchronization, etc. The weakness of the institutions of world governance makes it enormously difficult to synchronize a world that is increasingly out of control. Social innovation finds itself in a rudimentary state here.

Desynchronization is also related to uneven global unification (which makes us all present, but does not unify completely) and to the multiculturalism of our societies, in which different groups with distinct identities appear. In both cases, there is either a unification of time without a unity of place (the instantaneousness of communications and of financial markets) or a unity of place without a unification of time (multiculturalism). The tension between forces that unify but do not differentiate and forces of difference that lack the capacity or will to unify, between a time without place and a place without time, will continue to concern us until we can formulate modes of thinking that allow synchronizations that are not impositions (Innerarity 2009).

The collective nature of the time in which we live demands special synchronizations in order to regulate compatibility, cooperation, and competition. The role of politics is precisely to assure the cultural unity of time in the face of tendencies toward social disintegration, while simultaneously respecting the profound social pluralism that is also expressed as temporal pluralism. A "politics of time" would be a social innovation whose goal would be "identifying how different institutional orders work to different clockspeeds and imply different rhythms of social interaction" (Pels 2003, 209). Modern democracy is a complex game of balances within the realm of speed and leisureliness. Political pluralism is also reflected as temporal pluralism: the slow time of the constitution, the medium time of legislatures, the fleeting time of public opinion, etc.

That being said, how can politics strategize power over time? Is it possible to balance economic, techno-scientific, and media accelerations? How do we integrate the heterogeneity of innovations politically and socially? Democratic politics are greatly exposed to the dangers of desynchronization in the face of accelerated social and economic developments. The principal desynchronization between social systems is due to the disconnect between levels of economic, scientific, and technical innovation and our capacity for sorting them politically by integrating them into a logical social totality.

The democratic self-determination of society requires cultural, structural, and institutional assumptions that seem to be eroded by the social accelerations that dominant forms of innovation promote. The processes of innovation and acceleration, which sprang from utopian desire, were made autonomous at the expense of the hopes of political and social progress. It has now become clear that the acceleration of the processes of social, economic, and technological change depoliticizes to the extent that the synchronization of processes and systems is made more difficult, overburdening the political system's deliberative capacity, social integration, and generational balance.

One of our greatest problems derives precisely from the contrast between the speed of social changes and the slowness of politics. Governments are simply too slow in the face of the speed of global transactions. Neither education, politics, nor the law can withstand the pace of the globalized world. Their institutions progressively lose the capacity to organize the processes of technical and economic innovation. Governance becomes problematic. Confronting the complexity of decision making and the media pressure for instantaneousness, political institutions find their sphere of influence reduced, in the best-case scenario, to the reparation of the damages generated by economic and technological innovations.

The political system is faced with a serious dilemma. On the one hand, it must adapt to the accelerated developments of science and technology in order to integrate their innovations into the social system, but on the other hand, it is in no condition to keep pace with the velocity of the knowledge produced. While technology follows an enormously accelerated course, the speed of political processes is limited by their procedures. This is why the state, which arose as a revitalizing force in modern society, seems to be a force for social deceleration today. Administrations and bureaucracy present themselves as paradigms of slowness, inefficiency, and inflexibility. All the processes of debureaucratization or decentralization are motivated by this pressure to accelerate the decisions of public administrations. This desperate search for efficiency also explains the displacement of decision-making procedures from the area of democratic politics to other more agile, but less representative and democratic scenarios. This also explains that the areas of administration and governance are among those most pressed to realize meaningful advances in social innovation.

The dynamics of desynchronized innovation constitute a threat against politics to the extent that it represents a loss of a society's capacity for political self-regulation. There is a contradiction in the fact that democratic life presupposes self-government and yet we are aware that dominant time frames do not allow for self-regulation. There is real pressure to convert politics into a true anachronism, to remove political structure from the world: the most powerful conditions related to the determination of time are not democratically controlled or controllable. Because of this, some people announce "the end of politics"; others, as a response to the "ungovernability" of complex societies, recommend a "deregulation" that actually represents capitulation in the face of the imperatives of the economic movement. For this reason, our greatest challenge consists of defending temporal attributes—as well as the corresponding procedures for deliberation, reflection, and negotiation—in the democratic formation of a political will to counteract the imperialism of technoeconomic demands and the agitation of media time.

It is a question of knowing whether, despite the complexity of the contemporary world, a society can employ political action to configure its collective time, thus lending meaning to it and addressing the problems that arise from uneven accelerations. This is one of the primary realms for social innovation if we want innovation that works not against society, but within and for it.

3. The social character of innovation

The most common rhetoric of innovation reveals a lack of comprehension about what it entails: an unpredictable, rather minimal, and always social creation. There is no innovation without society so, strictly speaking, the very expression "social innovation" would be a redundancy. We could even question the appropriateness of a terminology that distinguishes technological or economic innovations from others that would have to be understood as strictly social. One could say that a technological innovation is a social innovation or, better yet, a series of innovations of various types. "All innovations, even when their nucleus is of a technical nature, are social innovations" (Vordank 2005, 43). Innovation only comes about in society and lacks meaning outside of an intersubjective space of endorsement and recognition.

Innovations are, from the outset, a social matter because they exist in a social context. Innovations are not injected into societies from the great beyond; they are the result of social practices and structures. There is a social context that favors them. Innovations are interactive products. No genius inventor produces them on his or her own. No matter how powerful or creative the individual genius may be, an innovation is not attributable to a solitary actor; it depends on the integration of diverse practices (which includes individual creativity, of course) which express the division of labor. Innovations interact socially with other innovations, in such a way that they condition or alter each other.

The identification or attribution of a novelty cannot take place outside of a context. It is not only a question of social context in which an innovation is registered, but the judgment that something is new or does not depend on previous structures, in other words, on expectations and collective and individual experiences (Weick 1998). Labeling something a novelty presupposes a social observer who classifies a deviation as a novelty based on a specific context's structures of expectation (Luhmann 1994, 216).

The unpredictable character of the novelty and its insertion into a society are two sides of the same coin; innovation is unpredictable because it is a social matter and no one can guarantee that other people will recognize a supposed novelty as such. The existence of new ideas is not sufficient to talk of innovation. An innovation takes place when the idea is transformed into a new product or service and accepted on the market. An innovation is real when it is produced but especially when it is recognized as innovative by other people, who make it their own, consuming it or investing in it, for example. There is a curious connection between discovery and its recognition as such (Simon 1994). The use of the term "discovery" tends to be used retrospectively. Labeling a novelty innovative requires a judgment that is independent of the system that created it. Acceptance by society is what determines whether we have an innovation or a mere passing idea. That is why innovation is the result of a social judgment that can only be made *a posteriori*. Accepting objective reality, after seeing that all attempts to define innovation or novelty fail, we must look to a society's communicative processes to determine what is understood by innovation. We will find that contents are taken into consideration, but under particular structural expectations.

The difference between creativity and innovation is found in the social nature of innovation. Inventions are one thing and innovations another. For there to be innovation, strictly speaking, it must be introduced in society or on the market and become a daily behavior. For changes in behavior to constitute a true innovation, they must occur on a large scale. For innovation to be innovation, it must be socially extended (Deutsch 1985, 20); otherwise, it would simply remain an idea. This is what Schumpeter was referencing in his famous affirmation that the inventor produces ideas, while the entrepreneur "gets things done" (Schumpeter 1947, 152). Innovation is the social dimension of creativity, which means it is a process in which individual creativity is transmitted, interpreted, transformed, and finally accepted or rejected:

> The topic of innovation is often discussed as if it referred to a unique event that marks the beginning of change and represents the sole sufficient cause of that change ... It makes much more sense to view the focal event—the innovation—as just one event within a continuous system-change or social-change. (McGrath 1985, 75)

Regardless of who creates the impetus for a particular innovation, the cooperation or at least the acquiescence of other actors is required. That is why innovative processes can be characterized as "network effort" (van de Ven 1988, 115), as a collective acquisition. Innovations require what is often called absorption, in other words, institutionalization and normalization (Rogers and Kim 1985, 102). That is why innovation is an eminently social event. Social innovations, to the extent they succeed, demand a relearning from all of society, which also implies a loss or devaluation of previously accepted abilities and knowledge (Nowotny 1989).

We can best see the social nature of innovations, their liberation from individual creativity, when we consider changes over time. Many novelties found their first successes in other fields, and they ended up being employed differently than originally expected. The most famous example of this in the history of technology is found in the case of the telephone, which Bell conceived for transmitting music, but Edison transferred to the field of oral communication (Rammert 1993, 233). The history of personal computers or cell phones is similar; expectations were for very low demand and minimal usefulness. That is why we should assume that the current form of many innovations is transitory, since there can be reinventions that modify them, and we still do not know what they might contribute. Innovations often have a fluid form. The object is rarely the same at the beginning and end of the innovative process. One of the reasons innovations can transform in this way is that the confrontation with new ideas foments a learning process in participants that leads to a modification of products and purposes, which are adapted to concrete necessities and interests. The same innovations can be employed for different things, and we can in no way determine or predict the unforeseeable uses that can also become part of the innovative process.

Even when the intentionality of an innovation was strongly predetermined, innovations rarely take the anticipated path. Innovative processes follow a logic that is neither predictable nor calculable, yet neither is it completely a product of chance. That is why it is difficult to establish inflexible cause–effect models to explain innovation, predict its path, make economic calculations, and control it politically.

Sociology has repeatedly revealed the extent to which innovations are subject to the flow of time. There is often a disconnect between their original meaning, the idea their creators had for them, and the use other people make of them, including later developments, combinations with other artefacts, and user reinterpretations that modify them over time. When it comes to determining if something is an innovation and what it entails, its consumption is as important as its production. Use and appropriation are what decide the success or failure of an innovative process. Creative variations or the breaking of the rules are necessary but not sufficient factors in the emergence of innovations. Only repetition and dissemination convert wild ideas, unusual practices, and new objects into social innovations. This reference to social expansion is even more intense in the case of social innovations since, given the fact that their diffusion depends upon assessment and collective acceptance, they cannot be unilaterally institutionalized. For this reason, social innovations are more dependent on context than technological innovations.

In any case, the theory of the diffusion of innovations (Rogers [1962] 2006) has long since revealed the extent to which clients and places of application contribute decisively to the development of innovations. This is extensive enough that we can note a "recursive process" (Asdonk, Bredeweg, and Kowol 1991) between innovation and diffusion. We can also conclude that thinking about innovation beyond the social conditions of realization and variation is an abstraction that does not do justice to the complexity of the phenomenon. Not paying sufficient attention to this complexity is the gateway to the failure of the politics of innovation. Recent investigations have revealed that innovation in research or in industrial sectors of the vanguard is not enough. We also need client demand or experiences of implementation, which constitute what some have called "the systemic character of innovations" (Fagerberg, Mowery, and Nelson 2005). That is why the processes of innovation cannot be understood in a linear and sequential fashion (from research to application and the marketplace) but must be interwoven with complex models of learning, in various senses and different combinations.

4. The innovation society

It is not possible to understand modern society without accepting the centrality that the institutionalization of innovation has acquired within it. Innovation has become a generalized reason for action. In practice, "ubiquitous innovating" (Braun-Thürmann 2005, 5) signifies the fact, unimaginable in other societies or other moments of history, that there are barely areas of modern society that cannot be observed from the point of view of what must be renovated.

Not all societies at all times have favored the new. Modern society has a special weakness for the new, and this inclination affords diverse dynamics of innovation in different social areas. Modern art demands originality, but not all transgressive proposals find a corresponding acceptance. Media news is steered by the value of novelty that they themselves create; in politics, principal actors must recognize politically relevant themes soon enough (in other words, before elections) in order to be able to channel them into the relevant decision-making processes. Similarly, in economics, since we tend to produce under conditions of scarcity, it is very important for businesses to distinguish their products sufficiently from those of the competition, etc.

This generalized demand for innovation is due to the fact that a long process of differentiation and professionalization has shaped institutions that are specialized in producing innovations systematically. Particularly in the arts and sciences, a dynamic has been created that commits to extending new and surprising information. While pre-modern innovation was seen as a deviation, exorcised as heterodoxy, or admired as genius, modern societies are constituted by institutionalizing the production of novelty. Without this process, realities we consider as constitutive as conscience, preferences, or freedom in general could not be understand.

The question this all presents is whether and to what extent it makes sense to do something to favor and promote innovation. The paradox is that if something is truly innovative it cannot be the result of an intentional action. By definition, the new cannot be known in advance; it would have to be the chance result of a discovery, not something deliberately pursued. Is there any way of getting around this contradiction?

In the first place, there are those who begin with the assumption that innovations are something that can basically be planned. If this were the case, then innovations would arise wherever there was an adequate and consistently applied plan to produce innovation. This presumes a functionalist conception of institutions and an idea that human action simply enacts concepts and theoretical models. It is obvious that the type of action designed to favor innovation cannot be the same as the rigid planning that would make sense when working toward other types of goals. Strictly speaking, innovation cannot be demanded or produced in a decisionist manner. We are capable of creating the necessary, but not sufficient, conditions for innovation to emerge and avoiding the routines or restrictions that make it impossible. In this sense, the negative formulation is the most common, but also the most logical, given the unpredictable character of what we want to promote. Creativity, which is the basic assumption of innovation, cannot be forced, and it makes no sense to determine what innovation should be achieved ahead of time. It seems much more logical to determine the conditions that increase the probability of innovations and to create those conditions (Wottawa and Gluminski 1995).

There is a corresponding debate about the role of the authorities regarding the policies of innovation. *Laissez-faire* principles suggest that industry should be given the task of innovation, while institutions should limit themselves to science and education. This would be the traditional division of labor. The government would only pay attention to innovation in a reactive manner, adapting legislation to new technological circumstances and compensating the negative effects that innovation would have on society as a whole. In a more interventionist approach, the state would control innovation, especially through large technological projects. Both views see politics as a cooperative power in a heterogeneous field. Government action has as many limitations as possibilities :

> The way the government intervenes is now more limited than ever to establishing frameworks for the contexts of research, development, production, and the application of new technologies for non-governmental actors, which are largely self-organized and follow their own designs. (Dolata 2004, 23)

In this sense, we recognize that the state and authorities are in no condition to plan complex processes of technological innovation, but they can establish general conditions for diverse innovative activities.

A special modesty is required when dealing with innovation in complex societies. Societies and social change can only be planned and governed to a limited extent. But in spite of the indeterminability of time frames and the content of innovative processes, it would be a huge mistake to abandon this process to chance because we are unable to plan it. Innovative processes are not merely economic processes; they take place in a broad context of institutional, structural, and political realities that also interact in regional and supranational spaces. Economic forces are not sufficient to "institutionalize" innovation. It is unquestionable that the authorities are able to make decisions that favor innovation, in culture, in civil society, in organizations and institutions. The question would then be to determine the structural conditions that must be created so the climate is favorable to innovation.

There are specific cultural elements—from public policies to long-term processes—that favor innovation. That culture could be summarized as a society open to learning, capable of questioning certainties, beliefs, and routines, and confronting the destabilizing effects of that process. Systems and societies that are focused on learning triumph over those that only learn with difficulty and prefer telling reality how it should be. The learning society also implies a new culture of organizations. Their demands for informality increase when they try to manage knowledge and innovation, which are areas that are hampered by hierarchical and sectorized organizations.

The true wealth of a society resides in its knowledge. The energy of its talents is incomparably greater than the force of material and all its possible transformations. What we call a knowledge or learning society is a type of society that does not compete for material resources as much as for the skills that have to do with knowledge in a very broad sense. From the outset, innovation consists of the ability to distance oneself from one's own routines, from what is known, from stereotypes, and not accepting what has been achieved. Innovation's greatest enemy is how well things are currently going. That is why innovation demands, from the beginning, a culture of risk, responsibility, and learning. This is the key to social vitality and the active role societies can claim. Innovation that comes from a risk culture and is willing to learn is a general imperative, a value that affects both managerial organization as well as the model of coexistence we must design, both in the forms of cultural expression and in public policies.

In a knowledge economy, innovation is promoted when we successfully configure systems of territorial innovation: "spatially concentrated managerial networks that have socio-cultural roots and are institutionally established, which enjoy special advantages of accumulation, recombination, and use of technical knowledge in selected technological fields" (Heidenreich 2000, 89). At a time of globalization, it does not seem to make sense to focus innovative strategies within the region or the nation. Technological, scientific, and cultural knowledge is produced around the world; innovations are consumed on a global scale. Spatial distances lose meaning with communication and transportation capacities. Even medium-sized businesses build global production and distribution networks. But surviving the global competition in a knowledge economy depends more and more on local resources in the form of knowledge, skills, relationships, and motivations that are not available to distant competitors (Cooke, Gómez, and Etxebarria 1998; Freeman 1991; Lundvall et al. 2002; Maillat 1995; Nelson 1993; Porter 1990; Storper 1997). This connection between the innovation society and the revalorization of local spaces must be understood and prioritized.

What is being produced is a convergence between the modifications of space and the dynamics of innovation. For some time now, the locality of innovations was considered a question of competition. The physical proximity of prime materials, the means of transportation, areas of increased population: all of this was considered favorable for the emergence of key technological industries. These competitive factors lose relevance when there is a decline in the type of economy focused on classic industry, such as the supply of prime materials and the corresponding labor force. This is the starting point for the theories of society that analyze the transition from the industrial society that focused on production to the postindustrial society that focuses on knowledge (Bell 1973; Stehr 1994; Knorr-Cetina 2000; Willke 2001). Nowadays, speed, price reduction, the expansion of communicative tools, and the possibility this all offers to create expert knowledge throughout the world make it possible that people who are not in physical proximity will be working on the same project or product.

It would, then, be a mistake to think that globalization voids the meaning of local space in favor of a de-territorialized global system of communications and exchanges. The process of globalization does not destroy locality; it affords it new meaning. While the development of innovations can be driven by the global division of labor, new networks are formed within a regional system of innovation.

We have overcome the belief in a unilateral and technocratic globalization where concrete places would disappear because of new global communications and technologies and knowledge would be reduced to mere information that would circulate throughout the globe as *flow*. We now talk about innovative places that are found in areas where globalization and localization processes come together. After undervaluing the local dimension of knowledge and human resources, knowledge, space, and governance have now achieved a new unity in knowledge societies. Territorial politics recently celebrated the theme of knowledge which is already being defined as a "knowledge turn of spatial analysis." The value of temporal closeness, confidence, and wellbeing has been rediscovered. Local networks no longer oppose the knowledge society. Quite the contrary.

Bibliography

Asdonk, Jupp, Bredeweg, Udo, and Kowol, Uli (1991), "Innovation als recursive Prozess : Zur Theorie und Empirie der Technikgenese am Beispiel der Produktionstechnik," *Zeitschrift für Soziologie* 20, 290–304.

Bell, Daniel (1973), *The Coming of Post-Industrial Society*, New York: Basic Books.

Braun-Thürmann, Holger (2005), *Innovation*, Bielefeld: transcript.

Castells, Manuel (2011 [1996]), *The Rise of the Network Society: The Information Age, Economy, Society and Culture*, Hoboken, NJ: Wiley-Blackwell.

Cooke, Philip, Gómez Uranga, Mikel, and Etxebarria, Goio (1998), "Regional Systems of Innovation: An Evolutionary Perspective," *Environment and Planning* 30, 1563–84.

David, Paul A. (1990), "The Dynamo and the Computer: An Historical Perspective on the Modern Productivity Paradox," *American Economic Review* 80/2, 355–61.

Dolata, Ulrich (2004), *Unfassbare Technologien, internationale Innovationsverläufe und ausdifferenzierte Politikregime*, Bremen: Artec-Paper 110.

Fagerberg, J., Mowery, D., and Nelson, Richard (2005), *The Oxford Handbook of Innovation*, Oxford: Oxford University Press.

Freeman, Christopher (1991), "Networks of Innovators: A Synthesis of Research Issues," *Research Policy* 20, 499–514.

—(1996), "The Greening of Technology and Models of Innovation" in *Technological Forecasting and Social Change* 53 (1), 27–39.

Future Commission, Friedrich Ebert Foundation (1998), "Economic Performance, Social Cohesion, Environmental Sustainability: Three Goals—One Path, " Bonn: Dietz.

Gillwald, Katrin (2000), "Konzepte sozialer Innovation," WZB discussion paper P00-519, Berlin.

Hauff, Volker and Scharpf, Fritz (1975), *Modernisierung der Volkswirtschaft: Technologiepolitik als Strukturpolitik*, Frankfurt: Europäische Verlaganstalt.

Heidenreich, Martin (2000), "Regionale Netzwerke in der globalen Wissensgesellschaft," in Johannes Weywr (ed.), *Soziale Netzwerke*, München: Oldenburg, 87–110.

Innerarity, Daniel (2009), *The Future and its Enemies: In Defense of Political Hope*, Sandra Kingery (trans.), Stanford, CA: Stanford University Press.

Knorr-Cetina, Karin (2000), "Die Wissensgesellschaft," in Armin Pongs (ed.), *In welcher Gesellschaft leben wir eigentlich? Gesellschaftskonzepte im Vergleich*, München: Dilema, 149–70.

Kondratieff, Nicolai D. (1935 [1926]), "The Long Waves in Economic Life, " *The Review of Economic Statistics* 17 (6), 105–15.

Luhmann, Niklas (1994), *Die Wissenschaft der Gesellschaft*, Frankfurt: Suhrkamp.

Lundvall, Bengt-Ake, Johnson, Björn, Andersen, Esben Sloth, and Dalum, Bent (2002), "National Systems of Production, Innovation and Competence Building," *Research Policy* 31, 213–31.

Maillat, Dennis (1995), "Territorial Dynamic, Innovative Milieus and Regional Policy," *Entrepreneurship & Regional Development* 7, 157–65.

McGrath, Joseph (1985), "Groups and the Innovation Process," in Richard L. Merrit and Anna J. Merrit, *Innovation in the Public Sector*, Beverly Hills, CA: Sage, 63–84.

Meyer-Krahmer, Frieder (ed.) (1998), *Innovation and Sustainable Development: Lessons for Innovation Policies*, Heidelberg: Physica.

Mumford, Lewis (1967), *The Myth of the Machine: Technics and Human Development*, San Diego: Hartcourt Brace.

Nelson, Richard R. (ed.) (1993), *National Innovation Systems: A Comparative Analysis*, New York: Oxford.

North, Douglass C. (1990), *Institutions, Institutional Change and Economic Performance*, Cambridge: Cambridge University Press.

Nowotny, Helga (1989), "The Sustainability of Innovation: A Preliminary Research Agenda on Innovation and Obsolescence," WZB-Schriftenreih P89-001, Berlin: Wissenschaftszentrum Berlin für Sozialforschung.

Ogburn, William (1922), *Social Change with Respect to Culture and Original Nature*, New York: B. W. Huebsch.

Pels, Dick (2003), "Unhastening Science: Temporal Demarcations in the 'Social Triangle,'" *European Journal of Social Theory* 6, 209–31.

Polanyi, Karl (1944), *The Great Transformation*, Boston: Beacon Press.

Polsby, Nelson (1984), *Political Innovation in America*, New Haven, CT: Yale University Press.

Porter, Michael E. (1990), *The Competitive Advantage of Nations*, New York: Free Press.

Rammert, Werner (ed.) (1993), *Technik aus soziologischer Perspektive*, Opladen: Westdeutscher Verlag.

Rogers, Everett M. (2006 [1962]), *Diffusion of Innovations*, New York: Free Press.

Rogers, Everett M. and Kim, Jouong-Im (1985), "Diffusion of Innovations in Public Organizations," in Richard L. Merrit and Anna J. Merrit, *Innovation in the Public Sector*, Beverly Hills, CA: Sage.

Sauer, Dieter and Lang, Christa (1999), *Paradoxien der Innovation: Perspektiven sozialwissenschaftlicher Innovationsforschung*, Frankfurt and New York: Campus Verlag.

Schaffer, Simon (1994), "Making Up Discovery," in Margaret A. Boden (ed.), *Dimensions of Creativity*, Cambridge, MA: MIT Press, 13–51.

Schumpeter, Joseph (1939), *Business Cycles: A Theoretical, Historical and Statistical Analysis of the Capitalist Process*, New York: McGraw Hill.

—(1947), "The Creative Response in Economic History," *The Journal of Economic History* 7 (2), 149–59.

Simonis, Georg (1993), "Macht und Ohnmacht staatlicher Techniksteuerung," in Herbert Kubicek and Peter Seeger (eds), *Perspektive Techniksteuerung*, Berlin: Edition Sigma, 39-57.

Stehr, Nico (1994), *Arbeit, Eingentum und Wissen: Zur Theorie von Wissensgesellschaften*, Frankfurt: Suhrkamp.

Storper, Michael (1997), *The Regional World: Territorial Development in a Global Economy*, New York: Guilford Press.

van de Ven, Andrew H. (1988), "Approaches to Innovation and Organizing," in Michael L. Tushman and William L. Moore (eds), *Readings in the Management of Innovation*, Cambridge, MA: Ballenger.

Vordank, Tino (2005), "Zur organisationalen Reziprozität von Diffusion," in Jens Aderhold and René John (eds), *Innovation: Sozialwissenschaftliche Perspektiven*, Konstanz: UVK, 33-48.

Weik, Elke (1998), *Zeit, Wandel und Transformation: Elemente einer postmodernen Theorie der Transformation*, München.

White, William (1982), "Social Inventions for Solving Human Problems," *American Sociological Review* 47, 1-13.

Willke, Helmut (2001), *Atopia: Studien zur atopischen Gesellschaft*, Frankfurt: Suhrkamp.

Winner, Langdon (1980), "Do Artifacts Have Politics?," *Daedalus* 109, 121-36.

Wottawa, H. and Gluminski, I. (1995), *Psychologische Theorien für Unternehmen*, Göttingen: Verlag für angewandte Psychologie.

Zapf, Wolfgang (1989), "Über soziale Innovation," *Soziale Welt* 1-2, 170-83.

11

The Governance of Smart Territories

The relationship between global and local environments is giving way to new realities, which are questioning some of the oversimplifications we had accepted that claimed an unqualified victory for the global. In the context of a knowledge economy, these new circumstances present new opportunities for the configuration of spaces, both urban and regional, around the idea of intensive work with knowledge. In this way, an economic geography of creativity is established that requires a significant number of modifications in the way territories are governed.

1. A new articulation of the local and the global

The first diagnostics about globalization suggested a teleology that was impervious to local context. It believed, implicitly or explicitly, that the global was defined by the suppression of the local and that physical spaces merged into a virtual whole. Its boldest proponents even claimed that geography had died and that distance had perished alongside it. Space, in the sense of a material substratum, seemed to have become nearly irrelevant. Some people deduced that time had destroyed space (Harvey 1990, 299), that we lived in an "atopic society" (Willke 2001) where "the place has been trivialized" (Luhmann 1997, 152).

At the same time, theories of globalization have trained us to contrast flows and locations, as if they were two separate and even conflicting territorial realities. It is true that the principle of territoriality is currently subject to a great uncertainty (Badie 1995; Innerarity 2004); financial cycles; commercial exchanges; the broadcasting of trends and images; population migrations; religious, cultural, or linguistic solidarities seem to weigh more than ever on the world's weak cartography. It is most likely an exaggeration to talk about the end of territories, but there is no doubt that the gravity of space has given way to a diffuse, ambiguous, and multipurpose territoriality. The global scene currently harbors an ensemble of political, economic, and social strategies that contradict the principle of territoriality. In general, the realities of mobility are imposed upon the realities of territorialization.

In any case, it is true that we are experiencing a relativization of distance, of close and far, that shakes fixed and stable localizations. Of course, globalization has destroyed the idea that social realities are constructed in delimited territorial units. We no longer believe politics, culture, and identity must be viewed as isomorphic, in other words, as coextensive realities within a territorial unit. Territories are no longer "container spaces" (Ulrich Beck), but locations that achieve diverse forms of self-articulation with the world according to what is in play. In any case, social realities can no longer be understood through comprehensive spatial categories.

The current discourse about globalization and its consequences is full of misunderstandings. One misunderstanding is that limits and differences disappear completely with deterritorialization. Those who claim that "the world is flat" (Friedman 2007) have not understood that the delimitation of spaces is only one phenomenon in the process of a new territorialization. The world is not "flat," but uneven and disparate, as is revealed, negatively, in examples of injustice and exclusion, but also in the competitiveness that is related to territorial differences. Space has not been rendered irrelevant, but diverse.

The inability to recognize the dialectical nature of global versus local realities and the tendency to consider relationships between actors in terms of absolute winners and losers has given rise to interpretations that do little in terms of explaining and less in terms of guiding. The idea that the global, in a type of zero-sum game, gains everything that the local is progressively losing is a categorical failure. Why should the local be seen as the sole form of territoriality while the global is viewed as nothing more than fluid, deterritorialized space? The global financial system would not exist without its specific locality in cities such as London or New York. We would be unaware of particular local cultures, catastrophes, and specific injustices if it were not for the fact that globalization has made us aware of them. Putting global issues on the same footing as capital or equating progress and civilization, on the one hand, with local issues, tradition, and territoriality, on the other, is an oversimplification that does not do justice to the complexity of the relationships between these two realities. It is also simplistic to see the local as a victim of uncontrollable external forces, as if the local could not generate any context of its own, since decisive events are completely beyond its reach.

Theories of deterritorialization view the local as equivalent to the territorial and the global as a process that makes space irrelevant. However, the imposition of global standards of rationality does not necessarily imply cultural standardization. Local cultures and global fluctuations should not be understood as opposites. The local is not a compensatory space for the global. Instead, global events emerge and are weakened or strengthened within local contexts. Edward Casey has proposed identifying locations as products of the encounters between different histories, a notion of place whose specificity is not derived from the mythical root of relative isolation but from "the absolute specificity of the mixture of influences that took place there" (2006). The particularity of a place is not due to a separation but to the way diversity has been synthesized.

The belief that the global presupposes dominion and dependence while the local represents tradition and continuity is a mistake since it denies the interaction between the global and local and thus ignores their creative evolution. In this sense, the fact that a territory is or is not threatened by globalization depends on its interactions with the global rather than its ability to protect itself from global flows. For that reason, being a place in the world is more a question of how to resolve this connectivity, rather than how to resist or close oneself off from it.

When the creation and circulation of knowledge in the current global economy is explored with greater subtlety, we discover that what has taken place is not so much the destruction of the local as its transformation. The place has stopped being a closed system. We are no longer as connected as people were in the past to locality as a source of information, experience, entertainment, or security. The place itself is no longer necessarily life's central location. In this context, communities do not disappear; they are freed from their dependence on a territory. The configuration of communities has been progressively uncoupled from spatial fields, from the "principle of spatial closeness" (Wiesenthal 1996, 5). With the disappearance of closed spaces, "the myth of neighborhood communities" (Albrow 1998, 257) also vanishes. Community should no longer be understood as a network of local relationships, like a neighborhood. Spatial connections are still real, but they are not the only type of relationship. Phones and computers make the construction of "psychological neighborhoods" (Aronson 1986) possible. We no longer belong to a single community; life is divided between a multitude of networks, none of which can claim to be exclusive. We live in relational and multiple spaces that make it possible to have commitments that are more open than when territory was a fixed, objective, and rigid element in the life of humans and societies.

This situation does not lead to the disappearance of places or complete freedom from them; instead, it affords us something that could be called an "individualized relationship with territory." Individually, these new realities mean greater diversity and freedom of choice than ever. The fact that we are progressively more able to live or remain at a distance from other people has made it easier to withdraw from the "centers" and from physical contact. The relationship with place is still important, but not in the traditional sense. Physical closeness to others no longer necessarily means being trapped in a reciprocal dependency. In the same way, physical distance does not equate to communicative distance. We can be very close to those who are far away and very far from those who are nearby.

This is the context that has produced a progressive recovery of place that corrects the incomplete reasoning regarding the space of flows. For some years now, there has been a change of perspective as a result of the convergence between city and region and what have been called "dense spaces" (Nassehi 2002). These spaces must be viewed and managed as a location of general competitiveness, the management of services, and the shaping of political will.

If it is true that "place matters" (Baraldi, Fors, and Houlz 2006) in the knowledge society and economy, this is due to the fact that new knowledge does not emerge just anywhere; economic agents are located in particular contexts and, as Polanyi noted (1957), they operate under institutional and cultural conditions from which they cannot be easily separated. Global players also make use of specific territorial conditions for the creation of knowledge. The restructuring of territories and cities does not depend only on the international flow of capital and information, but at the same time on the local actors who can support or impede this process. While the industrial economy was delocalized and benefited from global reorganization, the creative economy tends to be territorialized, to select its own spaces for the relationship between network and exchange.

In the face of certain stereotypes about globalization, a new concept of spatial development that was closer to the reality of knowledge societies began to take hold at the end of the 1990s. In contrast to the supposed irrelevance of concrete places and information society territories, there was an emphasis in the knowledge society on simultaneity and hybridization between concrete places and the flows that operate globally. Analyses based on a more elaborate articulation of global and local forces played a fundamental role in this broader perspective. Spaces stopped being obstacles to general virtualization and were viewed as stimuli for innovations. The advantages of specific places began to be compared to transnational competitiveness and mobility.

Spatial conditions also have a particular meaning in knowledge societies. It has been empirically proven that, in activities based on knowledge-intensive jobs, the relationship that actors have with space is more intense. In the debate about the geography of information and knowledge, there was a solidification of the truism that information and knowledge would in principle be ubiquitous in a global society, available anywhere and in any way. The fact that this is not the case becomes obvious when we distinguish between information and knowledge. Information is universally accessible but knowledge is connected to concrete contexts. What is transferable and available anywhere is information, while implicit knowledge can only be transmitted through personal interactions. Given that both learning and the exchange of specific knowledge depend to a large extent on the assumptions of direct personal communication, the specific conditions of territory, in spite of the global flow of information, not only partially persist but acquire a central significance for territorial development. Knowledge processes are processes of learning that are based on communication and that, therefore, need certain infrastructures that are realized in a location. A territory's capacity for innovation resides in the articulation of explicit present knowledge and the information that is obtained through global networks.

It is important to maintain the distinction between diverse types of knowledge, especially the distinction between codified and easily transferable knowledge and non-codified or implicit knowledge that can only be transmitted through personal contacts. Following this distinction, not all relevant knowledge is easily accessible, and the expression "global information society" is too superficial to describe the reality of contemporary society. While the concept of *information society* pointed toward global rootlessness, the idea of a *knowledge society* assumes a territorial reference. That is why, in contrast to the neoclassical fictions of homogeneous spaces and available information, we must also question the real distribution of knowledge, the "technological gap," the "digital divide," and new regional peripheries.

Structures and spatial localizations have not become obsolete with the mobility of goods, people, and information in favor of virtual flows. In spite of global connectivity, the concept of a center or local roots does not lose significance, even if it changes meaning. "When activities move beyond a digital space, they do so through a massive concentration of material resources, from the corresponding infrastructure to buildings" (Saasen 1998, 349). This is how Saskia Saasen criticizes the idea of "informational cities," understood as mere interchangeable connections that would confirm the preeminence of flows as opposed to places, an abstract urbanness within whose economy of space the centers would lose gravitational force in favor of pure virtual connectivity.

However, it is worth emphasizing that the local reality that is reasserted in the new relational economic geography is not the reality of traditional, closed, and self-sufficient local communities but of the open spaces that are part of a global system. The space that is currently being recovered, after the disappearance of abstract global space, is a space whose limits are not as clearly defined as those established based on concepts of competition, borders, or territorial integrity. The new spaces are less limited and exclusive, more multi-dimensional and open to connections and overlap. If a territory acquires a certain centrality, this is due to its ability to form relationships.

From this point of view, we can understand the value of the idea of proximity but also its limitations. Proximity is important because it facilitates face to face contacts that can develop relational capital and stimulate collective learning. We should not mythologize locality but consider it in the context of greater international contact because the exchange of knowledge can be carried out in different ways, not always or necessarily through proximity. Many studies have revealed that only a minority of small business clusters take advantage of collective local knowledge, while large companies learn through non-local relationships. An evaluation of the efficiency of technological parks reveals that spatial closeness does not automatically lead to greater contact between actors; spatial density is not the same as social density. Proximity does not automatically lead to the establishment of strong local networks. One source of competitiveness is a type of interaction we could call "relational proximity," which can be realized without too much concern about the distance between actors. Current innovative resources combine forms of urban mobility and stability.

That being said, since communication and transportation technologies make the concentration of people and products unnecessary, geographic closeness no longer means political or economic centrality. A new geography of centrality and marginality, a new "spatial economy of the center" (Saasen 1996) is being produced. The center and the periphery must be reconsidered there, in the same way we must revise categories of closeness and distance because physical proximity is not the only variable. As the theory of relational economic geography (Bathelt and Glückler 2002, 49) has emphasized, proximity is a concept that integrates many dimensions (spatial, cultural, institutional, organizational, virtual).

2. Forms of collective intelligence

Whatever the name used to characterize contemporary societies—post-industrial society, information society, or knowledge society—these concepts all point toward a profound change that has taken place in advanced countries in recent decades. They refer to the fact that information and knowledge resources have grown powerfully in comparison to material and energy resources. The production and transfer of knowledge now has great significance and plays a fundamental role in social, economic, and territorial development. The character of the time in which we live could be summarized by saying that humanity's great challenge is no longer dominating nature but making information and organization move forward in tandem. The enemy that must be fought is not so much poverty or fear, but ignorance. Our principal challenges have to do with knowledge in the broad sense, and the most decisive strategies are oriented toward the politics of knowledge, science, technology, innovation, research, and education. The true wealth of nations resides in their knowledge. What does this mean for territorial politics? What challenges does it present for government?

For some years now, there has been what we could call a *cognitive turn* in the conception of space and its planning and governance. In the European Union, the Fifth Framework Programme for Research unveiled the concept of territorial development based on knowledge. The goal of the Lisbon Strategy to convert Europe into a knowledge-based economic space has been translated into territorial governance with the idea of *intelligent territory* or *knowledge cities*. Knowledge has become a repeated concept within territorial studies and the practice of local governance. The principal challenge seems to consist of encouraging processes to create knowledge and apply it to economic activities.

Since the mid-1980s, European cities and regions have been increasingly adopting strategies to intensify knowledge-based programs of innovation. Innovative media, knowledge cities, technological parks, university campuses, learning regions, start-up networks ... all of them attempt to put in play a special relationship between space, knowledge, culture, and science. The function of "knowledge environments" is to soften individual risks, making operative resources available, and configuring resonance structures for innovations (Fürst 2001, 372). A knowledge territory is a dense series of interactions in which knowledge transfers are carried out or, at the very least, implicit knowledge and particular forms of common practice are shared (Matthiesen 1998). The formation of clusters serves to allow access to implicit, non-codified knowledge, which represents a strategic resource in the processes of innovation. In studies on the regional economy, we find some attempts to measure how territories are capable of exchanging "tacit knowledge" (Lever 2001).

We could summarize these indicators when it comes to measuring territorial intelligence in some way by pointing out that, in order for the creation, interchange, and use of knowledge to be effective, at least four factors are required (Growe 2009): 1) Infrastructures for the production and communication of knowledge, which means research and educational institutions; 2) Creative interaction between many groups of actors. This refers to the complex system of generally informal social contacts that make economic space a fundamentally relational space; 3) Constructive articulation of the endogenous and exogenous sources of implicit and explicit knowledge with cognitive territorial resources. Because of its codification and diffusion by communication technologies, much knowledge has become globally available. The opening of territory is important for economic success; territorial actors should be connected to broader interactions; 4) An optimistic attitude that is fulfilled in a climate that stimulates curiosity and a positive disposition toward risk.

However, we must understand exactly what we mean when we talk about something like *collective intelligence*. First we must distinguish individual and collective knowledge because organizations and territories create specific knowledge in addition to the knowledge of their members that is even greater than the sum of the knowledge of the members of the group. It is one thing that people in territories learn and another thing that territories learn, one thing that actors cooperate and another that institutions learn.

We often think that knowledge in an organization is simply the sum of the knowledge of its members. Of course, organizational competence depends on the knowledge of its members. But in the same way that an unorganized collection of geniuses and Nobel Prize winners does not constitute an intelligent organization, neither does an increase in degree holders automatically produce an intelligent society. Having institutions that are dedicated to knowledge is not enough to ensure spaces of knowledge or territorial intelligence. The specific conditions required so that the relationship between diverse intelligent institutions can create an intelligent territory are met when intelligence is transformed into social ability within the territory's framework.

When dealing with matters that have to do with collective dynamics, there is always the question about whether the whole is greater than the sum of its parts, whether there is something supra-individual—the system, the organized totality, an emerging phenomenon—that can "be reduced to the intentions of the individual participants" (Heintz 2004, 3). Emergencies are discussed precisely when there are general properties that cannot be reduced to the characteristics of their parts. A knowledge society is not a society in which there are more experts, but a society where the system is expert. It is not enough for individuals to learn and innovate; it does not do much good for citizens to acquire new competencies as long as the rules, routines, and procedures—in other words, organizational and public intelligence—prevent taking advantage of new competencies. Changes are only realized when structures, processes, and collective rules are also modified. Territorial knowledge is more than the mere accumulation of existing knowledge, in the same way that an intelligent organization is intelligent because of the synergy that is produced in its systems of rules, institutions, and procedures, not by the mere summing up of personal intelligences. The creation of knowledge is the consequence of communicative acts or, stated another way, a relational good.

This points us toward a difficulty that has to do with the emerging character of collective intelligence, in other words, with the fact that it is something that does not emerge unfailingly even when certain measures are adopted, and it may not appear in the short term. Collective intelligence stems from long processes whose results are not assured. Both the configuration and the governing and structuring of networks are difficult. Social capital is not something that can be truly created or controlled. "A cluster cannot be constructed. It has to grow" (Koch 2007, 202). The processes of the configuration of collective knowledge are complex; they demand long-term perspectives and have little visibility. This means we must be especially cautious when it comes to trusting the models of indicators, which do not reflect collective knowledge as much as the visible results of that knowledge.

The emerging character of properties like shared intelligence is due to the fact that there are no magical or universal formulas for the configuration of learning processes and collective innovation. Knowledge-based urban and territorial politics should be exactly contextualized in relation to the concrete capabilities and problems of each territory. This expressly contradicts the idea that it is possible to transfer the experiences of "icon regions" like Silicon Valley or the idea of recuperating modernization based on a previous model such as the one found in Eastern Europe after 1989, for example. The specific conditions for success are not precisely reproducible. As with territories, we cannot forecast the behavior of highly complex systems. The dynamics of innovation cannot be predicted precisely; this lack of foresight is part of the emerging nature of all new knowledge, an indetermination that is emphasized by the growing difficulty of governing complex realities.

It is true that the ability to attract talent creates a regional advantage. This is what we mean by the term "sticky place" (Markusen 1996): these are locations that have the spatial ability to attract and retain talent or innovative businesses. But we should not overlook the limitations of this type of politics as if they were automatic magic formulas. The diffusion of the creative model has frequently balanced the playing field and encouraged all territories to respond in a similar fashion. On the other hand, the construction of cultural infrastructures does not simply guarantee cultural revitalization, and cultural creation often flees from those formatted and planned cultural sectors. If we want to be creative, we cannot simply use commonplace procedures that have been successful in the places we recognize as especially creative. To be creative, we must place creativity itself in play.

3. Geography of creativity

The paradigm of the information society, which was dominant during the 1980s and a good part of the 1990s, resulted in essentially setting technological infrastructures in motion. Urban and territorial policies opted for the construction of technological and research parks, frequently in remote locations, isolated from cities. Concrete locations, urban spaces, and city centers were considered vestiges of a general process of globalization and virtualization. Social spaces were progressively reduced to an accidental locality meant to serve the hardware of the means of information and communication. For a number of years now, however, the debate about territorial conditions for the creation of knowledge and the capacity for innovation is no longer reduced to the field of new technologies and has achieved a more intense territorial and urban significance.

The evolution of the knowledge society is modifying the articulation of "hard" and "soft" factors of competitiveness. The importance of the factors of competitiveness that constitute "non-market linkages" (networks, confidence, social capital, etc.) is being revealed. The "soft" factors of competitiveness are no longer considered accidental or secondary, remnants of economic rationality understood in a neoclassic manner. While traditional analyses about regional development were almost exclusively focalized on industry, clusters, and companies, the idea of "knowledge environments" encourages us to pay more and more attention to the cultural factors of social life and the qualitative meaning of social structures in economic processes. We are realizing that many non-commercial elements are found at the center of the economic development of territories.

The theory of competitiveness has long been a pure theory of costs, according to which businesses located themselves wherever the costs of production and distribution were most favorable. The "hard" factors of competitiveness, like infrastructures or the labor market, were key factors in the localization of businesses. The homogenization of these factors, especially within the European Union, has made territories distinguish themselves by "weak" factors like image, free time, or housing options, cultural or ecological criteria, human and social capital. While the traditional point of view suggested that a place's attractiveness was due to economic advantages, there is now an emphasis on questions relative to lifestyle and cultural amenities. The point of view that was typical during the industrial era was that places grew either because they were on transportation routes or because they were close to the natural resources that had encouraged establishing the business in that area in the first place. On the other hand, the theory of human capital asserts that the key to growth is not cost reduction but ready access to very educated and creative people. We must move from low costs to high creativity. In the knowledge economy, creative potential is fundamental for the growth and success of cities and territories.

One of the main reasons for this change in perspective comes from theories such as Putnam's theory of social capital (2000). The concept of social capital was introduced because of the realization that the structure of social relationships had an effect on economic processes. This refers to the resources that emerge from more or less institutionalized relationships in which forms of recognition are established. It also references confidence, cooperation, and solidarity as the basis for social relationships. The analysis of social capital focuses on the fact that social networks create value, and we can invest in them (Putnam and Goss 2002, 8).

However, if technological determinism was blind to social factors of competitiveness, the theory of social capital presupposes an idea of community that does not mesh very well with contemporary individualism. It also rejects the collective benefits of personal creativity. In contrast to Putnam, we could say that some traditional social categories like self-sufficiency, coherence, stability, and agreement now work against prosperity, which requires openness and weaker connections. This is the point of view contributed by Richard Florida's theory of creativity. We were used to analyses by Max Weber or Daniel Bell that located the strength of societies in their efforts, at a distant remove from pleasure and enjoyment. Bell even blamed the hedonism of the 1960s for having a negative effect on innovation and economic growth.

In the face of these views, diverse theories of creativity have been appearing in recent years; the most famous of them is by Richard Florida (2005). While the first half of the twentieth century was impressed by physical transformations and the implementation of technological or engineering miracles, in the second half, the most important transformations are found in social environments and new cultural forms. In the new knowledge economy, where information and knowledge are the tools of production and prime materials, creativity constitutes a comparative advantage for businesses, individuals, and territories. The new indicators of a creative territory would be the three "T's": talent, technology, and tolerance. The greatest economic growth is taking place in areas that are tolerant, diverse, and open to creativity, given that these are the places where all kinds of creative people want to live. Florida affirms that creators are more likely to move, and they search for places where they can best satisfy their needs. They are people who prefer individuality, self-expression, and plurality, and they seek these characteristics at work, in their cities, and in social relationships.

In spite of the class-conscious language that Florida employs, the inventory of the type of people who constitute this "creative class" is wide ranging. The group includes people who are employed to resolve complex problems, to invent new solutions, beyond routine and repetitive issues of production. Creative people are "symbolic analysts," experts, knowledge workers, professionals, and technicians, whose task consists of providing "meaningful new forms." They are scientists, engineers, creators, educators, musicians, whose function is to create new technologies or new contents. What fundamentally distinguishes creative people from everyone else is what they are paid for: while some people are paid to carry out an established plan, creative people are paid to create new ideas, products, and procedures.

If we were to detail some of the characteristics of the new knowledge production or what we could call the conditions of creativity, I would emphasize three characteristics: their non-exclusivity, their heterogeneity, and their informality. Let us take a look at each of these characteristics in turn.

In the first place, we would have to emphasize the *non-exclusivity* of the production of creative knowledge. While the traditional production of knowledge was concentrated in closed spaces and in delimited interactive systems (such as universities and businesses) or in interactions between experts, new forms of knowledge are developed in spatial contexts that are more open and complex, less exclusive, with a combination of diverse modes of knowledge. The knowledge society is characterized by some new modes of knowledge production that are differentiated from the traditional concept by the fact that they are not exclusively developed in academic institutions, but in more heterogeneous contexts and in communication networks that are more open. This is how new forms of the expression of expert and common knowledge arise, as well as specific processes for the creation and circulation of knowledge. That is why we need to create relationships between universities and businesses or the public and private sectors.

Creative knowledge and innovation take place in contexts that are characterized by strong *heterogeneity*. The knowledge of intelligent territories is characterized by their hybridization, diversity, and contrasts. Instead of belonging to a closed circle of experts formally recognized as such, knowledge is produced in an open arena of actors who collaborate or compete among themselves. This is the reason for the creative strength of cities or urban spaces, since cultural hybridization is a phenomenon that is intensely realized in cities. Urban spaces or metropolitan areas with a high degree of social, ethnic, and professional diversification constitute rich reserves for the interactive production of knowledge. Cultural plurality is a factor of innovation. Sociologists have always defined cities as a place for strangers, the most appropriate space for developing a culture of difference. Harboring a full range of richness and poverty, cities are spaces where different modes of life, cultures, and conceptions of the world have managed to coexist and have simultaneously carried out the most productive exchange we know. Cities are key locations for the mingling brought about by the displacement of human beings, who are then exposed to connections and novelty. At the same time, the city creates a space for differentiated lifestyles, and that space is needed for the culture's innovative power. This is one of the reasons why some people have claimed that being open to immigration is key to innovation and economic growth (Zachary 2000). In any case, the potential of urban diversity is not automatic; it requires certain conditions in terms of social cohesion. Otherwise, we would merely have a juxtaposition of diversities that, in practice, would signify exclusion and inequality, as we see in so many European cities.

In the third place, creativity is produced in contexts of *informality*. Research about innovation networks has revealed that these networks do not work without occasional personal encounters. This connects with the idea of heterogeneity since, if anything characterizes a city's dense spaces, it is that they are places of otherness, of unforeseen encounters, experiences that are unexpected, anonymous, full of crowds and a diversity of resources (Innerarity 2006). Cities are chance generators of novelties, personal contacts, the exchange of opportunities and knowledge. The idea of the creative city urges us to discover the value of those forms of life that spring from chance, movement, and creation. The challenge of territorial politics consists of creating the conditions for creativity, accepting that unplanned practices will arise that make unforeseen and improbable encounters possible because, in the end, the city means other people (Ascher 2007). This reality encourages those who govern and town planners to be humble since creativity is neither planned nor programmed. Creativity, whether it is artistic, social, technological, scientific, or urban, arises from places where it was not expected, even though its emergent nature does not free us from working to establish the conditions for its improbable appearance.

4. Governing the knowledge society

The idea of territorial development based on knowledge has many implications for government and ways of articulating decision making. In the same way that conditions of competitiveness have changed enormously in the networked, complex, and interdependent world of knowledge societies, classic forms of government (market and hierarchical) are also overburdened, as are its instruments (prices and authority). What we are seeing is that, since it deals with collective learning, government relationships are not subject to hierarchical or central control.

Nowadays, we are faced with the undermining of hierarchy as a fundamental organizing tool for societies. Complex systems cannot be governed from a hierarchical apex, which would imply a simplification that does not match the richness, initiative, and skill of its parts. Handling elevated complexity creates numerous problems that overcome any hierarchical strategy: the person who is supposed to make a decision is unaware of the temporal dynamic of complex systems. Decision-makers generally do not have all the information, do not include temporal developments in their calculations, and when they do, they tend to favor linear extrapolations. They ignore side effects and exponential developments. They usually think of events as cause and effect, rather than as networks or circular realities. They are most concerned with details and immediate effects, undervaluing connections and panoramic points of view. The solutions they adopt, based on everything-or-nothing extremes, can aggravate the problem. An intervention that is sharp on detail would mean a necessary loss of the general vision that is so necessary for governmental tasks. It is in the interest of all democratic governments to avoid the burden that results from assuming unshared leadership.

A networked world demands relational governance. Networks require more complex instruments like confidence, reputation, or reciprocity. These new formations demand institutional innovation in the processes of governance and reject classic administrative routines. The new governance points toward a form of coordination among political and social agents characterized by regulation, cooperation, and a horizontal approach.

Reflections about local and multilevel governance have revealed the growing importance that local political networks have as soft forms of government. The inclusion of relevant actors is now seen as a more reliable formula for the resolution of problems given that it expands and better uses required knowledge, summing up competencies and their potential for democratization. New forms of governance point toward more cooperative procedures and a greater demand for participation, a combination of public and social elements.

In a knowledge society, there is less willingness to accept decisions adopted hierarchically or with little transparency. There is a demand, on the contrary, for new forms of participation and communication. This was suggested by the World Urban Forum of 2004, organized within the framework of the United Nations Habitat program, which alluded to a consensus about the decisive importance of involving civil society in governance, especially at the local level. The local level is highly self-organized. Given its proximity to the public and the smaller size of the problems it confronts, it is the arena where increased public participation is most likely. The local level is an experimental field for testing new cooperative procedures.

Governance is less concerned about having ready-made solutions for any possible problem. Its focus is, instead, on developing skills for problem solving. The political system is thus faced with demands for preparing ("enabling" or "empowering") citizens (Giddens 1989). Putnam (1993) has summarized this demand in the concept of local social capital, where the quality of public life depends to a large degree on the norms and networks of commitment. Haley describes "governance capacity" as a public good or as the most important infrastructure of civic life (2002), a "soft" infrastructure that accompanies the "hard" infrastructures of physical networks, social services, and legal guarantees.

In the new knowledge economy, economic processes presuppose a social system that works. The relationship between politics, the economy, and civil society is an important factor in territorial competitiveness. The economic development and competitiveness of a territory depend on having the social capital of actors secure the availability of information, competencies, resources, qualified workers, financing. All of this is influenced by structure, governmental form, the stability and dynamics of social relationships, or what is now called institutional capital. In this sense, we can affirm that the city is called on to be a place of reconciliation for economic, ecological, and social realities.

Bibliography

Albrow, Martin (1998), *Abshied vom Nationalstaat: Staat und Gesellschaft im Globalen Zeitalter*, Frankfurt: Suhrkamp.

Aronson, Sidney H. (1986), "The Sociology of Telephone," in G. Gumpert and R. Catthcart (eds), *Inter/media: Interpersonal Communication in a Media World*, Oxford: Oxford University Press, 300–10.

Ascher, F. (2007), "La ville, c'est les autres," in *Airs de Paris*, Paris: Centre Georges Pompidou, 269–71.

Badie, Bertrand (1995), *La fin des territoires*, Paris: Fayard.

Baraldi, Enrico, Fors, Hjalmar, and Houlz, Anders (2006), *Taking Place: The Spatial Contexts of Science, Technology and Business*, Sagamore Beach: Science History Publications.

Bathelt, H. and Glückler, J. (2002), *Wirtschaftsgeographie: Ökonomische Beziehungen in räumlicher Perspektive*, Stuttgart: UTB.

Donzelot, Jacques (2009), *Vers une citoyenneté urbaine? La ville et l'égalité des chances*, Paris: Éditions rue d'Ulm.

Florida, Richard (2005), *Cities and the Creative Class*, New York: Routledge.

Friedman, Thomas (2007), *The World is Flat: A Brief History of the Globalized World in the Twenty-First Century*, London: Penguin.

Fürst, Dietrich (2001), "Regional Governance – ein neus Paradigma der Regionalwissenschaften?," *Raumforschung und Raumordnung* 5–6, 370–80.

Giddens, Anthony (1989), *The Third Way: The Renewal of Social Democracy*, Cambridge: Polity Press.

Growe, Anna (2009), "Wissensalianzen und regionale Wissenskonzepte als Bausteine zur Nutzung von Wissen und Metropolregionen," in Ulf Matthiesen, *Das Wissen der Städte: Neue stadtregionale Entwicklungsdynamiken im Kontext von Wissen, Milieus und Governance*, Wiesbaden: Verlag für Sozialwissenschaften, 323–42.

Harvey, Davis (1990), *Spaces of Hope*, Edinburgh: Edinburgh University Press.

Healey, Patsy (2002), "Urban Governance Capacity in Complex Societies: Challenges of Institutional Adaptation," in Göran Cars (ed.), *Urban Governance, Institutional Capacity and Social Milieux*, Aldershot: Ashgate, 204–25.

Heintz, Bettina (2004), "Emergenz und Reduktion: Neue Perspektiven auf das Mikro-Makro-Problem," *Kölner Zeitschrift für Soziologie und Sozialpsychologie* 56, 1–31.

Innerarity, Daniel (2003), *La sociedad invisible*, Madrid: Espasa.

—(2006), *El nuevo espacio público*, Madrid: Espasa.

Koch, Tobias (2007), "Regionen werden von Menschen gemacht," *Brandeis Neuland: Das Wirtschaftsmagazin der Regionen* 1, 198–294.

Lever, W. F. (2001), "Correlating the Knowledge-base of Cities with Economic Growth," *Urban Studies* 39 (5/6), 859–70.

Luhmann, Niklas (1997), *Die Gesellschaft der Gesellschaft*, Frankfurt: Suhrkamp.

Markusen, Ann (1996), "Sticky Places in Slippery Space: A Typology of Industrial Districts," *Economic Geography* 72 (3), 293–313.

Massey, Doreen (2006), "How to Get From Space to Place in a Fairly Short Stretch of Time," in Steven Feld and Keith Basso (eds), *Senses of Place*, Santa Fe: School of American Research Press, 13–52.

Matthiesen, Ulf (1998), *Die Räume der Milieus: Neue Tendenzen in der sozial- und raumwissenschaftlichen Milieuforschung sowie in der Stadt- und Raumplanung*, Berlin: Sigma.

Nassehi, Armin (2002), "Dichte Räume," in M. Löw (ed.), *Differenzierungen des Städtische*, Opladen: Leske, 211–33.

Polanyi, Michael (1957), *The Tacit Dimension*, London: Routledge.

Putnam, Robert D. (1993), *Making Democracy Work: Civic Traditions in Modern Italy*, Princeton, NJ: Princeton University Press.

—(2000), *Bowling Alone: The Collapse and Revival of American Community*, New York: Simon & Schuster.

Putnam, Robert D. and Goss, Kristin A. (2002), "Introduction," in Robert D. Putnam (ed.), *Democracies in Flux: The Evolution of Social Capital in Contemporary Society*, Oxford: Oxford University Press, 1–19.

Saasen, Saskia (1996), *Metropolen des Weltmarkts: Die neue Rolle der Global Cities*, Frankfurt: Campus.

—(1998), "Zur Einbettung des Globalisierungsprozesses. Der nationale Staat vor neuen Aufgaben," *Berliner Journal für Soziologie* 3, 345–57.

Wiesenthal, Helmut (1996), *Globalisierung: Soziologische und politikwissenschafliche Koordinaten eines unbekannten Terrains*, Max-Plank-Gesellschaft zur Förderung der Wissenschaften e. V. Arbeitsgruppe Transformationprozecce in den Neuen Bundesländern an der Humboldt-Universität zu Berlin, Materialien 96/1.

Willke, Helmut (2001), *Atopia: Studien zur Atopischen Gesellschaft*, Frankfurt: Suhrkamp.

Zachary, Pascal (2000), *The Global Me: New Cosmopolitans and the Competitive Edge – Picking Globalism's Winners and Losers*, New York: Perseus Books.

Index

AAAS *see* American Association for the Advancement of Science
access to information 11
accountability 88
accounting 128
　global 115
administrations 170
Adorno, Theodor 149
advertizing 7
advisers 74
agora 89
AIG *see* American International Group
American Association for the Advancement of Science (AAAS) 94
American International Group (AIG) 114
Anrodmache 77
Anthropology from a Pragmatic Point of View 20
appropriation 57
archives 19, 147, 148
art
　modern 175
arts 142, 155
attention 14
authority figures 51
automatism 7

Bacon, Francis 43, 75
bailouts 111
balance sheets 110
balanced scorecard 8
bankruptcy 112
banks 102, 105, 110, 132, 134, 135
　central banks 114
　regulation 102, 103, 104, 105
Barnes, Julian 26
　Flaubert's Parrot 26-7
Basel Accords 105
　Basel II 106
Bell, Alexander Graham 173
Bell, Daniel 194

Bentham, Jeremy 51
bio-politics 69
books 18, 19
Borges, Jorge Luis 18
　"The Congress" 18
Bourdieu, Pierre 24, 54
brokers 135
budgetary policy 102
bureaucracy 170
businesses 134

calculation procedures 35
Callon, Michel 93
capital 186
　institutional 198
capitalism 136
　modern 132
　seventeenth-century 132
causality 123
Chief Scientific Adviser (UK)
　code of practice 73
cities 195-6, 198
citizen science 82
citizenship 33
class 56
classification 19
climate 83, 90
Clinton administration 102
cognitive capabilities 39
cognitive competence 71
cognitive expectations 37
cognitive maps 12
collective decision making 131
collective learning 85
Commission of the European Communities
　White Paper on European Governance (2001) 73
common sense 55
communication 44, 169
　technology 10, 188
communications 178

global 178
competition
 global 177
competitiveness 141, 193, 194
complexity 13–16, 17, 25–6, 28, 39, 82, 108, 197
computers 15
Comte, Auguste 53
"Congress, The" 18
consciousness 148
consensus 91
consensus conference 91
construction of information 9
constructive interpretations 23
constructivism 74
contingency 25
control 48, 51, 52, 60
corporate governments 37
corruption 132
creative inaccuracy 151–4
creative people 194–5
creative will 145
creativity 28, 141–58, 172, 176, 192–6
 authentic 148
 Florida's theory of 194
 individual 173
 learning 147–51
 rhetoric 151
 theories 194
credit 134
 derivatives 122
 institutions 108
credit rating agencies 108, 109, 110, 122
crisis situations 101
 global 102
cultural lag 163
cultural reality 47
culture 177
cyberspace 6

data 8–9, 69, 81, 90, 152, 153, 158
 analysis 126, 152
 circulation 154
 management 152
 processing 153
 storage 155
data supply networks 12
databanks 10

decentralization 52
decision making 77, 93
 collective 131
dedifferentiation 59
Deleuze, Gilles 24
Democritus 133
deregulation 164
derivatives 122, 123
 markets 114
Derrida, Jacques 22, 24
desubjectivization 145
desynchronization 168, 169
determinism
 technological 194
deterritorialization 184, 185
Diderot, Denis 19
différance 22
differentiation 175
digital revolution 155
disorder 17–28
diversity
 urban 196
division of labor 37, 38, 76, 89, 126, 154, 156, 171, 176
documents 19
dot-com bubble 112
double-entry book-keeping 8
Dunyach, Jean Claude 142
Durkheim, Émile 130

ecology 113
economic crisis of 2008 101–17, 119, 124, 125, 131, 132, 135
economic decisions 76
economic instability
 global
economic productivity 65
economic reality 47, 130
economic science 125
economic values 68, 126
economics 125–7, 129, 175
 mathematization 125
 models 126–7
 political 126
 theory 127, 128, 164
economists 127, 129
economy 119–36
 global 85, 90

industrial 186
interpretation 122
mathematization 156
regional 190
Edison, Thomas 173
elitism 94, 144
emergencies 191
emergency 28
Enron 128
entropy 17
environment 60, 69, 76
ethics 130
Euripides
   Anrodmache 77
Eurobarometer
   "Social Values, Science and Technology" 66
European Union (EU) 43, 114, 115
   Fifth Framework Programme for Research 189
   governance program 91
   international agreements 43
   Lisbon Strategy 189
   treaties 43
exchange of information 10
experiences 36
experiments 84–5, 90
experts 66, 71–5, 82, 87, 89, 90, 91, 92, 93, 195

false alarms 22, 27
fashion 142, 143
finance 84
financial crisis of 2008 *see* economic crisis of 2008
financial governance 113
financial innovation 104, 106–7
financial instability
   global 113
financial institutions 37
financial markets 104, 114, 131, 133, 132, 135, 169
   global 107
   regulation 69, 104, 105
financial services 110
financial system 105–6, 116, 122
   global 109–10, 113, 184
Flaubert's Parrot 26–7

Florida, Richard
   theory of creativity 194
food production 85
food security 83
Foucault, Michel 18
   The Order of Things 18
France 128
Freud, Sigmund 24
Friedrich Ebert Foundation
   Future Commission 167
functionality 7

G20 115
GAAP *see* Generally Accepted Accounting Principles
GDP *see* Gross Domestic Product 121
Generally Accepted Accounting Principles (GAAP)
   agreements 115
genetic code 83
genetic engineering 76
genetic modification 84
geography
   economic 188
global accounting 115
global competition 177
global crises 102
global economy 90
global events 185
global finances 104
   depoliticization 119, 109–10, 184
global information society 187
global society 187
global warming 85
globalization 107, 111, 170, 177, 178, 183, 184, 185
   commercial 111
   financial 111
   risks 114
   stereotypes 186
   theories 183
goods
   circulation of 154
Google 10
governance 70, 116, 170, 183–98
   financial 113
   global 107
   structures 115

government 69, 71, 73, 104, 169, 176, 197
　agencies 83, 85
　institutions 65
　opposition parties 90
greed 131, 133, 135, 136
Gross Domestic Product (GDP) 121
Groys, Boris 143

Habermas, Jürgen 150
Hall, Donald 5
health 83
Heidegger, Martin 6, 146
heterochronies 168
history 50
homogenization 56–7, 59
Hume, David 133

identity and citizenship 166
IFRS *see* International Financial Reporting Standard
ignorance 33–4, 36, 39, 40, 41, 42, 54, 153
　collective 39
　rational 14
IMF *see* International Monetary Fund
indeterminacy 24
industrial economy 186
industrial societies 7, 54
infinite regress 22
informality 177
information 153, 186
information society 155, 192
information technology 10, 110, 162
informative design 12–13
infotoxication 5
infotrash 5
innovation 33, 68, 143, 144, 147, 195
　desynchronized 170
　economic 163, 164
　financial 104, 106–7, 119
　political 167
　politics of 174
　processes 176
　radical 148
　rhetoric 171
　social 38, 161–78
　technological 163, 164, 165
　technological–economic 167

innovation society 174–8
inspiration 146
instability
　economic 113
　financial 113
institutionalization 173
intelligence
　collective 189–92
　cooperative 113–17
　creative 145, 148
　social 70, 113
International Financial Reporting Standard (IFRS)
　agreements 115
International Monetary Fund (IMF) 115
internet 19
　search engines 19
intersubjectivity 146
interventionism 103
inventions 172
investment banks 135
investor confidence 111
investors 107–8
Invitation to a Beheading 19

Kallas, Siim 73
Kant, Immanuel 6, 20, 22, 23, 28, 41
　Anthropology from a Pragmatic Point of View 20
Keynes, John Maynard 130
Keynesianism 101
Kierkegaard, Søren 24, 147
Kondratieff, Nikolai
　Wave Theory 162

labor force 178
Lacan, Jacques 24
laissez-faire principles 176
language 23
law 104, 106
laypeople 90
learning 35, 67, 70
　collective 70, 85
　paradox 149
　processes 36, 192
learning society 177
legal principles 81
Lehman Brothers 114

liberalism 133, 132, 135
librarians 18–19, 21
libraries 18–19, 147
literature 19
living conditions 167
loan risks 105
lobby groups 73
localization 178, 184

machine translation 21
Mannheim, Karl 49
markets 125, 126
    globalized 161
Marx, Karl 130, 161
mass production 156
mathematicians 124
mathematics 121, 123, 130
    economics 126
    models 123, 129
mathematization 123, 156
    economics 125
media 12, 76, 94, 95
    relationship with science 94
media news 175
mind maps 19
minded search 14
mobility 184
modern art 175
modernization 59, 60
monetary policy 102
money managers 135
moral theology 22
mortgages
    subprime 103
multiculturalism 168–9
museums 147

Nabokov, Vladimir 19
    Invitation to a Beheading 19
natural resources 163
nature conservation 83
neoliberalism 102
neo-Marxists 48
New Economy 120
new media 7
new technologies 35, 50
Nietzsche, Friedrich 27, 146, 147
non-experts 91, 92

normality 146
normative expectations 37
norms 22, 23
novelty 142, 145, 146, 171, 172, 196
nuclear energy 84

objectivity 86
observation 9
OECD *see* Organization for Economic Co-operation and Development
Ogburn, William 163, 165
order 17–28
Order of Things, The 18
Organization for Economic Co-operation and Development (OECD) 161
originality 175

panopticon 50–1
parliaments 73
Pasteur, Louis 146
patterned evasions 22
peace accords 165
physical violence 55
physics 126
Plato 65
pluralism
    political 169
    temporal 169
plurality
    cultural 195
Polanyi, Karl 130, 166
political action 88
political advising 71–5
political decisions 73, 92
political disputes 72
political institutions 76
political issues 83
political principles 81
political system 103, 113, 119
politicians 65, 74, 76, 77
politics 59, 66–9, 72, 75, 76, 77, 86, 90, 91, 95, 104, 106, 115, 119, 129, 170
    territorial 178
pollution 83
Popper, Karl 130
Porphyrian tree 19
postindustrial societies 49
power 51, 52–7, 65–77

power relationships 57, 67
  theories 51
private sector 48
probability 39, 121, 122
processing information 12
professionalization 175
protest movements 90
public consciousness 83
public controversies 89
public life 198
public opinion 42, 85, 90, 93–5, 169
Putnam, Robert
  theory of social capital 193–4

qualifications 35

randomness 17
rational ignorance 14
rationality 53
regulation 48, 116, 125
regulators 104, 115
repetition 23–5
resources 189
responsibility 82, 111–13
  social 113
rhizome 19
rights 82
Rio Declaration on Environment and Development 43
risk 40, 84, 109–10, 120–1, 122, 132
  collective 120
  ecological 119
  financial 119, 123
  global 121
  management 124
  prevention 69
risk analysis
  mathematics of 121
risk assessment 44
risk society 92
rules 21, 22, 23, 26
  breaking 26
rumor 81, 82
rumorology 82

Schelksy, Helmut 7
Schumpeter, Joseph 161, 162
science 40, 42, 44, 47, 48, 49, 50, 51, 53, 56, 59, 60, 68, 71, 74, 75, 76, 81–95, 155, 168, 170
  advances 88
  economic 125
  relationship with media 94
  relationship with society 87
  self-regulating 88
  social integration of 93
  social relevance 87
  social role 90
  socialization 89
science and technology *see under* science *and* technology
"Science for All" 94
sciences and humanities 166
scientific autonomy 84, 87, 88
scientific citizenry 82
scientific civilization 48–52
scientific infrastructures 76
scientific knowledge 4, 52, 53, 54, 55, 59, 60
scientific opinion 72
scientific progress 53
scientific research 35
scientific truth 93–5
scientification 88
scientists 76, 83
search engines 19
securitization 111, 114
self-determination 169
self-interest 132
self-observation 70
self-organization 28
self-reflection 74
self-regulation 120
Sen, Amartya 129
shareholders 112
side effects 85
Silicon Valley 144, 192
skills and values 166
Smith, Adam 129, 130
social action 50, 53, 88
social capital 191, 193–4
  Putnam's theory of 193–4
social cohesion 162, 196
social constraints 51
social critics 59
social evolution 52, 59

social experiments 83
social hierarchies 58
social manipulation 48
social organization 52
social power 68
social reality 59
social relationships 56
social sciences 65
social structures 58
social systems 89, 168
social theories 52
social theorists 48
"Social Values, Science and Technology" 66
society 75, 82
    global 187
    relationship with science 87
sociologists 54
sociology 173
software designers 5
"sticky place" 192
Stiglitz-Sen-Fitoussi Commission 128
stock market 107
storage 10
Sturm, Hermann 6
subjectivity 145, 146
subprime mortgages 103
synchronicity 168
synchronization 169

talent 194
Taylor, Frederick Winslow 161
technological civilization 48–52
technological determinism 194
technologies of humility 43
technology 3, 10, 35, 42, 47, 48, 49, 50, 51, 55, 60, 71, 91, 153, 162, 164, 166, 168, 170, 194
    communication 188

transportation 188
territorialization 184
theorists 52
Third World 168
tolerance 194
transfer of information 11
translation
    machine 21
transparency 10, 111
transportation technology 188

uncertainty 39, 40, 44, 85
unemployment 162
    insurance 165
UNESCO *see* United Nations Educational, Scientific and Cultural Organization
United Kingdom
    Chief Scientific Adviser 73
United Nations Educational, Scientific and Cultural Organization (UNESCO) 94
United Nations Habitat program 197
universities 37
unlearning 149
unpredictability 157
urban diversity 196

Wave Theory, Kondratieff's 162
Weber, Max 36, 49, 130, 132, 194
welfare state 67, 103
White Paper on European Governance (2001) 73
Whitehead, Alfred 8
Wittgenstein, Ludwig 21, 24
women's suffrage 165
world economy 85, 102
World Urban Forum 2004 197